WHO ARE
CHINA'S
WALKING DEAD?

A personal journey into the strange world of
communist culture and officialdom

By Kay Rubacek

LIBERTY HILL PRESS

Liberty Hill Press
2301 Lucien Way #415
Maitland, FL 32751
407.339.4217
www.libertyhillpublishing.com

Printed in the United States of America.

Cover design & interior formatting by Better World Studios
Editor: Louise Stevanovic

Paperback ISBN-13: 978-1-6322-1479-9
Ebook ISBN-13: 978-1-6322-1480-5

To my parents, parents-in-law, grandparents,
and great grandparents for escaping communism
in Russia, China, and Czechoslovakia and for teaching,
by example, the importance of not compromising
the values of family, freedom, and liberty.

Contents

Thank You

This book was possible only because of the willingness of numerous Chinese Communist Party insiders to speak honestly and openly during interviews for our movie, *Finding Courage*. I am forever grateful for their trust.

May their courage and humility inspire more people to find value in their own lives and experiences—both the good and the bad—and share them with others.

Preface

We were filming a family who was torn, both emotionally and physically, between California and Northern China. One woman, our main character, was a former high-ranking journalist for Chinese Communist Party's (CCP) state-run media. Now living in exile, she was trying to free her brother who was serving a thirteen-year Chinese prison sentence for "printing pamphlets," while simultaneously trying to prevent a morgue in China from cremating the remains of her sister, who had been murdered by the CCP.

It was a complex story.

A year into filming, the story suddenly became more intriguing and far more complex when this woman's husband (also a high-profile Chinese journalist, but who was still living and working in China) decided to secretly film a visit to the labor camp where the sister had been killed. And then he gave his undercover footage to our small documentary filmmaking team.

It was a score for us. Not only had we gained access to the private life and archives of a family with high-ranking connections in China and a compelling story, but we now had exclusive and rare footage from China, including clear footage and audio of a meeting with the director of a Chinese labor camp, who provided shocking admissions about the ordeal of inmates not only in her camp, but in correctional institutions across China.

Kay Rubacek interviews Guangsheng Han for the movie, *Finding Courage*.

This windfall forced us to expand our movie project from a short ten-minute portrait of one courageous woman to a feature-length documentary about this woman and her family's tragedy and triumph against the world's largest and most brutal totalitarian regime—the CCP.

But there are many sides to every story.

After many long days of interviews with our story's protagonist— Yifei Wang, the former Chinese journalist—despite her riveting tale and all the evidence we had to prove her case, we had no one to tell the other side of the story—the story of the antagonist, the CCP.

I already knew from experience that it would be next to impossible to get an interview with any of the existing CCP leadership about any human rights abuse in China. And with much of Yifei's story being related to the persecution of Falun Gong—the popular spiritual group that the CCP targeted for elimination in 1999—it would be absolutely impossible. Because, while Chinese officials are able to mention some of the CCP's conflicts by name, the persecution of Falun Gong is an absolutely forbidden subject in China.

I had a deep fear that without including the CCP's motives and actions in the film, Yifei's courageous story might be sidelined by critics as "one-sided," or worse, mislabeled as "propaganda." That fear drove me to pore over scores of official CCP documents—speeches, books, television news, newspaper reports, advertisements—anything I could get my hands on, and could get translated into English, to look for a solution. I had to find a voice for our story's bad guy.

But all the official CCP words were an immense disappointment. I found them to be thickly veiled in a sticky sugar coating that hid the truth behind lies so big that the general public wouldn't look past the shiny outer layer before swallowing them whole, like poison-filled candy. I found no CCP words I could use in the movie that revealed the truth in a way that could be understood by a Western audience, without a huge amount of dull context and boring explanations that would send them to sleep before Yifei's story ever had the chance to enthrall them.

Over and over again, I watched the undercover interview with the labor camp director that Yifei's husband had smuggled out of China. I'd never seen anything like it. The director was a real CCP representative in a CCP uniform. She spoke without a script. She yelled at Yifei's family with CCP authority, but she also stumbled and fumbled and became lost for words. Like all CCP members and officials, behind all the pomp and bureaucracy of the Party, she was a human being and I found her words to include more truths than all the official CCP speeches and documents.

So I decided to look for more CCP officials like that labor camp director.

We did find a few CCP insiders in China who were willing to speak to us, but the risk to them and their families was far too great. Their lives could be taken at any moment by the CCP. So despite their willingness, we refused, and we began to seek out regime defectors who had already left China.

We did find many, but they refused to be interviewed for a variety of reasons, including personal safety and the safety of their family members who were still in China. But surprisingly, a vast majority of them seemed to see little value in their stories and couldn't understand how their words would be helpful to our film, which was being made for a Western audience. However, with luck on our side, over a period of 18 months, we found and interviewed close to thirty CCP insiders, including a handful of particularly high-ranking officials.

I had expected their interviews to help bring a close to the story of Yifei and her family in our movie *Finding Courage*—which it did—but meeting them presented a whole new problem. They introduced me to the *Walking Dead*.

> **Behind the stars of CCP officialdom, life is a human pressure-cooker that has, over decades, hardened the skin of many and destroyed the flesh of many more.**

The stories and revelations that came from these CCP insiders constantly challenged all my assumptions and turned my years of research upside down. Then, after watching our movie, viewers were not only moved by Yifei and her family's courage, but also by the courage of the small number of CCP insiders who appeared for only a few minutes in our film. And our viewers often wanted to know more about their stories too.

But the insiders' stories are hard to show on camera, and without access to film independently in China, visuals are extremely scarce. So, like our movie, this book first began as a single article about what we had learned from CCP insiders during the making of our movie, and eventually it grew to a full length book about the culture created by the CCP and its effect upon those who carry out the CCP's operations.

In the eyes of ordinary Chinese citizens, CCP officials have status, power, and money to get things done in China. Without their consent, nothing will be done. And with their consent, almost anything can happen.

But in the eyes of the officials themselves, day-to-day living is like being slowly boiled alive. Behind the stars of CCP officialdom, life is a human pressure-cooker that has, over decades, hardened the skin of many and destroyed the flesh of many more. And the souls that do remain often barely recognize themselves.

Each chapter of this book is a thread that ties together the insights and experiences of these CCP insiders around one subject—from China's astounding environmental and food problems to the unexpectedly glaring interiors of China's CCP prison camps. But while one thread binds each of the chapters together, other threads unwind and unravel the opaque veil that shrouds the bizarre reality of the CCP's operations, as these insiders reveal the ghostly world of CCP culture and officialdom from within its Marxist core.

Kay Rubacek, New York, August, 2020

"The High-Ranking Official," *Youqun Wang, PhD*

Key lieutenant to powerful leader, Wei Jianxing (1931–2015), who was head of the CCP's Internal Investigatory Unit and a member of the Politburo Standing Committee—the CCP's highest echelon—accompanying him to top secret meetings and drafting his speeches; Officer, Supervision Division of the Central Commission for Discipline Inspection of the CCP; Officer, Laws and Regulations Division, Central Commission for Discipline Inspection of the CCP; Doctorate of Philosophy (Law), Renmin University of China.

"The Senior Official," *Hao Ye*

Highest ranking positions held: Deputy Chief, Public Security Ministry; Police Commissioner.

"The Army Colonel"
Baigen Li

People's Liberation Army Colonel; People's Liberation Army Soldier.

"The PSB Official &
Labor Camp Director"
Guangsheng Han

Chief and Party Secretary of the Justice Bureau in Shenyang City; Chief
and Party Secretary of Shenyang City Prison Management Bureau;
Chief and Party Secretary of the Re-education Through Labor Bureau;
Committee Member for the Central Commission for Discipline Inspection
of the CCP; Committee Member of the Shenyang Political and Legal Affairs
Commission; Shenyang CPPCC Standing Committee Member.

"The Propaganda Official," *Sanpu He*

Administrative Officer, Propaganda Department of the CCP Henan Provincial Committee; Distribution Officer, Henan Propaganda Magazine; PLA Soldier; CCP Red Guard.

"The Chinese Professor & CCP Model Student" *Patrick Ling, PhD*

Doctor of Philosophy (Research in China Studies, Religion and Faith), University of Technology Sydney; Master Degree in Engineering; Master Degree in Applied Mathematics; University lecturer; Secretary, CCP Youth League Committee and Party Branch Secretary for Teachers (Department of Mechanics), Changsha Railway Institute, CCP Secretary, Department of Mechanics Branch, Fosha University.

"The Judge"
Jinghua Zhong

Former presiding judge for criminal cases and later presiding judge for civil and business cases at the Intermediate People's Court of Wenzhou Municipality, Zhejiang Province; Human Rights Lawyer.

"The Secret Agent, 6-10 Officer, & Police Officer," *Fengjun Hao*

Police Officer, National Security Agency, Tianjin City Public Security Bureau (Tianjin 6-10 Office).

"The Journalist"
Junmei Wu

Public Opinion and Sentiment Analyst, Journalist, Hubei Channel of People's Daily Online; Television Director, Hubei Television; Documentary Director.

"The Celebrity Artist"
Guimin Guan

Nationally renowned celebrity singer; Level A performer according to the CCP's Ministry of Culture, which designates performers as either Level A, B, or C. Level A is reserved for a limited number of exceptional artists.

"The Diplomat"
Yonglin Chen

First Secretary Consul for Political Affairs in the Chinese Consulate in Sydney, Australia; Political Diplomat, Chinese Embassy in Fiji.

"The Heart Surgeon"
Hong Yuan

Cardiac Surgeon, First Affiliated Hospital of China Medical University, Liaoning Province.

"The Businessman"
Michael Lee

Australian-Chinese businessman; Retailer; Import/export wholesaler;
"Red descendant" targeted as overseas espionage asset.

Other former CCP officials and CCP members who contributed to the
research for this book, but have chosen to remain anonymous.

CHAPTER 1

Meeting the Walking Dead

"We lost truth a long time ago," he said. He then laughed. "It is extremely miserable."

I returned his laugh with a broad smile until the English translation of what he had said came into my ear a few seconds later. My smile disappeared.

"People there don't live like real humans," he continued, "they live like walking corpses. It's a world for ghosts, not for humans."

"Hold on," I interrupted, doing something that I religiously avoid doing when conducting an interview. "Translator," I called out loudly so they would hear me through the interviewee's microphone. "Did you translate his last sentence? I'm not getting his meaning."

"Walking corpses . . . walking ghosts," the translator stammered, obviously tired from well over an hour of continuous translation from Chinese into English. But now was not the time for a break.

"Walking dead?" I asked, trying to maintain a calm exterior while my mind was racing.

"Yes, that's correct," replied the translator.

I looked back at the interviewee. He was the highest ranking communist official we'd been able to get on camera so far. He was the first in charge of modernizing the technology of the CCP's Public Security System (that oversees police and citizen control). The technology has since helped turn China into one of the most highly controlled and surveilled countries on the planet.

I watched him as he continued to speak, momentarily ignoring the translation. He spoke without anger or remorse, but his tone showed a sense of apathetic disregard for Caucasians. He looked at me as if to say: You should understand what I'm talking about— you all should, but you don't. And I don't expect you ever will.

That was one of our first on-camera interviews with a former high-ranking CCP official in New York, back in 2016. In subsequent interviews with more officials and CCP members, I would casually mention how someone had used the term, "Walking Dead," to describe the state of Chinese people under CCP rule today. Then I'd be closely watching for their response. And from former officials living on opposite sides of the world, who had never met each other, who worked in completely different departments in China, who were born in different generations and grew up in different regions, none of them batted an eye at the mention of the term. I had hoped it would be an anomaly and that I could thereby justify ignoring the term, but to my alarm, the concept of China's Walking Dead was a norm to them.

"Oh yes, I have published several articles about that," said a Chinese professor, who is also a doctor of philosophy, and a former CCP model student.

> **"You know, in China, sometimes I was drunk and then did [heart] operations on people."**

"Yeah. Walking Dead," nodded another CCP member in broken English. He leaned toward me, as if to avoid the cameras and to

2

indicate we were now speaking off record.

"I have some thoughts," he continued, "but they are probably useless for your interview." I encouraged him to continue.

"You know, in China, sometimes I was drunk and then did [heart] operations on people." I gulped, but he nodded and shrugged his shoulders. He had been a heart surgeon and worked most of his life at a large, prestigious hospital in China, particularly famous for organ transplantation operations.

"And policemen—drunk, and then go to their job."

I raised my eyebrows and lowered my chin. With wide eyes I searched his face for any hints to grasp his meaning.

"Yeah," he said, "drunk, play mahjong all night, the whole night, and then go to work."

He was dead serious.

"Where was this?" I questioned.

"Everywhere, everywhere, everywhere," he said waving his hands. "Being in that environment is like being in a big vat of dye. Over time it will change you. Gradually you will lose your true self, your soul, or your spirit. That will die. That's the Walking Dead."

He leaned back in his chair and began talking in Chinese again, talking and talking ... but at that moment I felt I'd entered a world that I couldn't leave—not until I could fully understand what he meant.

For the last five years I've tried to forget the Walking Dead. I couldn't bear to use such a ghastly term to describe my fellow human beings in any country, let alone the interviewees who had given me their trust. It was too difficult a term to unravel for an audience in a world of political correctness, and so full of cultural distortion and depravity that I chose to ignore it. And my decision felt justified because the Walking Dead didn't fit the frame I needed from these interviews for our movie, *Finding Courage*,[1] which up until now, had been my task at hand.

But I feel a growing weight of responsibility bearing down on my shoulders. Scores of translated CCP documents and interview transcripts sit in boxes in my office. Over 50 hours of recorded interviews with former Chinese communist officials and CCP members and operatives have, until now, sat unused. It had been challenging to find willing interviewees, and it took time and patience during the interviews to build their trust and overcome cultural, knowledge, age, and gender differences. But eventually, the overwhelming majority warmed to my questioning and spoke sincerely and candidly. Their lived experiences, their truths, are rarely told in Chinese or Western media. Their stories are too foreign for those who don't understand, and too disturbing for those who do. And worse, their guilt, remorse, distress, failure, and despair, were overshadowed by an overwhelming hopelessness. And without hope, I felt obliged to hide these stories, rather than pour more sorrow upon the world. We already have enough.

But today I do see a hope and a purpose in sharing these stories.

As pro-communist, socialist, globalist regimes—especially China—seek to expand their oppression worldwide, and as the beacon of the Free World, America, is on the brink of losing its foundation of personal liberties and succumbing to socialist control, understanding the poison that created China's Walking Dead may help us save ourselves from their fate. And I truly and dearly hope that it is not too late to awaken many of the Walking Dead from their poison-induced slumber.

CHAPTER 2

A New Puzzle

We were well over an hour into our interview when he finally started making eye contact with me.

His thin grey hair was brushed neatly across his scalp, framing an oval face that had seen many battles over his 80-plus years of living. He wore a neat colored shirt beneath a vest and light coat, which I never saw him remove. Occasionally his eyes would spark with an intensity that drew my curiosity, but also made me shiver.

This Senior Official had been Police Commissioner, Class II, and Deputy Chief at the Ministry for Public Security in China's capital, Beijing. The Ministry was where the soldiers set out from before descending on the square where they killed a yet-to-be-disclosed number of innocent students.

"Every day I was at Tiananmen. The Ministry was like the heart of the Tiananmen incident."

Like most Chinese, he used the regime's term "incident" (short for *political incident*) to describe the bloody massacre.

"The soldiers ambushed the students from the Ministry," he stated. "I was there. I knew. I saw it all. I saw everything. The night of the massacre, I was at the Ministry of Public Security. I saw how the CCP deceived the people and how it allowed the military to march into the square."

Up to this point, I'd only heard the testimony of victims of that massacre. They were students, parents, or media reporters. Even a few former soldiers had come forth to testify, but they too saw themselves as victims. They felt they had no choice but to pull the trigger on their brothers and sisters that night. Now finally, I was sitting face to face with an official who had been in a position of power within the regime. Someone who had grown up among the madness of Mao Zedong and the Communist Party's first stage of socialism in China, who had survived it well enough to climb the ranks, with power to order others to pull the trigger against their fellow citizens.

I knew I could learn a lot from him, if only he would trust me.

"Since the days I started remembering things," he recalled, "I have been struggling against landlords, persecuting and suppressing the counterrevolutionaries, the war to resist U.S. aggression and aid Korea (the Korean War) . . ." He went on and on, listing suppression after suppression on his hands until he ran out of fingers. Our young Chinese translator couldn't translate the names of many of them.

". . . the Great Famine, the Four Cleanups, the Great Cultural Revolution . . ." Clearly, he didn't think those suppressions were "great," yet he still used the communist term of choice: *Great*. No truthful terms for such brutal events are allowed under the regime. Even those who have left the regime continue to use the regime's words and phrases. The regime's cultural roots have dug in deep.

Suddenly his eyes sparked and he looked at me squarely.

I was a young, white, female documentary director, ignorant of the operations of China's totalitarian system under the CCP, but desperate to understand. I was trying to hide my naivete, but he had immediately seen right through me. He had been trained for

Hao Ye, "The Senior Official."

"Can people from the West understand the concept that a nation is a tool to suppress its people? You can't."

decades to identify potential enemies of the regime.

He burst out laughing.

I didn't know how to respond.

"You don't understand *struggle*, do you?" he asked me.

"No."

"These are the things the West cannot understand."

He pointed at me. "Can people from the West understand the concept that a nation is a tool to suppress its people? You can't."

He threw his hands outward and laughed even harder.

He was right—I didn't understand what on earth he was talking about.

His words were confusing, even with the simultaneous English translation streaming directly into my right ear via a small wireless headphone system that we'd rigged up to be able to lull the interviewee into forgetting that I didn't understand Chinese. It wasn't just his language that was foreign. He spoke of, and from, a completely foreign culture.

It is a culture where names of grandeur are given to bloody massacres. A culture where only the state decides what is *truth*. A culture in which black is periodically, and often suddenly, renamed white (or white renamed black). A culture where bloodshed is required—and fully justified—against anyone who dares to remember the color or properties of the old "black."

Yet this was a culture that I *wanted* to be familiar with, and could no longer avoid. It was part of my own history.

My grandparents and great grandparents knew of this culture from escaping persecution in Russia during the beginning of the Soviet Union, but they passed away before I was ever interested enough to ask. My father and stepmother lived it in China and then fled as communism's red hand tightened its grip upon the vast nation. But my father had refused to discuss his youth in China, except for fragmented memories that he would speak of only after a late night and a few empty wine bottles.

I learned the most from my parents-in-law, who told me some of what they lived through when Soviet communism ensnared their beloved Czechosolvakia, eventually forcing them to flee to avoid imprisonment or worse. But they had not been part of the system. My family had all been merely oil in the gears, and later part of the remnants of "unwanted" peoples, who were fortunate enough to have escaped another inevitable human liquidation had the Berlin Wall not come down.

But despite the fall of the Berlin Wall in 1989 and the break up of the Soviet Union, the crimes or criminals of communism have never been tried. In schools, we are taught the evils of Nazism, but never the evils of communism. Communism didn't die after the Cold War or with the fall of the Soviet Union. Communism renamed itself as socialism and continued to breed and evolve in the shadows, and in China, where it proactively fueled other totalitarian regimes around the world. In America—the ultimate enemy of all communist regimes—socialists have successfully carried out an American cultural revolution and now control the education system, from the Common Core education system, to almost every college campus, and their shadow over American liberties is growing darker and darker.

Today, China is the best example of communism I can learn from. And it doesn't require learning the Chinese language, it requires learning a new culture—the culture created by the Chinese Communist Party that justified the periodic killing of millions of innocent people. This is a culture so thickly veiled in cultish dogma and twisted double-speak, that few academics bother to continue digging beyond its outer layers.

These thoughts were flooding my mind as I looked back into the eyes of the jaded Senior Official. He sat opposite me, opposite two cameras, two cameramen, and a wall of lights to keep him from fading into the black backdrop behind him. He was unfazed by the attention, or my questions. It had been almost two hours of interviewing, simultaneous translation, and patronization toward me, and I was struggling to hold my fraying confidence together.

But then, as if he sensed my distress, his tone softened and he began to talk to me as if a grandfather might talk to his granddaughter:

"Let me put it this way," he said. "In the United States, a presidential election is held every four years. Since the founding of the nation, the U.S. government serves its people, and power is limited by the system. American people have the right to own guns. If the government fails to do its job, the people have the right to protect their interests. These are part of the founding principles since George Washington." I nodded and wondered if he knew just how close the U.S. system was to succumbing to a new breed of socialism and losing these founding principles.

"On the contrary," he continued, "Marx, Lenin, Stalin, and Mao understood the concept of a nation as a tool for suppression. Marxism defines a nation as a tool for suppression. A nation exists for that purpose. This is fundamentally different from the West. You can't expect the Chinese regime to not suppress its people, because, by definition, our nation suppresses our people through force. Those are the rules!"

By definition, our nation suppresses our people through force . . . A nation exists to suppress its people. . . . These words were circling in my mind. I needed time to let them sink in.

"They didn't bother to hide it, they said very frankly that they kill. So how could you still expect them not to?"

"The perspective you have chosen for your research is wrong," he said, shaking his head.

I didn't want to hear those words, but I sincerely appreciated his candor and the fact that he didn't just walk out on the interview.

"You are too kind," he softened. "It is difficult for Western people—who are very kind—to truly understand such evil. If you are not evil to that extent, you can't grasp the true horror of the cruelty in China."

"These things are written clearly in the regime's theories. So if you expect that the regime won't persecute or kill, you just haven't studied their theories well enough."

He was right. I had barely scratched the surface of their theories, and he'd studied them his entire life.

He continued, "If they told you in writing, and in no ambiguous terms, that they are going to kill you, how could you not believe it? They didn't bother to hide it, they said very frankly that they kill. So how could you still expect them not to?"

He burst out laughing again. I faked a smile in an attempt to hide my discomfort.

He laughed harder.

"The problem is not with the regime," he was pointing directly at me again. "The problem lies with you."

"The CCP is evil by its very nature. How could you expect it to be anything else?"

Was he right? I wondered.

Despite a decade of studying modern-day China, the CCP, and its crimes, had my research really been off course? I had sought out these Party insiders to help fill a gap in our film—to provide the last piece of the puzzle that would give our audience an insight into how the CCP operates. I wanted them to explain how it is possible for such a regime to still exist today, and treat its people so brutally.

However, this insider adjusted the course of my quest and made me start digging deeper. I still needed the answers to my original questions, but it was no longer a matter of insider testimonies providing the last puzzle piece to complete our movie. This insider hadn't given me that piece of the puzzle I had wanted. He had given me a whole new puzzle entirely—and every piece of it was blood red.

CHAPTER 3

Two Layers of Skin

"No, no, no! This is wrong," a former Chinese judge told me less than 30 minutes into our interview. My assumptions were being turned on their head, and it wasn't the first time. I was hoping he'd say on camera what I thought to be true based on observation, research, and witness and victim testimony—that China had no rule by law, only rule by power.

Jinghua Zhong, "The Judge."

"It's not that China has no law," he corrected me in a kind but firm, very judge-like manner. "On the contrary, China has lots and lots of laws. When you go and read some of the laws you will see that they are very well written and very fair."

The Judge had spent five and a half years as a presiding judge for criminal cases in China and another six years as a presiding judge for civil and business cases. He had conducted significant research on the differences between the CCP and U.S. legal systems, and he had my full attention.

"There are two main differences between the judicial and legal systems of China and the United States," he explained. "First, China uses the civil law system, which uses statutory law, similar to countries like Germany and France. Hundreds of articles are codified for both criminal and civil law. The law is decided by the People's Congress, so you just have to do things according to the codified law. Whereas the United States, Britain, and Australia use the common law system. They look at how similar cases were dealt with in the past, so their cases are tried based on precedent. They are two different kinds of judicial and legal systems."

"The second, and most distinguishing feature of the Chinese system, is that it lacks any independence. Of course, official Chinese media and propaganda claim that its legal and judicial system is independent, but in actual practice that is not so. When countries adopt an independent legal system, their society can have fair trials, and individuals can have relatively fair outcomes in those trials. But when you don't have that, then you won't have fairness or justice."

The Judge's words reminded me of another interviewee who summed up the same concept by saying, "It's as if you are both the sportsman and the referee. No one supervises you except yourself. That's the CCP. It supervises itself."

I soon realized that the Judge's lesson in law was not about the law itself, and that to understand law in China, I couldn't get lost in the details of the operations. The details really don't matter. All that ultimately matters is the biggest player, the most influential referee, what they want, and the stakes they are willing to play to get it.

The Judge repeated a communist cultural phrase to help me understand how Chinese judges think about the system:

"We have a saying in China: The law is just words on paper. Every man can act with discretion."

> ## "Our Propaganda minister often told us to think about why our propaganda tasks always have *two layers of skin*."

I couldn't follow him. As a Westerner and a sinophile, I was proud to be able to recite numerous popular proverbs of ancient Chinese wisdom, from Lao-tzu to Confucius, but I was ignorant of the modern Chinese sayings born of the communist culture.

The Judge paused to think how to express it in a way I could understand. He said: "We also use this phrase: To say one thing but to do another."

Ah. Now *that* I understood. But according to my Western, Christian upbringing, that meant acting without integrity, being dishonest. Imagining a systemic requirement of dishonesty throughout a vast nation's legal system brought an eerily dystopian picture to mind.

In another interview, a former CCP official from a provincial Propaganda Department used a different phrase to explain the concept from the view of his department. "In the Propaganda Department," he said, "our Propaganda minister often told us to think about why our propaganda tasks always have *two layers of skin*."

I first had to confirm that with the translator. Yes—he did actually say "two layers of skin."

The Propaganda Official continued, "We were told we had to think about why propaganda and reality are disconnected. We had to know that they were disconnected."

> ## "Truth is the most precious thing. That's why we should ration it," Lenin had said.

The man squirmed in his seat as he spoke in front of the cameras. Or perhaps the squirming was a reflection of his mind being twisted back into the complex labyrinth of communist thinking that he'd been trying to get away from since escaping the system.

"The Propaganda Department is not afraid to say that black is white," he elaborated. "They just say it. And they say it repeatedly. They've done it for decades already. They continue to lie like this, so you follow them very easily and completely. It is very easy to become brainwashed."

He looked how I felt. Depressed.

The CCP has learned well in its study of Marxism-Leninism. "Truth is the most precious thing. That's why we should ration it," Lenin had said.

"The Chinese people cannot see outside, cannot hear outside. All you see and hear is what the CCP wants you to know. You cannot jump out of that environment," he continued.

"It was only later that I really understood why it has two skins. Because the propaganda cannot tell the truth. If it did tell the truth, the CCP would be finished immediately. Therefore, it must continue to lie and cover up the truth."

A nation that systematically trains its officials—its elites—to lie, cannot value honesty or integrity at all. And the most insidious aspect was that another euphemistic term had to be swallowed to soften the moral blow to the human soul.

Chinese officials and CCP members understand that a second layer of skin is essential and justified. It is required not only to conceal reality, but as a wall between one's mind and one's soul—to ensure that no moral code of integrity or honesty itches between them.

But not everyone is able or willing to accept this second layer of skin, as I found out the next day, when I interviewed another former CCP member.

"I often couldn't stand how the CCP ran society. I couldn't stand it at all," he exclaimed with anger rising in his voice. "However a lot of other people seemed oblivious to it. They didn't think what the CCP did was abnormal."

He was waving his arms emphatically as he spoke. Every line on his face reflected his words and meaning. He seemed to have no second layer of skin. I admired how freely he spoke—more freely than any other former CCP member I'd ever met.

As if recognizing my thoughts, he suddenly became self-conscious. He paused and asked if he was being too emotional.

I encouraged him to speak as freely, and however he wanted.

Sweat had begun to blister on his brow.

He lowered his arms and continued more slowly,

"Sometimes I even thought I was insane. Why were other people completely numb to the things that I thought were terribly bad?"

He looked at me with deep sincerity and waited, but I had no answer.

CHAPTER 4

Department P

"You need to know something about the media within the CCP system," said a former CCP journalist who had spent years working for one of the largest state-run media organizations in China. "In China, all media are controlled by an office called the Publicity Department."

I'd heard different names for this department.

"Is it the Publicity Department or Propaganda Department?" I questioned the translator.

I had asked this same question of numerous Chinese journalists, some of whom had been at such a high level in Chinese society that they were regularly called upon by the CCP whenever interviews were needed with famous national officials visiting their city. They told me that the department name used to be translated to the Propaganda Department in English, but later it was changed to the Publicity Department because it sounds more acceptable in the West.

"Did the Chinese name change when the English translated name changed?" I asked for clarification.

"No."

"Okay, we're going to use the original translation: Propaganda

Department." I decided against the status quo of many Western media who chose to parrot the CCP's sugar-coated euphemisms.

Junmei Wu, "The Journalist."

"So," continued the Journalist, "up in the higher level in the central government there is the Central Propaganda Department, and in each state there is the State Propaganda Department. Similarly, in each city there is a City Propaganda Department. Our job is to serve the needs of the Central Propaganda Department."

In a separate interview with the former Propaganda Official, he further explained the hierarchical structure:

"The Propaganda Department is in charge of disseminating the ideology of the Communist Party. Each year the CCP's Central Committee Propaganda Department will gather with the propaganda ministers of each province for a meeting—the Central Work Conference—to set the next year's political tasks. They convey the political tasks and standards required for publishing on radio, television, newspapers, cultural publishing, and other publishing and programming."

"They order the propaganda ministers to implement it in each province. The ministers go back home and hold meetings with the city and district propaganda ministers to pass on the order from the central government. These district ministers go back home and hold the same meeting with the county level ministers who do the same thing."

This hierarchy in the propaganda department seemed consistent with the intensive planting of the CCP's deeply rooted branches into every level of all social structures in China.

For years before these interviews, my communist propaganda vocabulary had been limited to visuals only. At the mention of the words "Chinese propaganda," highly stylized paintings would immediately spring to mind: rosy pink cheeks, shiny black hair, and bright white shiny teeth in "glorious" smiles—or an expression of deep hatred.

"Most people liked the posters for their composition and visual content . . . This allowed the political message of the posters to be passed on in an almost subconscious manner."

When researching for the film, *Finding Courage*, I had ordered a bright red book full of such posters, printed in China by a German publisher in 2011.[2] The book cover has two titles, one in English and one in Chinese.

English Title:
Chinese Propaganda Posters

Chinese Title:
***Warmly Celebrating the
50th Anniversary of the Founding of the CCP***

The book's poster curation skews toward the Chinese title, with more surface smiles than public venom.

A sinologist, Stephan R. Landsberger, who owns the world's largest collection of Chinese propaganda posters, describes their appeal in one of the three introductory articles in the book:

> "Most people liked the posters for their composition and visual content, and did not pay too much attention to the slogans printed underneath. This allowed the political

message of the posters to be passed on in an almost subconscious manner."

"These works created a kind of 'faction,' a hybrid of 'fact' and 'fiction,' stressing the positive and papering over anything negative."

I put an elastic band around the book's hard cover and stuck a Post-it note on the front with *"Warning!"* written on it. Should an unsuspecting reader take the book from my library shelf, I wanted them to consider the context of the content before they flicked through the colorful icons that revere the CCP, and before they become glazed and giddy—like most unprepared Western viewers—by the outer skin of the CCP's propaganda.

We had included a moving collage of CCP violent-struggle campaign posters in our *Finding Courage* documentary. A soldier helps a preteen girl steady her pointed rifle. A young woman with a red headscarf determinedly aims a hand-held missile launcher. I saw bayonets, swords, bombs, fists, men, women, children, anger, and hatred. Yet when I showed the sequence to a work colleague, he saw bright color, power, and dynamism.

"Those colorful posters really get my attention," he said. "Can't you show them longer in the movie? I like looking at them. I want to look at them longer."

After deliberation, we increased the duration of the collage in the movie from three seconds to five seconds. And in the end, we removed the boisterous color and made them black and white.

"The CCP's propaganda is very effective. It's had a lot of practice," said the Propaganda Official. "Now it is more subtle and tries not to be so obvious."

So while the propaganda skins have evolved to accommodate new technology, the inner bone structure and flesh and blood of the propaganda's goals haven't changed since the time when

Mao's cheeks were given their first pinky poster-glow.

"The propaganda is based on Marxist-Leninist theory," explained the Propaganda Official. "Lenin said, the working class can't possibly have Marxist-Leninist thought spontaneously, so the CCP must rely on indoctrination, otherwise the public cannot automatically agree with following the CCP. It must rely on indoctrination."

> **"Controlling public opinion is the same as caging up citizens like animals. Their goal is to not let you know the truth, to not let you talk."**

Lenin, with full faith in the power of socialism, really believed that the majority of us are *useful idiots*—fools who cannot think or make worthy decisions for ourselves; dispensable sheep that require the leadership of an elite group of thinkers to be able to fully function as human beings.

So, according to socialist elites, without masters, we the regular people are merely "idiots." But with them as our masters, we become "useful idiots."

Marx stated it rather plainly in the *Communist Manifesto*:

> "They [the general public] cannot represent one another, they must themselves be represented. Their representative must at the same time appear as their master, as an authority over them, as an unlimited governmental power, that protects them from above, bestows rain and sun shine upon them."

"So," continued the Propaganda Official, "the propaganda must make things upside down. It makes right into wrong and good into bad. It does this continuously, from the beginning of your life until the end of your life. The CCP relies on this."

In a later interview, another CCP insider compared the CCP's propaganda department to a cage:

"Controlling public opinion is the same as caging up citizens like animals," he said. "Their goal is to not let you know the truth, to not let you talk. 'I keep telling you lies to make you keep following me. In the end I will harm you and you won't even know.' "

And the CCP's propaganda stronghold keeps getting tighter.

"Media and education are the two areas that are controlled more strictly now."

"Media and education are the two areas that are controlled more strictly now," said a former CCP journalist who we interviewed after she defected to the West in 2015. "I feel like the control is getting more and more strict."

The Journalist recalled a recent order her media office received before she defected. It came from the head of the CCP's *People's Daily* media organization—one of the largest media networks in China:

> "Both the official public media and 'independent media' (i.e. unofficially controlled media) must be strictly controlled. We must control the rights of speech."

In 2014, a photograph from a CCP journalist training session was leaked and posted onto the popular Chinese microblogging site, Weibo, where it was captured before being deleted by CCP censors. It was taken from an extensive training session required by the CCP for Chinese journalists to complete in order for them to be able to pass a newly revised examination to renew their

(Source: China Digital Times)

official press credentials.

The session's focus was on the Marxist view of journalism and was designed to ensure that CCP journalists are clear on the difference between news and propaganda, as well as their place in the world of the CCP's propaganda state.

China Digital Times, a California-based bilingual news website covering China, translated the points on the slide into English.[3] The points read as follows:

1. News focuses on information, Propaganda on format.
2. News focuses on originality, Propaganda on repetition.
3. News focuses on fact, Propaganda on opinion.
4. News focuses on the timely, Propaganda on timing.
5. News focuses on communication, Propaganda on manipulation.
6. News focuses on balance, Propaganda on spin.

"When I first stepped into this field of journalism, and again whenever I started a new job, and whenever we had a meeting," continued the Journalist, emphasizing the repetitive nature of the education of CCP journalists, "we were told that our company's propaganda mission was a political task, and that's the most important thing. Our job is to propagate the CCP."

"The most important job is monitoring the reputation of the CCP among the people. Once opinion or speech is identified as unaligned with the CCP's ideology, the media will control these by either eradicating their voice or offsetting it."

I wondered what *offsetting* included.

As I went back through the interview transcript with the Propaganda Official, I noticed he used CCP cultural euphemisms to explain the concept of offsetting:

"We're told to use positive guidance and to reduce the negative effects. Positive guidance must be in line with the interests of the Communist Party. Negative things are anything that damages the image of the Communist Party; anything that reveals its mistakes or crimes. These negative reports must be suppressed."

But that was still confusing. I needed to understand the concept in plain English.

"What the Communist Party fears is exposure," he explained further, giving me better clarity. "You cannot mention, you cannot report. If something negative happens in the community, the report should immediately make it lighthearted and try to cover it up. If something bad happens in China, you must instead report about something bad happening overseas to suppress the things happening here."

Then I understood. And I'd already seen it done again and again.

For example, in late January 2020, when the CCP Virus (COVID-19) pandemic started ravaging China's city of Wuhan, my friend in New York received a distraught call from her family members living in Shandong, China. They were terrified for her life. They knew nothing of the pandemic outbreak in China, but they'd been told by CCP media that America had a disastrous outbreak of the flu that was taking lives across the country. They asked her to return to China to be safe with them.

Of course, there was no crazy flu outbreak in the United States at the time, and the pandemic from Wuhan was yet to hit America, but CCP officials were actively suppressing news about the pandemic and putting Chinese people at risk. Leaked directives from the CCP Propaganda Department (translated and published by *China Digital Times[4]*) gave me a firsthand example of how the CCP controls the nation's narrative:

> Content related to the pneumonia of unknown cause in Wuhan must follow information issued by authoritative departments. To prevent false reports from causing panic, do not write conjecture, do not quote foreign news media, do not link to SARS. *(January 8, 2020)*

> Regarding the Wuhan novel coronavirus, authoritative government information shall prevail. Control push message notifications. *(January 15, 2020)*

> Regarding reports related to the Wuhan epidemic situation, promptly publish official information and scientific epidemic prevention knowledge, in order to prevent panic. *(January 22, 2020)*

> Regarding the Wuhan novel coronavirus, use standard content sources, do not republish unverified information from self-media, do not independently aggregate or edit, do not alter headlines. *(January 22, 2020)*

The Propaganda Official tried to give me another example, but he was still talking in CCP-speak:

"Anyone who stands on the side of the people cannot be used by the Communist Party."

"Our department had an official who was sent to work at a particular newspaper as an editor. He found some illegal fundraising and so he reported it, which caused some reactions from people. So the man was dismissed and transferred to another place and also criticized."

Caused some reactions? I wondered what that meant exactly.

I wrote the *reaction* euphemism in my notebook. I'd heard phrases like that a lot—so vague, so tame, and giving nothing away to someone unversed in CCP cultural language. I was starting to recognize and understand parts of this foreign language, but I wondered how I could convey it to an audience.

The Propaganda Official must have noticed the perplexity on my face. He thought harder and then offered me a more graphic illustration:

"Here is a story. We have a Public Security Bureau (PSB) Chief who has a patron official protecting him—a Vice Governor who is known for being very reckless and acting lawlessly. One day, the PSB Chief took his patron out drinking, and afterward, while the Chief was driving his patron home, he hit a person on the street. He hit a man who was riding his bike with his twelve-year-old son. The child was killed instantly, but the bike and the man were caught on the side of the car. The Chief kept driving for a few miles more, dragging the man and his bike along the road. The man's skin and flesh were ripped off his body and the man later died."

That was horrific, but it wasn't the point of his story.

"At the time there was an editor at the local newspaper, and he followed this event closely and reported it. It became big news. The public was very angry at the PSB Chief and the central government found out about it. So the Chief was given the death penalty and the public settled down. But the editor of the newspaper was fired from his position because he didn't keep things quiet. The CCP won't allow such a person to be an editor."

"Anyone who stands on the side of the people cannot be used by the Communist Party. You must obey the Party. Your reports must be consistent with the Party. You cannot write your own words, you can only report according to the requirements of the Party."

"The CCP keeps power by two points," he concluded, "propaganda and violence—the pen and the gun—both are indispensable."

CHAPTER 5
Progress vs Creativity

The former Propaganda Official was particularly uncomfortable in front of the camera.

"I thought we would have a rehearsal," he said to his friend in Chinese, who was translating my questions. "But now she's suddenly asking me questions without a rehearsal and I don't know what to say."

Sanpu He, "The Propaganda Official."

I knew he was complaining about my interviewing approach.

> **"For Chinese people, their political lives were more important than anything else. Because if you can't survive your political life, you are done for."**

I do provide general topics in advance, but not specific questions and he felt uncomfortable and unprepared—which was what I wanted. It might not seem the kindest approach, but I found it to be the best way to get them to be sincere on camera.

Chinese officials are notorious for being stiff and robotic on camera, or for speaking through a fixed—often contextually inappropriate—smile, regardless of the topic. I was curious to know why.

In an earlier interview, the Senior CCP Official had commented on this type of behavior:

"For Chinese people, their political lives were more important than anything else. Because if you can't survive your political life, you are done for. Not just you, your entire family and extended family are affected. If it were just you, it would be okay. But if you were to make a political mistake, your entire family is doomed. That is a deeply sad truth for Chinese people. One could easily be labeled an enemy and that's the end of you. You'd lose your job, your money, your home, and your children won't be able to find a school."

A younger, but higher-ranking official, who I interviewed months later gave a different explanation as to why CCP officials speak so rigidly. Since this Official had at one time been a speechwriter for even higher ranking officials I was particularly interested in his comments on this point.

"They are afraid of saying the wrong thing. Even I have not gotten rid of that habit yet," he said.

The High-Ranking Official had now lived for two years in the West, but throughout our interview he did indeed look afraid to say the wrong thing. He maintained an odd, steady smile, regardless of whether he was describing hideous murder, corruption, or imprisonment. It made it very difficult to present him on camera to a Western audience, who would be confused by a smile that didn't match his words.

Youqun Wang, PhD, "The High-Ranking Official."

Over the course of three hours of interviewing, while his words seemed more open than most officials, his face almost never betrayed his rigid plastic smile to reflect his true emotions. Old habits die hard.

"There is a Chinese saying: Words are no small matter," he said. "It means that if you say one thing wrong, you risk losing your entire political career. One mistake and you'll be persecuted. So everyone is extremely cautious, very scared of saying the wrong thing. Everyone makes sure they always stay within the boundaries set by the regime. They won't dare to cross them even a bit. This fear is stifling the Chinese people."

He described how shocked he was when he first witnessed a congressman speaking at a rally in public—*without a written speech!*

"He was so eloquent," said the High-Ranking Official. "American officials are able to speak in public fluently without a script. But this is unthinkable in China. Chinese officials have such rigid minds."

"In the U.S., different ideologies clash and create sparks, leading to varied and rich outcomes," he explained. "But in China . . . No one is allowed to think outside the box."

"Chinese leaders, when they are given their script, they can read fluently from them. But without the script, they'll begin stuttering like, 'um, um, um . . . um, um, um. . . .' "

He suddenly laughed rather boisterously.

I enjoyed this moment of genuine emotion as his plastic smile melted away. I sensed the complex but gratifying relief he must have felt standing on American soil, being allowed to witness and mentally compare the abilities of his former political superiors to the American congressmen and congresswomen.

He stopped laughing and composed himself. His smile hardened again.

"Chinese people live in all kinds of stifling mental boundaries and boxes," he said. "They have no freedom in their minds."

The brief moment of joy was over.

I expected him to continue talking about freedom of speech, but he spoke instead about mental freedom, something that I've always taken for granted growing up in the West.

"The most distinctive feature of a college education in China is that it does not permit innovation. Since coming to America, this is the greatest difference, in my opinion," he continued.

Innovation? I wondered. I was yet to grasp the connection between communist culture and a lack of creativity.

"In the U.S., different ideologies clash and create sparks, leading to varied and rich outcomes," he explained. "But in China, everything is tightly controlled. They only allow one point of view, one perspective, one belief. Everyone must follow that. No one is allowed to think outside the box."

A-ha! No wonder so many Chinese businesses have grown out of shamelessly ripping off foreign brands. I giggled to myself, thinking of the ridiculous copycat brands that operate freely in China as parasites on Western creativity:

KFC vs OFC / KLG / KFG

Pizza Hut vs Pizza Huh

McDonald's vs Mcdnoald's

Nintendo Playstation vs Nintendo Polystation

Starbucks Coffee vs Sunbucks Coffee

Burger King vs Burger Madam&Sir

Superman vs Specialman

Johnnie Walker whiskey vs Johnnie Worker whiskey

Heineken beer vs Heinmekem beer

Corona beer vs Cerono beer

Crocs shoes vs Corcs shoes

Orio cookies vs Borio cookies

Nike brand vs Hike, Mike, Knie

Olay vs Okay

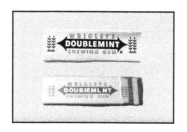

(Source: China Uncensored)

Wriggleys Doublemint gum vs Wrlgleys Doubiemlnt

Sharpie permanent marker vs Skerple permanent marker

Under Armour sportswear vs Uncle Martian sportswear

Walmart vs Wu Mart

Adidas vs Adidos

Prada clothing vs Prapa clothing

Calvin Klein vs Calvim Klaim

Beats by Dre headphones vs Deads by NANI headphones

Jack Daniels Tennessee whiskey vs Johns Daphne Tenderness

Redbull drink vs Ridbull drink

Marlboro cigarettes vs Maolboea

Oh, the list goes on. . . . And that's only the laughable branding stolen by CCP-cultivated, small business operators. The list of intellectual property stolen by larger CCP operations is far more serious and far too long for this book.

Karl Marx didn't believe that human thought is capable of creativity and innovation.

Stealing intellectual property—especially from America—is a safe norm in communist culture, but freedom to innovate is not allowed under Marxist rule.

Karl Marx didn't believe that human thought is capable of creativity and innovation. He believed that we are products molded solely by our environment and economic situations. He preached that because we are incapable of finding peaceful methods to change our lives for the better, we must "naturally" fight with violent revolt in order to improve our lives.

Conspirators of Marxist revolutions most often target impressionable, moldable youths to be revolutionary drivers. Their youthful vigor can be amplified to physically crush opponents, while their natural drive to question, create, and innovate can be crushed and reformed into a narrow, Marxist viewpoint that will prove very hard to unlearn.

History provides many examples, such as during Lenin's and Stalin's "scientific" revolutions upon Russia. These murderous men utilized Russian innovation and then crushed it in their Marxist quest to create a shiny new socialist society of machines and their masters.

After the first stage of mass industrialization was complete—and after they had bred a whole new class of young engineers—the senior engineers who had been essential in the scientific industrialization process were publicly humiliated and destroyed.

But the new, young engineers stayed. They had been molded by Marxist revolution. Their minds had been turned away from the "old" methods of scientific research and discovery. They had been reformed and taught to scorn the "old ways" and thus never knew what they were missing. Innovation and creativity, for, or by an individual, was replaced with "progress." And progress could only be defined by socialist elites. The regime set the rules of discovery and nothing could exist outside of these rules.

One of my most intriguing interviews was with a former celebrity singer from China, who was one of the CCP's indoctrinated youths. He had been "born and raised" by the CCP, and had been taught that the CCP was never wrong.

"In China, arts and entertainment are basically one and the same, and the purpose of the arts is to serve politics. This is expressly stated by the CCP."

"That was a deep-seated mentality that we always had," the Artist explained. "We always tried to find excuses for the regime. That's the way we felt. We were brainwashed to think like that."

As a famous artist promoted nationally by the CCP, he told me about the strict boundaries that communist culture placed on creativity.

"In China, arts and entertainment are basically one and the same, and the purpose of the arts is to serve politics," he said bluntly. "This is expressly stated by the CCP. The CCP clearly states that you must play the role of the CCP's mouthpiece. If you refuse to do that, the CCP will ruin you—ban you from your career. There are just too many artists and performers who have to rely on the CCP to survive. The CCP doesn't care if a few refuse to obey."

The Artist had not been banned from his career in China, but had eventually chosen not to obey and fled China. However, the CCP followed him to America and worked hard to ban him from any artistic performance or teaching work. After a few years of being unable to work as an artist, he took a job as a janitor. He decided that being a janitor held more dignity and integrity than rejoining the Party.

"The CCP praises with one hand and suppresses with the other hand," he said. "The performers who obey are handsomely rewarded and those who refuse to obey are demoted and subject to all kinds of ill-treatment."

"Your whole life is in their hands. You can be arrested on any kind of fabricated charge. And after you are in jail and can't endure

Guimin Guan, "The Celebrity Artist."

their torture, you admit to the charges they force on you. Then they broadcast to the public that you have behaved well in prison and will be released. They do this to make you obey. In the end, you yield to them."

He described the CCP's elaborate political structure that artists are required to follow in order to receive national publicity:

"Performers are designated Level A, B, or C, as evaluated by the Ministry of Culture. This system was established after 1987. Level A represents the highest and is at the national level. The evaluation process is tough and very strict. And if you sing songs the CCP doesn't like, there's no way you would ever qualify."

He had been designated a Level A performer.

"Every government branch has a designated culture division. For example, the military has a culture division that falls under the political division. The General Political Department of the military has its own culture division. The major military divisions and the major branches of the military all have their respective culture departments and divisions. There are CCP officials positioned in all of these places."

Years ago I had learned the extreme emphasis communism places on inculcating culture. But I soon learned that the culture the CCP values is not the creative freedom and expression we foster in the West. It is a political culture to which artists must adhere to and create for.

"If you are a talented individual who gets ahead by relying on yourself, they [the CCP] will train and develop you so they can use you to praise them," continued the Artist. "They use you to strengthen their rule, basically to whitewash them."

"When you are part of that system," he said regretfully. "You really don't sense there's anything wrong with it. You just feel that you are praising your mother country—it's one and the same—so you give your all and they encourage you."

The Artist's guilt and sorrow for being a tool in the hands of the regime was not unique among our interviewees.

However, the high-ranking former speech writing official was completely unapologetic in his summation of how creativity is stamped out by the CCP:

"You are forced to tell lies. It won't work if you don't tell lies. As a result, everyone becomes a liar."

"After you are persecuted and tortured through political movements, one after another, what do you become in the end? You become someone incapable of thinking independently and speaking the truth—you are a tool for the Party."

All the officials and many of the CCP members had at some point recognized themselves to be merely CCP tools or weapons to be used at the CCP's disposal.

The High-Ranking Official had existed near the top echelon of CCP officialdom for decades and wanted his message heard loud and clear. He didn't mince his words:

"The two things the CCP can never tolerate are independent thinking and speaking the truth. Telling the truth is forbidden. Anyone who still has some sense of independent thinking in him or who is willing to tell the truth is unable to survive under the CCP. You are forced to tell lies. It won't work if you don't tell lies. As a result, everyone becomes a liar."

Ironically, that was one of the most truthful statements I heard.

CHAPTER 6
Money-Law and Constitution

"In China, everything—including the court system and the government—is controlled by the CCP. It's not that the CCP and the government exercise dual control of the court," stated the former CCP Judge.

I was jolted by his choice of words: "the CCP and the government." *Aren't they one and the same?* I asked myself.

It is commonplace for Western media to refer to Chinese authorities or the CCP as "the Chinese government." I didn't understand the distinction. I was yet to find out how these two entities are strategically and intimately intertwined because the Judge was continuing his monologue, which required my undivided attention:

"China is run by one party, the Chinese Communist Party, which rules the nation like a dictator. Since the CCP violently seized the nation, it has always said that the law is a tool of the ruling class. So it says that it can use the law to suppress anyone it deems an enemy. And anyone that opposes the CCP is an enemy."

It was becoming more and more apparent that learning the operations of any aspect of China today required a lesson in politics.

"The CCP has the final say on everything. The government must obey the CCP, the court must obey the CCP, the Congress must obey the CCP, enterprises, civic organizations must obey the CCP. The CCP has presence and influence in every system and every corner. The CCP has monopolized all the power of this nation."

"For example, a CCP Committee is often assigned to work alongside the court. The Committee may give a directive, an opinion or even order the court to handle the case a certain way. The court is not allowed to comply with the law in that instance. The regime's authority is above the law."

"When did you realize this?" I asked him, assuming he had either gradually or suddenly awoken to a dystopian nightmare, like millions of Americans who have only gradually woken to the quiet, yet systematic Marxist takeover of their country.

The Judge corrected me again:

"It's not like what you have suggested, that I gradually found out about this over time. No." He was kind, but emphatic.

"This was clearly written in China's legal textbooks," he explained. "It was only after 1978, after China began opening up its economy, that they changed direct wording like that to make it look less obvious. In Chinese we say: It was exposing too much bone."

Our translator explained the bone saying as being similar in meaning to the English phrase *thinly veiled* meaning not hidden well enough or too transparent. I understood. The CCP is infamous for its lack of transparency.

"So gradually they changed the old words in the textbooks, but the meaning and purpose haven't changed. They've always treated the law as just a tool to control society and smash any opposing forces," concluded the judge.

In subsequent interviews, the other former CCP officials gave rather different perspectives:

> # "In China, the law is only for people who are low-class—those who don't have any connections with people in high positions or don't have strong relations in society."

"In China, the law is only for people who are low-class—those who don't have any connections with people in high positions or don't have strong relations in society. Those are people who have little network." That was said by a former CCP diplomat.

Low-class? I raised my eyebrow.

"In China, the law is not important," he continued, "everything is about personal relationships. If something bad happens to you, you don't think about going to the police or to the court. That isn't a Chinese person's first thought. They first think: Do I know an official in the police? Do I have a friend in the court? Or a friend of a friend in the court? If I can find that person I can bribe him to solve the problem."

Corruption happens in all countries, regardless of the political system, but bribery is not the first solution for most people living in the Free World.

Another Official provided a vivid comparison:

"A few years ago, my wife took her driving test here in the West. Her mother happened to be visiting from China at the time and she kept insisting: 'Take money for the examiner! You need money for the examiner! How will you pass the test if you don't bring any money?!'"

The Official raised his voice as he got into the story, and was now gesticulating broadly, but he was not smiling.

"I was quiet at first," he continued with an intense seriousness, "but eventually I had to say something." He raised his voice again as he delivered the punchline:

"'You don't know!' I told her. 'If she gives money to the examiner she will fail! Not only will she fail, she might even get charged! To do anything in China requires 'gifting.' Nothing will work in China if you don't do that. But in other countries bribing is abnormal.' Only then did her mother stop insisting."

"You don't give tea or cigarettes or liquor anymore. No top wine anymore," explained another Official. "Now bank cards are used as a direct gift. On any occasion, officials collect many bank cards. He can put them into any of his accounts or into any of his family's bank accounts—the money can be directly transferred into the personal account of anyone you like. It's very convenient."

The Judge concurred on this aspect of China's unwritten money-law, quoting another modern communist culture saying, "The way China is today, if you have loads of money, you can, like how the Chinese say it: You can solve a lot of problems with money."

"Money will make the devil turn millstones," said the High-Ranking Official in his interview. The translator further explained his meaning as: "With money, you can do anything."

The High-Ranking Official had held a national post where he was responsible for actually writing national laws at the Laws & Regulations Office within the Central Commission for Discipline Inspection (the CCP's national department for regulating the behavior of CCP members and officials).

"What actually are China's laws and regulations?" he asked me rhetorically.

I shrugged my shoulders.

"They are tools for getting a promotion and a tool for making money."

It was another unexpected answer.

"You need to write books to interpret the laws and regulations, so when you finish drafting a set of laws or regulations, the interpretations will then be published into books."

I was slowly realizing the massive scale of China's socialist quasi-government operations, and its extreme overregulation and red-tape bureaucracy.

"These books are then sold all over the country and they are bought with public funds. These books can earn you a lot of money," he laughed.

"Did you sell your books directly or did your office handle that?" I asked him, before realizing what a silly question it was.

"No," he laughed again. "The books are sold by the Laws & Regulations Office. The Office makes the money from the book sales and the office rewards us with part of the earnings. So, in terms of work benefits, the Laws & Regulations Office provides rather excellent employee benefits!"

Then he stopped laughing.

"Laws and regulations are tools for deception."

"Laws and regulations have become tools to serve four purposes."

He listed them on his fingers:
1. Getting a promotion
2. Making a fortune

3. Persecuting one's enemies
4. Deceiving the public

"For example, if someone wants to persecute you, they can use laws and regulations however they see fit. Someone may be guilty of a serious crime, but as long as they have a friend in a high position, the laws and regulations don't apply to them. Likewise, someone may be innocent, but if they have enemies in high places, the enemies can use laws and regulations as a tool to persecute."

He spoke with such certainty that I assumed he had been on the giving or receiving end for each of the purposes.

"Lastly, laws and regulations are tools for deception. Officials can claim that they have written so many laws and regulations that they will handle affairs by law. They say that they will rule the country by law, run the government by law, etc. They speak about law all the time but these are all lies."

"I was an official both within the party system and the government. I couldn't even protect myself using the laws and regulations I wrote, let alone other Chinese people." He spoke with authority, but with a sense of defeat. "There isn't any hope for China to realize rule by law."

The High-Ranking Official repositioned himself on his black chair, straightened his navy suit, adjusted his narrow glasses, and wiped his shiny forehead. He then began listing departments on his fingers. I didn't know if they were departments of the government or the CCP. Perhaps few know the difference, or perhaps the difference is irrelevant.

"The Party controls legislation. The Party controls enforcement. The Party controls supervision. The Party controls public security. The Party controls the procuratorate. And the Party controls the courts. The heads of each of those national departments are members of the Political & Legal Affairs Commission, which means they must obey the leadership of the Secretary of the

Political & Legal Affairs Commission. In essence, they are one and the same—they cannot operate independently because of the rule that subordinates must obey their superiors."

"Which rule?" I interrupted.

"All departments must yield to the leadership of the supreme ruler of the CCP Central Committee." That was a rule. "This is the discipline of the Party," he stated.

Could that be the only rule that is consistently maintained in China today? I wondered.

He continued, "The CCP's Constitution sets forth that:
- The subordinate must obey the superior.
- The individual must obey the collective group.
- The minority must obey the majority.
- The entire Party must obey the CCP Central Committee."

I believed the Official, but due diligence compelled me to check the CCP's Constitution for myself.

The same section of the official English translation of the CCP's Constitution from 2002 reads:

> Individual Party members are subordinate to Party organizations, the minority are subordinate to the majority, lower-level Party organizations are subordinate to higher-level Party organizations, and all organizations and members of the Party are subordinate to the National Congress and the Central Committee of the Party.[5]

The English translation from 2017 reads the same, except the thinly veiled "subordinate to" has been replaced with "defers to," which does expose much less bone.[6] I began a collection of CCP cultural euphemisms and placed *'defers to'* into it.

This hierarchical mode of operation—where lower ranks

unconditionally follow the decision of the rank above them, who in turn unconditionally follow the decision of the rank above them, and so on—is called Democratic Centralism. It was formalized by Lenin, and the CCP uses it as its basic principles of operations.

Analyzing the CCP's Constitution proved it to be a dark swamp of filthy euphemisms and muddy lies, covered in mock green moss to hide the depths of its deception. It mostly consists of communist terminology that requires a dictionary for the uninitiated. But be warned, if you read it at face value, without knowledge of the CCP's "two layers of skin" education, you're likely to be taken for a dupe—or a "useful idiot" as Lenin put it—because you'd likely, and incorrectly, think the CCP actually has a heart, and that the interests of its people are at its core.

Here are some examples from the CCP's Constitution:

> "In leading the cause of socialism, the Communist Party of China must continue its commitment to economic development as the central task, and all other work must take an ancillary role and serve this center."

The actual inner skin meaning can be translated as: The CCP's primary goal is to get rich. Nothing is allowed to impede this goal. Nothing. Period. For example, terminal harm to citizens, workers, and the environment can be (and has been) overlooked or bypassed for the sake of achieving wealth.

From the CCP's Constitution:

> "The Communist Party of China represents...the fundamental interests of the greatest possible majority of the Chinese people."

So, in reality, the CCP does *not* represent the interests of *all* Chinese. For example, this statement allows the CCP to justify dehumanizing minority groups and targeting them for elimination, which they have done in many forms over the past decades.

From the CCP's Constitution:

> "China is currently in the primary stage of socialism and will remain so for a long time to come . . . it will take over a century. . . . The Party's highest ideal and ultimate goal is the realization of communism."

This says to Chinese people: Do not expect the CCP to change in this lifetime, or in the lifetime of your children, or your grandchildren. So don't complain about anything. What you have now is the best you're going to get, so be grateful for it, and seek no alternative.

From the CCP's Constitution:

> "The Communist Party of China shall promote long-term prosperity and stability in Hong Kong and Macao and achieve the reunification of the motherland in conformity with the principle of "one country, two systems."

There is no inner skin meaning on this. The outer layer of skin has been removed. It is now clearly unveiled as a lie since the CCP essentially abolished the "one country, two systems" in Hong Kong in May 2020.

From the CCP's Constitution:

> "The Communist Party of China shall uphold its absolute leadership over the People's Liberation Army and other people's armed forces."

That's a rule set in communist stone, taken from the words of Mao's little evil book: "Our principle is that the Party commands the gun, and the gun must never be allowed to command the Party."

From the CCP's Constitution:

> "Leadership of the Communist Party of China is the most essential attribute of socialism."

The inner skin meaning is: Socialism cannot be achieved without the CCP's complete control. Therefore, the CCP must absolutely remain in power.

From the CCP's Constitution:

> "The Communist Party of China shall uphold an independent foreign policy of peace, follow a path of peaceful development... defend world peace, work to build a community with a shared future for mankind, and advance the building of a harmonious world of lasting peace and common prosperity."

The inner skin meaning is: The communist concept of peace is vastly different to the West's concept of peace. It is a term used to deceive. In the words of Vladimir Lenin: "The preaching of 'peace' in the abstract, is one of the means of duping the working class." And: "As an ultimate objective, 'peace' simply means communist world control."

From the CCP's Constitution:

> "The Party exercises overall leadership over all areas of endeavor in every part of the country."

The inner skin meaning is: Every person and entity in every part of China must unconditionally obey the CCP.

This last example about overall leadership, as well as the first example about economic development, are the keys to unlocking the decision-making priorities of the CCP. The goals of these two points can be summarized as:

Absolute national control and *money above all else*.

Thus, any action at all that helps maintain these goals is completely justified, and any other aspect of the constitution can be undermined if it is for the sake of achieving these two goals. This equates to the reality that any aspect of anyone's life in China can be undermined for the sake of achieving *absolute national control* and *money above all else*.

I was beginning to understand what a former Chinese secret agent had meant when he told me in an interview:

"There is no bottom line for political cases in China. You don't have to consider any form of morality, conscience, or give any second thought to your behavior."

The Secret Agent had spoken very plainly, very matter-of-fact, as an officer required to take out enemies of the state.

He said:

"It doesn't matter what methods you use to achieve something, as long as you can resolve the issue."

I used to wonder: *How can Chinese people tolerate and carry out such brutal torture and killing of each other?*

The CCP's Constitution now made it crystal clear. The goals of *absolute national control* and *money above all else* trump any and all other promises made in the constitution. Nothing is more important than these goals, not even human life.

That is wild. I thought.

But there was another constitution that niggled in the back of my mind.

There is a constitution for the government and country called the

MONEY-LAW AND CONSTITUTION

"Disruption of the socialist system by any organization or individual is prohibited."

Constitution of the People's Republic of China. That constitution is generally the most widely known and commonly referred to.

In *Article 1*, it states very clearly that the CCP is in control of the government and the country and that nothing or no one may change that:

> "The socialist system is the basic system of the People's Republic of China. The defining feature of socialism with Chinese characteristics is the leadership of the Communist Party of China. Disruption of the socialist system by any organization or individual is prohibited."[7]

So there are two constitutions of China: one for the Chinese Communist Party and one for the People's Republic of China. Similarly, there are two flags of China: one for the Chinese Communist Party and one for the country. There is also a government of China. The government, the constitutions, the flags—they were all created for and by the CCP. They are all completely and utterly hostage to the CCP and its constitution, which itself is hostage to the CCP's absolute goals.

What about elections and voting? I wondered.

China has elections, but they are also completely beholden to the CCP. The term "election" in CCP culture is a euphemism. It is merely an outer skin meaning to give the appearance of an election but without any real election process. It is a lie.

"We, the Chinese people, actually call elections 'rubber stamps,'" explained the former Secret Agent. "Elections are like the decorations of a house, they don't play any significant role. All elections are fixed. They are single-handedly arranged by the CCP."

It suddenly struck me. The Senior Official that I had interviewed much earlier had been right when he had pointed to me and said: "The perspective you have chosen for your research is wrong."

His words had hurt my pride, but they had cleared my vision. They shook me out of my comfort zone and spurred me to dig deeper.

It was futile to study the operations, formalities, and legalities of China's enormous red-tape bureaucracy that requires massive big-brother-government and mass citizen involvement and participation. It was like trying to study the behavior of bank tellers being held hostage at gunpoint, and ignoring the loaded weapon pointed at their temples—as if their actions and behavior were the same as if they were working freely and by choice.

Every single position, person, law, book, task, and form in China is hostage to one small group of people: the elites who are able to hold the reins of the CCP entity and survive long enough to do its bidding. And all of China must obey. And obey they do.

Is it irony or fate that in 1949—the same year that the CCP took control of China—George Orwell published his famous dystopian novel, *1984*?

Orwell wrote:

> "Every record has been destroyed or falsified, every book rewritten, every picture has been repainted, every statue and street building has been renamed, every date has been altered. And the process is continuing day by day and minute by minute. History has stopped. Nothing exists except an endless present in which the Party is always right."

According to the CCP, it is infallible. And although the CCP may not call itself Big Brother, the reality of Orwell's society and that of the CCP are eerily parallel.

CHAPTER 7

Little Brown Birds

At about five inches in length and weighing less than an ounce, the Eurasian tree sparrow is a little brown bird, with a short black beak, a cheerful chirp, and no defense against the bigger birds that want it for dinner. The sparrow pecks at grain and seed and lice and spiders and centipedes and other little bugs it can find to eat.

"According to ancient Chinese books," explained a former CCP role-model student, "within the food chain, sparrows eat harmful insects, but they also eat rice crops. So as long as you protect the rice crops, you will be fine."

The thought of little birds tweeting and flying about was a pleasant distraction.

"When I was little," he continued, "society was eliminating four pests or four 'evils.' Sparrows were deemed a pest, so it was decided to eliminate all the sparrows."

Sparrow-cide? That just sounded stupid. It had to be an error. I wondered if the translator wasn't keeping up with the incredibly fast speech of this very articulate man who had always been an active thinker. He had been touted as a model for CCP students in his youth, gained master degrees in engineering and applied mathematics, and later received a doctorate of philosophy in China Studies in the West. He was able to apply for the official title of Professor in China, but instead chose intellectual freedom outside the Mainland, so I chose to call him the Chinese Professor for short.

The Chinese Professor had warmed up in the interview and was now pouring out his memories at such a fast rate that it required intense concentration on my part.

"But the CCP wants to do things differently to the old ways. So it wants to destroy all the sparrows," he said.

"That's ridiculous," I blurted out, stopping him in his tracks. But he barely took a breath and responded immediately:

"It's not that the CCP doesn't know that destroying sparrows will cause problems. This is the CCP's methodology. It wants to use these methods to add continual *struggle* to people's lives. So you are told it is necessary to eliminate sparrows."

> **"Why did everyone agree to kill the sparrows?" "At that time, people had been brainwashed by the CCP to just the right degree."**

Again, the term *struggle*. That word would continue to trouble me for years to come. But for now, I just couldn't get past the little brown birds.

"I don't know this story," I told him. "You have to explain it to me."

He described lines of trucks piled high with mountains of dead little birds.

It sounded so absurd, but he was telling the truth. Fact-checking his story later proved how ignorant I was of one of the worst environmental disasters in history.

Where is the media and educational materials on that? I thought. Especially now, when political environmentalism is a top priority global agenda item in public education, why aren't we taught about the results of perhaps the most extreme environmental catastrophe ever?

"Why did everyone agree to kill the sparrows?" I asked the Professor.

"At that time, people had been brainwashed by the CCP to just the right degree and they believed everything the CCP said."

It was true. And I found no shortage of primary evidence:

I looked at full-color posters declaring death to those nasty, pestilent, evil sparrows. I watched black-and-white, yet clear-as-day footage of public parades, complete with sign boards and model animals on posts, calling for death to the little birds. I saw the "gloriously heartwarming" activity of people of all ages working together to bring death to the little birds.

I saw men and youths aim and fire at them with pistols and slingshots. I searched for evidence of the birds shot down by balls or bullets but I didn't find any. Perhaps the precision of China's 1950's weapons were not accurate enough for untrained peasants to shoot the tiny targets very well, or perhaps no evidence of that method of killing exists because a bullet going through a little brown bird would leave little more than a little, bloody mess.

Mostly the masses yelled and screamed at the sparrows. People became living scarecrows, swatting at the birds with long sticks and branches. As soon as a little bird perched anywhere to take a rest to calm its pounding heart and catch the breath in its tiny lungs, the masses would scream and yell and swat and

CCP poster: "Exterminate the four pests!"
(Source: Chineseposters.net)

"Eliminating the last sparrow"
(Source: Chineseposters.net)

"Everybody must get to work to eliminate the sparrows"
(Source: Chineseposters.net)

harass again—over and over and over—until the little bird finally dropped dead in the dirt from exhaustion. One by one, they all dropped dead. And this happened again and again and again, all across the nation.

In the excitement of their success in the struggle against nature, masses of people gathered sparrow upon sparrow and tied their little bodies together, forming long, brown, feathery braids.

In single file, the braids were presented to seated communist officials who recorded the official count of the dead to report to higher authorities. The larger the number of dead birds, the greater the praise from the CCP. It is likely that those areas that didn't present enough dead little birds were somehow penalized, but I didn't search hard enough to find any evidence to prove that.

Perhaps some unlucky little birds were only exhausted and not dead. If they did awaken, being tied together, they would eventually die of hunger. Or perhaps they would be crushed, or suffocated beneath the giant sparrow hills that were driven off in rows of trucks into the sunset of a communist heaven.

There is no exact number of how many sparrows were originally living in China in that year of 1958. But it is estimated that hundreds of thousands were killed. Had there been a sparrow for each person in the nation, there would have been more than 600 million. But by the end of the same year, very few sparrows remained.

"Then what happened?" I asked the Professor.

"The next year, the crops were destroyed by insects. All the crops in all the places without sparrows had barely a single grain of food to harvest. Insect borne disease became severe and people had to starve again."

I learned what Chinese people do not learn and are not allowed to learn in China:

Up to 45 million[8] men, women, and children died of mass starvation in the devastating famine that followed the sparrow-cide. It was far worse than an environmental disaster. It is the worst recorded mass starvation in history. Yet in China, this is not taught. It is not even spoken of. And although we in the West have relatively easy access to information about it, it is hardly even common knowledge here.

> **A human being who is beholden to communist culture is prevented from using terms that value honesty above political needs. So they call the mass starvation of millions of people a "natural disaster."**

The disaster was compounded by man-made socialist design. New and untested agricultural policies were imported from Soviet Russia, and throughout China all farmers were mandated by the CCP to use the new Soviet farming techniques. It was another Marxist method to struggle with nature, and to destroy the old time-proven methods and implement the new.

The new techniques were a complete and utter failure, and compounded the problem created by the sparrow-cide.

Worst of all—and what is never mentioned in China—there was food and grain piled high in many large storehouses. And it was intentionally left to rot, or was exported to other countries as foreign aid to give the false perception of a booming Chinese economy.

Of course, CCP officials didn't starve. They fed themselves, while millions of citizens were forced to die slowly and painfully from malnutrition and starvation, desperately eating anything they could—from dirt and sawdust to leather, and even family members who were either murdered and eaten, or exhumed and consumed from their graves.

I am wrong to say that the sparrow-cide and famine are not spoken of in China. It is allowed to be mentioned, but only within the confines of the communist language and culture, which I came to learn doesn't require any honesty or accurate representation. Therefore, such a disaster can only be mentioned as a euphemism—a more pleasant-sounding word that waters down or hides the truth.

In the sparrow-cide example, a human being who holds honesty as an integral value in their culture would describe the famine as a mass starvation of millions of people, or something to that effect. Yet a human being who is beholden to communist culture is prevented from using terms that value honesty above political needs. So they call the mass starvation of millions of people a "natural disaster." Yes—a *natural disaster*.

Chinese history books, teachers, and therefore students refer to this period in history as: *The Three Years of Natural Disaster*. And with a benign term like that, teachers have been taught to disassociate honesty from truth, and this has been passed on to generation after generation of Chinese students who have grown up to be the mainstay of Chinese society. They not only don't know the real cause behind the tragedy of the little brown birds, they believe that it was never a tragedy at all.

CHAPTER 8

Parasite

The American Heritage Dictionary defines a parasite as:

> *An organism that lives and feeds on or in an organism of a different species and causes harm to its host; or*

> *One who habitually takes advantage of the generosity of others without making any useful return.*

The Cambridge Dictionary offers an additional, disapproving definition:

> *A person who is lazy and lives by other people working, giving them money, etc.*

"The CCP lives like a parasite," said the Chinese Professor and former CCP model student.

Thinking about a political regime as a parasitic organism seemed like a bizarre concept, but the Professor took me on another journey toward a new understanding.

"This situation began a long time ago when the CCP connected a CCP position to every other position of power. Within the system, the levels match. For example, a Military Chief has a CCP equivalent position: Chief Party Secretary. A Regiment Commander has a CCP equivalent position: Regiment Party Secretary."

"What is the difference between them?" I asked.

"They are two different positions—the Commander is in charge of commanding, but the CCP Secretaries actually manage the entire military."

"So the secretaries run the show?" I asked, realizing he was not describing the stereotypical female typists of the West.

Patrick Ling, PhD, "The Chinese Professor and CCP Model Student."

"There is a CCP Committee above them and the CCP Committee Secretary is above them. The Chief and the Commanders [non-CCP positions] are only Vice Secretaries or Standing Committee members. They would never receive a secretary position."

My face must have shown my confusion.

"Every single level has two troops—every single level." He emphasized. "And between these two troops, they always emphasize that the CCP is the leader. So the CCP always has the final say."

"Why do they do this?" he asked me. Perhaps he had read my mind.

He then answered himself, "They require that everything must be done according to the CCP's ideology, so every position has to be connected to the CCP at its foundation."

"It's all-pervasive," explained another former CCP member who had spent his life working as a heart surgeon at a CCP hospital. "China's Communist Party system controls every system."

I couldn't help but think of a Hollywood sci-fi dystopia. It was the only popular analogy I could quickly visualize, thanks to the lack of public education about socialism. I pictured one system succumbing to another as a dark web descended down the spine of every entity, every organization, every operation, tying each to the other, before extending toward every individual comprising the masses of the general public.

Hong Yuan, "The Heart Surgeon."

> **"In China, you can't just form an organization because you want to. You have to be approved by a leader. They have to be in charge of your leadership, ideological guidance, management, and regulation."**

"Take my hospital for example," continued the Heart Surgeon. "There are three tiers of Communist Party Organization. First, there is a Party Committee controlling the hospital as a whole. Next, for each major department, including the Department of Thoracic Surgery, the Department of Cardiac Surgery, the Department of Urology, and the Department of General Surgery, and so on, these all have a secondary organization called the General Communist Party Branch. Then, under that, within each department, there is a regular Communist Party Branch. These are the three tiers of the Communist Party Organizations."

Communist Party branches aren't just a requirement for state operated entities. For example, a 2016 CCP news report states:

> "Since the nation opened up its market in the late 1970s, Party branches have existed in foreign companies. Now over 40,000 foreign companies are operating in Shanghai. GE's [General Electric] headquarters in Shanghai has fourteen Party branches and over 600 Party members."[9]

And it isn't just businesses, government, legal, and law enforcement operations that require parasitic CCP leadership attachment.

"In China, you can't just form an organization because you want to," stated the Senior Official. "You have to be approved by a leader, an authoritative organization. They have to be in charge of your leadership, ideological guidance, management, and regulation."

I looked at the Heart Surgeon sitting in the interview chair opposite me. After researching the activities of CCP branches in businesses and other operations in China, I hoped that the surgeon would be able to give some tangible examples of what CCP branches actually do beyond enforcing CCP thought control.

"How do they help you?" I asked the Surgeon. "What do they do for the hospital?"

"We don't need them, they need us!" he retorted. "They need us to help them do things. They control us. They control what we can say. What they require us to do are things that are outside of what our jobs are—things unrelated to treating patients. The more things we do for them, the more time we waste. Overall, they are harmful and provide no benefit to citizens."

"If they are part of the hospital, don't they have to care about the patients you treat?" I asked. I still couldn't grasp that the CCP didn't actually *do* anything outside of enforcing Party rule.

He shook his head at me. "They don't care how we doctors treat patients. They don't care about these things."

"Then what do they care about?" I prodded.

He paused and narrowed his eyes.

I had told him early in the interview that it would be most useful if he could speak in a way that would help Western people understand his experience. With me being in my early 40s this educated man would have assumed I was familiar with the Tiananmen Massacre of June 4, 1989. Everyone in their 50s, 60s, 70s in the West saw the footage of tanks rolling into the square that night and students being shot. Following that, thousands of Chinese students were provided safety and refuge in Western countries. Had I been younger, it's quite possible I might have been unaware of that tragedy and he might have chosen a different example.

"Let me give you an example," he began. "After the June 4 Tiananmen Square massacre in 1989, the student movement was labelled a violent uprising against the regime. Because some of our hospital staff had supported the student movement, the staff were all under immediate investigation and all CCP members at the hospital were forced to re-register with the CCP."

Having to re-register sounded completely benign. I imagined checking some boxes, signing some forms, paying some fees. But the CCP is not a social club from which one can come and go. It is closer to a secret society or a cult, where Party membership is sacred and hard won, and all succeeding members must pledge the solemn oath as written in the CCP's Constitution:

> "It is my will to join the Communist Party of China, uphold the Party's program, observe the provisions of the Party Constitution, fulfill the obligations of a Party member, carry out the Party's decisions, strictly observe Party discipline, protect Party secrets, be loyal to the Party, work

hard, fight for communism for the rest of my life, always be prepared to sacrifice my all for the Party and the people, and never betray the Party."

Having to re-register with the Party meant that your loyalty to the Party was now under suspicion. It meant that you may be accused of the ultimate dishonor: betraying the CCP. It then means going through a process of interrogation, thought examination, intense personal scrutiny, re-education, and active devotion to prove your renewed and re-strengthened loyalty to the Party, which can take any amount of time. And if you don't succeed at it, you face imprisonment and the loss of all Party benefits, from a steady wage, to health care, to education for your children, and housing for your family.

The CCP demands and enforces complete obedience from its members.

> **"For Westerners this type of thing is inconceivable, but for a Chinese person, this is a very normal thing. Because as far as the CCP is concerned, whether or not it can control the lives of all its citizens is its top priority. As for the life and death of its citizens, it doesn't care."**

The Surgeon continued his story:

"I was a young doctor working in the patient ward at the time. I received phone calls from the Emergency Room calling for doctors to go to the Emergency Room to treat patients. But all the doctors had been called away from the Emergency Room to undertake political studies and re-register with the Party. They were not allowed to go to the Emergency Room. There were no doctors in the Emergency Room!"

"So if a patient was very ill, even if they died there, no one would care."

He saw me grimace.

"For Westerners this type of thing is inconceivable, but for a Chinese person, this is a very normal thing. Because as far as the CCP is concerned, whether or not it can control the lives of all its citizens is its top priority. As for the life and death of its citizens, it doesn't care."

Parasites rely on their hosts to survive. They embed themselves either inside or outside their hosts and exploit them, feed on them, reduce their health, and modify their behavior. Some parasites cleverly rely on their hosts to carry out activities that they would have otherwise had to do for themselves. In the case of bedbugs, lice, and fleas, since they rely on their hosts for food and transportation, they don't have to worry about flying or walking anywhere to find their next meal. Instead, they take advantage of easy food and shelter and focus all their attention and energy on reproduction.

Some parasites are *social parasites*—social insects that parasitize colonies of other social insects. One type of social parasite found in some ant colonies is a forceful slave-maker.

For example, the Polyergus ant raids other ant colonies, steals their unborn ants, and either eats them or chemically imprints them so that they become fully integrated with the society of their enslaver. These slave-maker parasites cannot function without their slaves. They rely on having at least 90 percent of their workforce being slaves to gather food and feed them, tend to the queen and young, and defend their nest. The slaves will even carry the slave-makers to a new nest if they need to move.

The slave-maker parasites may not be capable at basic survival

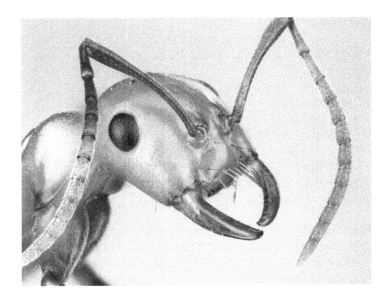

Polyergus "slave-maker" ants use their sharp sickle-like mandibles on any workers who resist enslavement.
(Source: Public domain image by Alex Wild)

tasks, but they are particularly good at raiding other colonies. They use their sharp sickle-like mandibles on any workers who resist enslavement. They also have particularly large glands from which they can release secretions that pacify new slaves or cause their targets to fight each other instead of the enslaver.

The Chinese Professor's use of the term "parasite" to describe the Chinese Communist Party's embedment into its nation host of China and its people no longer seemed like a far-fetched concept.

CHAPTER 9
Dear Mother

"Those who were shocked by the June 1989 Beijing massacre and repression of pro democracy demonstrators should not have been. Such cruelty and mass killing are a way of life in China. Indeed, no other people in this century except Soviet citizens have suffered so much mass killing in cold blood as have the Chinese."

~ R. J. Rummel, Author of *Death By Government* (2017)

According to a recently (2017) declassified secret diplomatic cable from Sir Alan Donald, the then-British ambassador to China on the eve of June 4, 1989, student protesters on Tiananmen Square were told they had one hour to leave before the military came in. But after only five minutes, armed personnel carriers (APCs)—military tanks—attacked them.

"Students linked arms but they were mown down, including soldiers. APCs then ran over bodies time and time again to make 'pie' and remains collected by bulldozer. Remains incinerated and then hosed down drains...

Four wounded girl students begged for their lives but were bayoneted. A 3-year old girl was injured but her mother was shot as she went to her aid as were six others who tried...

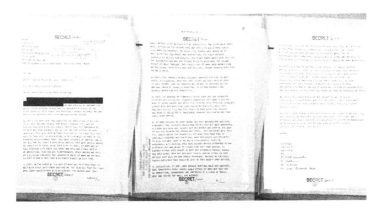

Declassified secret diplomatic cable from Sir Alan Donald, the then-British ambassador to China on the eve of June 4, 1989.

(Source: Public domain)

1,000 survivors were told they could escape via Zhenyi Lu [road] but were then mown down by specifically prepared M/G [machine gun] positions. Army ambulances who attempted to give aid were shot up . . .

Estimate of civilians dead: 10,000."

This account is said to have been provided by a reliable source who "was passing on information given him by a close friend who is currently a member of the State Council," and who had previously proven themselves "careful to separate fact from speculation and rumor."[10]

Ten thousand is the highest and most official death count of the Tiananmen Square massacre to date. Yet, despite the enormous number of eyewitness accounts, live news footage, and photographs of death and destruction at the time, the CCP still calls it "that political event" and refuses to discuss it. The "event" doesn't exist in China's history books.

"If I have to shoot 200,000 students to save China from another 100 years of disorder, so be it."

In a rare public admission to foreign media soon after the massacre, former Chinese official, Jiang Zemin—who strongly endorsed the massacre and who would later rise upon its blood to become the next Chinese dictator and initiate the nationwide eradication of peaceful Falun Gong meditators—gave journalists his comments on the Tiananmen Massacre:

"We don't think it's a tragedy," he said calmly and without any hesitation in front of unsmiling Western and Chinese media with their cameras and notepads. He seemed to smirk as he continued, "The Tiananmen event was a counterrevolutionary riot attempting to overthrow our Communist Party and socialism."

Watching his statement in archival footage,[11] I found his demeanor and heartlessness far beyond creepy.

Former Chinese dictator, Deng Xiaoping, commented on that "event":

> "If I have to shoot 200,000 students to save China from another 100 years of disorder, so be it."

The concept of "disorder" in CCP terms is vastly different from what we know and experience in the West.

Digging deeper into the news archives of the days that came after the massacre, we found footage that never appears in news reports in the West. It would be too confusing to include it in reports that commemorate the loss of life on that day. Yet, footage of one particular memorial event that was staged on Tiananmen Square, not long after the massacre, became etched in my mind:

Thousands of unarmed soldiers stand upright and stiff in spotless uniforms and perfect rows on a grey day on the freshly cleaned square. Beside them stand preteen boys and girls in white and blue clothes, each with the signature red scarf of the CCP Youth League organization tied neatly around their little necks.

Four preteen girls in crisp white shirts, red ties, and red skirts reaching just above their knees walk solemnly toward a front stage. They are observed by CCP officials and military leaders, and surrounded by CCP media cameras and reporters. The girls carry a giant memorial wreath to the front stage and then bow, leaving their heads low as the cameras stay close on their synchronized movements.

A middle-aged female soldier stands motionless—and emotionless—before an enormous pile of wreaths and flowers that extend well up above her head. She is poised with an impressive military rifle diagonally across her body. The rifle sports an overly large red bow, like a decorative ribbon on a gift, on its middle section. The bow is almost the size of her head. It would be comical if the whole situation wasn't so sinister.

A small number of carefully selected parents cry uncontrollably in front of a framed photograph of a young male. Cameras draw in close to capture their extreme and miserable display of grief.

This memorial filmed by CCP cameras is a show-memorial. It is a facade. And all the actors upon the square must act out their roles.

The show-memorial is the outer skin of the Tiananmen Massacre—the euphemistic visual propaganda to calm and appease the masses, and lay blame on the students who "rioted" on Tiananmen Square and "deserved to die."

At this show-memorial, the CCP "memorialized" a small number of soldiers who died on June 4, most likely by their fellow soldiers—but no one dares think that, let alone say it aloud.

**The CCP's
show-memorial
on Tiananmen
Square in 1989.**

(Source: Screenshots taken from CCP television footage)

> ## "A considerable part of the population are severely brainwashed by the CCP, poisoned to a very deep level. They think that the CCP's murdering of people is correct."

Nationwide, every Chinese person, at every workplace, school, and organization, was required to watch the CCP "news" of this show-memorial to learn that the "students killed the soldiers in a political event" on Tiananmen Square, and that the soldiers were heroes of the Party and of the people.

In the following days and months, every Chinese person across the nation saw and heard of students being arrested, sentenced, and imprisoned for being involved in the political event.

"A considerable part of the population are severely brainwashed by the CCP, poisoned to a very deep level," explained another Official. "They think that the CCP's murdering of people is correct. They think the CCP did the right thing on June 4th 1989. They think the students who 'made trouble' deserved to be killed."

That is a rule of socialism. Socialists believe that people can, will, and should be killed for the sake of socialist goals.

At the close of the show-memorial on Tiananmen Square, thousands of elementary school students hold their red scarves with both hands at a unified height above their heads.

In a practiced ritual, they chant in unison:

"We love the Chinese Communist Party!"

A young boy and girl at the front of the stage scream with extreme zeal into microphones that thunder their voices far and wide. The masses repeat their cry.

"We love the socialist motherland!" they yell.

The sea of red babes on the square return their call:

"We will continue on the cause of communism!"

All of the CCP insiders we interviewed had something to say about the indoctrination they experienced in their youth.

"In China, the brainwashing is very subtle. You complain about it, but you still always discipline yourself according to the CCP's rules."

"I've struggled to get rid of the brainwash and I don't want my child to be brainwashed like all the others," said one insider.

Another said:

"When I was in middle school, pretty much everybody had to join the CCP Youth League. It is the backbone force of the CCP, the CCP's backbone army. Only after you join the Youth League can you join the CCP later on. Only after you join the CCP party can you get promoted in your adult career."

An older insider said, "In school, my teacher told me there were three big steps in life:

Step 1: Join the Young Pioneers CCP organization.
Step 2: Join the Youth League CCP organization.
Step 3: Join the CCP.

"I was the first to join the CCP out of my class. I was extremely proud. My love for the CCP . . . my thoughts had always been with the CCP."

Another Official said:

"In China, the brainwashing is very subtle. When we go to elementary school we are encouraged to become young communist pioneer members with a red scarf. We are given a rank of one or two stripes and those who aren't members will be upset. That's brainwashing. Later you find yourself just following the CCP. You complain about it, but you still always discipline yourself according to the CCP's rules."

The testimony from these insiders was bringing the concept of indoctrination—of being "raised by the Party from birth"—to life in my mind. And the footage from the CCP's show-memorial gave it an outer skin of living color.

A younger CCP worker, in her 40's, explained what current indoctrination was like for her young child growing up in today's China:

"In preschool, kids are required to recite socialist political philosophy. When the kids go to elementary school, they are required to join the CCP Young Pioneers organization to stay close to the CCP's ideology. If he doesn't or can't join, he will be viewed as abnormal. He may be lonely and isolated from his peers because others will think he makes no effort to improve his position in life. Then in secondary school, only if you become a CCP Youth League member will you have hope of a good future."

"All the CCP's philosophy and political indoctrination are formed during these stages. Under this form of education, everyone more or less loses some of their respect for universal values."

"Children cannot understand Marxist philosophy," said the Chinese Professor, "so they make you understand and make you say: 'I am the successor of communism,' which is basically saying that I will definitely follow you when I grow up. They also take an oath: 'I will definitely follow the CCP when I grow up.' "

The CCP follows what Lenin had said: "Give me just one generation of youth, and I'll transform the whole world."

"When we are in kindergarten we sing their songs, we watch their movies," said another insider. "There are events, programs, slogans. It's all, 'Without the CCP there would be no New China' and 'Our blood is CCP culture,' 'Loving your motherland means loving China and loving the CCP.' From kindergarten we are educated that *China*, the *motherland*, is the same as the *CCP*. So this is what we think."

"Because the CCP always tells citizens how good it is," explained another insider, "whenever the Communist Party is mentioned, people have come to associate it with warmth, as if it was their own, dear mother's love."

The visual of the sea of red babes on Tiananmen Square holding their blood red scarves and calling loudly for their beloved socialist motherland sent a chill down my spine.

The strength and persistence of this feeling was reinforced by one of our translators when we stopped for a break during an interview. She rushed out from the translation room, clasping her chest.

"That's what it's like for me!" she exclaimed. "I've been living outside of China for years, and I hate the CCP, but I still feel it. When I hear the term *CCP* I instinctively feel a warmth in my chest, as if I was thinking about my own mother."

Her face was twisted into a terrible frown, revealing a deep sense of personal violation and complex guilt for still feeling a loving warmth toward her lifelong persecutor.

He'd been taught since birth that his captor's happiness was above his own happiness.

"I've been taught to feel this since I was young. It's so uncomfortable to recognize that I still have these uncontrolled thoughts and feelings that were put into me by the CCP."

As an outsider, it was hard for me to understand the depth of this love and warmth toward the CCP, knowing the unforgivable oppression and manipulation it had subjected these people to against their wills.

Are their feelings like that of a hostage who begins to love his kidnapper? I wondered.

CCP poster: "We love the motherland" (Source: Chineseposters.net)

The Stockholm Syndrome I'd read about in stories is defined by Encyclopedia Britannica as:

> "The psychological response wherein a captive begins to identify closely with his or her captors, as well as with their agenda and demands."

It elaborates:

> "Psychologists who have studied the syndrome believe that the bond is initially created when a captor threatens a captive's life, deliberates, and then chooses not to kill the captive. The captive's relief at the removal of the death threat is transposed into feelings of gratitude toward the captor for giving him or her life."

> "The survival instinct is at the heart of the Stockholm

syndrome. Victims live in enforced dependence and interpret rare or small acts of kindness in the midst of horrible conditions as good treatment. They often become hypervigilant to the needs and demands of their captors, making psychological links between the captors' happiness and their own."

I began to view those subjected to the poison of the CCP culture in a different light.

Were they captives of a brutal captor of a nation? Did they have to adapt and prioritize the happiness of their captor over any personal happiness to survive? Is that the reality of the socialist policy of submitting to the "will of the majority"? I wondered.

In a later interview, the Chinese Diplomat described how his father was killed when he was three years old for speaking to a higher authority on behalf of his fellow villagers. For his actions, he was tortured for a week and then released, only to die at home shortly after.

"At the time I never thought much about that," said the Diplomat. Later, as a young man he "appreciated the Communist Party because I was born in a village and was taught I should appreciate the Communist Party for giving me a chance to enter university."

The CCP murdered his father, yet he thanked the regime sincerely for allowing him to get an education because he'd been taught since birth that his captor's happiness was above his own happiness of

"These methods have created a mass of ignorant people brainwashed by China's propaganda. If the interests of these ignorant fools are seriously jeopardized, then they would become a violent mob."

having a father in his life. And the CCP had no concern that its child was now fatherless, because the regime had already placed itself as both mother and father of the nation and all its children.

A former CCP Labor Camp Director gave a more current example:

"Recently a CCP magazine published an article criticizing the concept: 'Love for the country does not equal love for the CCP.' It says this concept is wrong."

I had to do a double take on his words. It was a typically convoluted communist cultural way of saying: A CCP magazine was making clear to the public that to love China, you must love the CCP.

"The article explains that the CCP came *before* China—that the CCP came first and then came China—so if you want to love China, you *have* to love the CCP," said the Labor Camp Director.

"What kind of logic is that?" he asked me.

There's no logic to that, I wanted to say, knowing that China existed for thousands of years before the CCP ever surfaced. However, my Western logic was equating logic with *truth*. In communist culture, logic and truth are not required to be associated with each other.

The Labor Camp Director continued:

"How many years has the CCP been around? How many years has China been around? They just use this kind of deceptive concept of reversing the truth, inverting black and white to fool people. They have created a sustained deception of the masses by creating and changing history and facts, and switching right and wrong."

He had been outside of China for more than a decade, and had time to think outside the box of the CCP culture and question all the CCP baby mash he'd swallowed since birth.

"When information is not balanced and you don't have access to any other information, people believe it. These methods have created a mass of ignorant people brainwashed by China's propaganda. If the interests of these ignorant fools are seriously jeopardized, then they would become a violent mob. Very few of them would use peaceful, logical reasoning to promote democracy or rule of law."

Now I was understanding the venom behind attacks I had seen and had received when speaking out about abuses against Chinese citizens by the Chinese Communist Party. These attacks had come from Chinese citizens themselves—most often a mob of them with a barrage of verbal or online nasty name-calling that included labels, such as *anti-China, anti-Chinese, racist,* and so on.

These mob-like attacks seemed bizarre. Why would Chinese attack anyone trying to protect their fellow Chinese?

Yet, these mobs now have a name, *wu mao,* which is translated as *50 Cent Army* in English. Some of these mob "soldiers" are volunteer CCP patriots; others are paid a few cents (hence the name, *50 Cent Army*) by the CCP for every angry post they make online to attack anyone critical of the regime. A large portion of this army are tech-savvy youths. They are the red babes who have today matured under the molding hands of the CCP.

Another insider further explained the red babes' behavior:

"If your brain is like a computer and the data that is put into it all comes in from only one source, then the results you get from your brain will all be in that same direction."

My brain had to process his analogy for a moment before it made sense.

"After Chinese people have been brainwashed for a long time, everything they think about, their decision-making processes

...they all come from what they learned from the CCP. They automatically think that way," he said.

"Education in China is very scary," said another CCP member. "In Chinese university education, more than half the time is spent studying the CCP's things. In a situation like that how can young Chinese people learn the truth? They cannot."

I watched a British TV news program from 2011,[12] where a Western reporter interviewed a small group of 20-year-old Chinese students from a prestigious university in China. He asked them about their views on China's political system in comparison to the political systems of the West. The students all agreed as one of them explained their point of view:

> "[Winston] Churchill said, I don't know if it's his exact words, but he said: 'Democracy might not be the best thing, but it's the best choice so far.' Also for China, the Chinese government and the political structure of the Chinese government might not be the best thing, but it is the best thing for China and we don't see any possible alternatives to the current government. So of course we will support it because it is the stabilizer, it is the protector of this country . . ."

At this point in the television interview, the student's serious expression lightened. Her eyes brightened and she revealed a warm smile as she spoke about her *protector*.

> ". . . it is the protector of this country, which is so vast that it's embedded with problems, with conflicts, and we're just lucky that there is someone there taking care of it."

Back in 1989, at the CCP's show-memorial upon Tiananmen Square, the sea of red babes, with red scarves held high above their innocent minds, would never know that merely days before, the bloody red "pie" of thousands of their older brothers and sisters was ground and minced by their Dear Red Mother in the very same place where they now stood and called for her.

And by the end of that fateful year, the regime had further reiterated its all-powerful constitutional statement of: "The socialist system is the fundamental system of the People's Republic of China." It further propagandized that statement with a new poster that read: Only socialism can save China, Only socialism can develop China.

That year, a segment of Chinese people had tried to escape their captor. They had failed and suffered the consequences. Those who remained either closed their tearful eyes to the hope for hope, or swallowed the CCP's false narrative and continued to carry the weighty red flag for the regime.

Regardless of their inner turmoils, the entire population became bound ever tighter to the Communist Party's determination to survive upon them.

CHAPTER 10

Ad Break No.1

2016 CHINESE ARMY RECRUITMENT
COMMERCIAL[13]:

Low, tense music.

Close up on two male hands wearing pristine white
gloves against a black background. One gloved hand
adjusts the glove of the other hand. His sleeves and chest
are partially visible. Army green. Shiny gold buttons.

A soldier's gloved hand rests on his shoulder. His
youthful mouth and chin are out of focus. The fine detail
of his soft white gloves are in focus. The soldier moves
his hand downward to reveal a gold badge attached to
the shoulder of his uniform.

Two gloved hands reverently holding a Chinese army hat
raise the hat upward. The torso of the soldier's uniform
is visible. A single star is embossed in his golden belt.

The soldier places the hat on his neatly shaven short-
back-and-sides haircut.

Extreme close up: gloved finger tips stroke across the soldier's chest and reveal a shiny red flag badge.

Music tension rises. Red glow of flaming embers fade in and out behind big, bold, flame-filled Chinese characters.

A deep Chinese militaristic voice begins to boom:

MILITARY VOICE:
Keep your mission in your mind
Have your enemies in your eyes...
A war can break out anytime
Are you ready for it?

Young soldiers ready their weapons, from fists to guns to missiles, to tanks and aircraft. Bombs explode.

Music pounds to a heavy beat.

A Chinese rap musician spits out words, hard and fast, as a chorus of voices call back to him:

RAPPER:
Are you afraid?

CHORUS:
NO!

RAPPER:
Are you scared?

CHORUS:
NO!

RAPPER:
Just wait for the order!

CHORUS:
KILL! KILL! KILL!

I shuddered listening to the translation of the aggressive-sounding lyrics in the Chinese army recruitment commercial. It was so far removed from the army recruitment ads I grew up watching on television in the West, which glorified the act of protecting human life—not taking it.

The Chinese rap words went on and on. "Even if the bullet passes through my chest . . . The murderous spirit flares up . . . Just like the hammer and sickle, we join as one . . ."

"The murderous spirit flares up . . . Just like the hammer and sickle, we join as one."

For the final words of the song, voices call in unison: "KILL!"

And then the final words appear on screen: "It's the glory of your youth."

FADE TO BLACK

CHAPTER 11

Daughter, Go Watch the Slaughter

"On June 4, 1989, the day of the Tiananmen Square massacre, I was in the office of the Ministry of Public Security, the heart of the operations. My younger daughter was at home in Beijing. I told her to rush out to see it," said the Senior Official.

"To see what?" I asked, rather stunned by his admission.

"I told her to go see how the CCP kills its own people," he answered. "Otherwise she would regret it for the rest of her life."

I wasn't following his logic.

"I told my daughter the words of Lenin," he said, trying to help me understand. "Lenin said, 'One day of revolution is worth twenty years.' "

Now he's quoting Lenin! I sighed to myself. That did not help at all.

My only exposure to Lenin had been in selective quotes published in books or supposed Lenin quotes in random, untrustworthy memes that appeared in dubious internet searches. I was struggling to understand his story and he seemed to have little patience for ignorant interviewers who couldn't instinctively read the two skins of CCP cultural thinking at the same time.

Does one need to be a communist to understand a communist?
I wondered.

My grandmother would turn in her grave if she knew I was about to buy some of Lenin's original works in print. (She probably would be shocked to know that they are still in print.)

I'd been taught to never breathe the names of Lenin and Stalin and the Red Russians, unless they were in the context of condemnation of their evil slaughter of the Russian people and their destruction of the Russian culture and the Orthodox *Old-Believers* religion, who were the *White Russians*. But even then, it was best not to mention them at all. The names and deeds of the Reds bore the mark of the red devil himself.

Now, thirty years after my grandmother's death, I was drinking of the very poison she had prayed daily that we would never encounter. It made me uncomfortable, but I had to try and stand in someone else's communist shoes—I had to be able to think like a communist to be able to understand communist culture to the degree I felt was necessary.

The translator and the Senior Official were discussing Lenin's quote between themselves in Chinese. The translator had been in the West for over a decade and was never in the ranks of CCP officials.

"Your generation doesn't understand," the Senior Official told the translator as bluntly as he had been speaking to me.

"I told my daughter to hurry up and go see how the CCP kills its own people. Unless you witness it with your own eyes, you won't understand the extent of the CCP's evil nature."

I interrupted their conversation. We had already gone over our expected interview time and we had to focus.

"Why did you say that?" I asked the Official, trying to get to the bottom of why he ordered his daughter to watch the slaughter.

The translator mistranslated my question to: "Why did *Lenin* say that?"

The interviewee looked at me as if I'd never passed the second grade.

"Lenin was praising his revolution," he said with raised eyebrows. "One day of revolution equals twenty years!"

"No, no, no," I interjected, trying to keep my patience and save our conversation from degrading further into a comedic skit around the old game of *Chinese Whispers*.

"Why did he," I pointed to the Official but looked at the translator, "say that to his daughter on the day of the Tiananmen Square massacre? Why did he tell his daughter that she had to go and watch the killing?"

The translator quickly and correctly translated my question.

The Official huffed but willingly repeated himself, this time more slowly and clearly.

"I told my daughter to hurry up and go see how the CCP kills its own people. Unless you witness it with your own eyes, you won't understand the extent of the CCP's evil nature. Only if you witness how the CCP slaughters its own people can you truly understand the CCP."

The Official then turned to the translator to further explain why he quoted Lenin to his daughter. "To witness violent struggle firsthand is equivalent to twenty or thirty years experience of dealing with the CCP."

The translator and I both nodded. We finally understood this official's intention to awaken his daughter by requiring her to witness the coldblooded killing of brother and brother, and sister and sister by the order of the CCP. Perhaps it was the only way he could share with her a mere fraction of the bloodshed and anti-human behavior he had been part of throughout his decades of fighting for the CCP.

Hao Ye, "The Senior Official."

"You wouldn't really understand it if I just told you about it, would you?" the Senior Official asked, looking between the translator and me with his palms out and facing upward.

The translator nodded his head, but I didn't want to agree.

If no one could understand it even if they are told about it—

wouldn't that render my research futile? It would mean I wouldn't be able to understand the stories of China's Walking Dead, and therefore, anyone I tried to communicate these stories to wouldn't be able to understand them either.

Why should I bother? You can't understand. That was what this Official seemed to think, and why he seemed so apathetic to my questioning and so resistant to help enlighten me. Why should he bother trying to find words to express what he experienced—what life is really like for China's Walking Dead—if he knew I didn't speak the language of his CCP culture and if he believed I could never understand his life, their lives, without actually living it myself.

The Senior Official had been privy to the discussion and direction of the CCP elites. He had been required to carry out many CCP experiments upon the public, including the 1989 massacre. He himself had escaped the brutality that had fallen upon the general public time and time again, but his experience had eventually eaten through the two skins of the CCP's lies and his conscience had been exposed. It riled and revolted but was helpless. For decades he had barely slept and his health had declined terribly. Only when he finally felt there was no hope at all for China and Chinese people under the CCP did he reluctantly leave his beloved homeland. And now, although he wanted to expose the evils of his experience, Mao and Marx and Lenin still pumped through his veins. He still spoke their language although he despised it. It writhed and twisted within him. I wondered if he would ever inherit a new culture and be able to purge himself of the CCP's poison.

Was I now intentionally poisoning myself with the same evil in a futile attempt to understand the incomprehensible? I wondered.

I sat back and watched the translator ask the Senior Official his own questions in Chinese. The Official was rolling his eyes and shrugging his shoulders between his limited responses. The official kept me in the corner of his eye, watching me, as if he was chair-bound until I released him from his purgatory situation.

I looked down at my notepad and pretended to check off interview questions from my list. I didn't know what to think, let alone what to say.

Suddenly I remembered something.

"I have a story for you," I said to the Senior Official.

The translator began translating for me, but the Official responded with zero eye contact and even less interest.

"I was arrested in China in 2001 and held in an underground prison cell at the Tiananmen Police Station."

On Nov. 20, 2001, a group of peaceful protestors from 12 countries met—many for the first time—by the flagpole near the north end of Tiananmen Square. None were Chinese. Before coming to China to participate in the event, the author (back row, 5th from the left) knew of only three other people who would be there that day.

(Source: Minghui.org)

While the rest of the group began to meditate, the people in the back row raised a huge banner, which one man had hidden in his travel bag. The author's hand is visible holding the top of the banner behind the middle Chinese character.

(Source: Minghui.org)

Within 30 seconds, police had surrounded the group and used violence to remove them from the Square. The group had broken no law.

(Source: Minghui.org)

Suddenly I had the Official's full attention. For the first time, his eyes locked on mine, examining every twitch and flicker on my face. I was relieved to turn to the translator and break eye contact with him after some minutes of talking. The Official didn't break his stare on me as the translator retold my words in Chinese.

"I was arrested and abused and interrogated for 23 hours before I was deported from China. Why? For holding a banner on Tiananmen Square that said only three words: 'Truth, Compassion, Tolerance,' both in English and Chinese. I broke no law, but within 30 seconds of the banner being held up, both uniformed and undercover police were all over the scene, and within minutes I was in a police van heading to the police station where I was told that 'Truth, Compassion, Tolerance' are illegal in China. I was only bruised and pushed and pulled, but I saw others violently beaten and bloodied."

The Official's stare had softened.

I continued:

"I was held in a basement jail cell at the Tiananmen Square police station. The cell was squeezed full with more than 30 Caucasians from a dozen countries who I had protested with that day. White square tiles lined the cell walls and floor. A large single drain hole broke the tile geometry. I was left staring at the drainhole for hours. This was a cage where humans could be beaten into bloody pulp—or 'pie'—and the remains would quickly and easily be hosed off the walls and off the floor and washed down that drain hole."

"I had been followed by media cameramen who were aiming to recreate the truth into a fake story that would say how well the CCP treats its foreign visitors. I saw with my own eyes how the Chinese police were brainwashed by the CCP. My interrogators had yelled and screamed and coerced me to sign a confession that I had been paid by the CIA to protest on Tiananmen Square. I absolutely hadn't, so I absolutely refused to sign. I had a good management position back home, my boss and family knew about my trip, I had taken time off work and paid every cent from my own savings. If I hadn't wanted to do it from my own heart, no one would've been able to pay me enough money to make me do it for them."

A genuine expression of pleasure had taken over the Official's face, replacing his previously-fixed, jaded expression.

"Extraordinary!" he exclaimed.

There were only three words on that banner. Yet the Chinese people—who had been educated for decades in double-speak and reading between the lines to understand the terror of their ruling regime—immediately knew exactly what those words meant. "Truth, Compassion, Tolerance" are the tenets of Falun Dafa (also Falun Gong),[14] a spiritual discipline that had been immensely popular nationwide and then overnight became a hard-line enemy of the CCP under the dictatorship of Jiang Zemin in 1999.

The Senior Official also immediately understood. He suddenly began talking in heavily accented English, bypassing our translator and looking directly at me.

"It was a great thing when that event took place," he said. "You were heroes."

I smiled uncomfortably, unsure of how to receive his compliment.

He knew about the protest I had been a part of. The words "Truth, Compassion, Tolerance" have become synonymous with the Falun Gong spiritual practice, and once the group was marked for eradication in 1999, their moral tenets of "Truth, Compassion, Tolerance" were also to be destroyed. Displaying those three words on Tiananmen Square meant immediate arrest for Chinese citizens, but until that day in 2001, no one knew what displaying those words would mean for non-Chinese.

> **"I know in China, if you want to fight the CCP or fight the police, not one person or organization can do it. None . . . But this group of Falun Gong people—a group of ordinary citizens— dared to fight the Communist Party to protect their own beliefs. Their resolve was unbelievably strong."**

A former CCP People's Liberation Army Colonel told me in a later interview that he had attended a CCP Beijing Municipal Committee meeting in December 1999, two years before my protest. The meeting was called, *Summary Meeting to Reinforce the Fight Against Falun Gong*.

"They talked about how the eradication campaign was launched and what the nation's reaction was," said the Army Colonel. "The meeting focused on the current situation where tens of thousands of people kept coming to Beijing to appeal to the higher authorities. They kept trying to explain the truth about Falun Gong to the leading authorities, and continually went to Tiananmen Square to shout out: 'Falun Gong is good.'"

The Colonel said the meeting, which a reported 4,000 officials attended, was very interesting to him. As a communist cadre he thought to himself:

"I thought this was ridiculous. They were cutting themselves [the CCP] off from the masses. So many good people continuously went to Beijing or Tiananmen to seek an audience with the elites, and they weren't afraid of being arrested or imprisoned."

The former CCP Heart Surgeon was also observing the continual protests by Falun Gong practitioners at the time. He said in his interview:

Chinese citizens are arrested for holding banners on Tiananmen Square. The banners read: Truth, Compassion, Tolerance.

(Source: Faluninfo.net)

"This really got my attention, because I know in China, if you want to fight the CCP or fight the police, not one person or organization can do it. None. I was absolutely certain of this," he said emphatically. "But this group of Falun Gong people—a group of ordinary citizens—dared to fight the Communist Party to protect their own beliefs. Their resolve was unbelievably strong."

Instead of fear, the protests gave him a sense of awe. "I thought that if I wanted to seek spiritual power, that's what I would look for," he said.

The Colonel gave more insight into the unusual behavior of Falun Gong practitioners:

"The persecution [by the CCP against Falun Gong practitioners] was extremely severe, but all they [CCP officials] could say about practitioners was that they continued to go to Beijing, to Tiananmen Square, to shout out 'Falun Gong is good.' They couldn't even list a single case in which a practitioner had fired a shot, caused an explosion, created a fire, killed someone, beat someone, or even cursed at someone. There was not a single case like that at all. There were no negative examples of Falun Gong practitioners' behavior. I felt it was really ridiculous. For such high authorities, they had launched such a big campaign to imprison these good people, using such cruel measures, while no one resisted with force, only with words or speaking out facts. The whole meeting itself indicated to me that the campaign against Falun Gong was a failure."

My own experience in China had come and gone so quickly, and two decades had passed since then, so I hadn't even thought to mention it earlier to the Senior Official. But he was right. The experience had embedded itself in my being and in my psyche. What I had witnessed did provide motivation for my work and has been helpful in ending the argument with CCP apologists about "You don't know the truth because you haven't been to China and seen it."

Perhaps my one day of witnessing the CCP's violent revolution myself was worth twenty years of CCP study, but I don't want to give any credit to Lenin and his theories.

The Senior Official smiled broadly. "Without this experience you wouldn't be able to make a good film. You had to have this experience," he emphasized. "You *had* to."

A sense of relief flowed through my whole body. We were no longer standing on opposing sides of a deep, dark river. We had bridged an enormous cultural divide in a few moments. And if it could be done with this official, then I believed it could be done with others.

This was one of our earliest interviews and this small victory was the encouragement I needed to keep searching for more interviewees.

Two years later, I was leafing through *Time* magazine's "Best Nonfiction Book of the Twentieth Century," *Gulag Archipelago* by Soviet Communist forced labor camp (gulag) survivor, Alexandr Solzhenitsyn. I was moved by his opening words in the abridged version, which was written for non-Russians:

> "Yet I have not given up all hope that human beings and nations may be able, in spite of all, to learn from the experience of other people without having to live through it personally."

Solzhenitsyn's hope echoed mine. His words further strengthened my resolve.

Solzhenitsyn had written his gulag book for his fellow Russians, for people like my grandparents who were born and raised in the same turbulent years and in the same turbulent country as him. He had hoped to awaken them to the communist atrocities taking place beneath their very noses. But not everyone was willing to listen.

Did my grandparents ever read his book or had they chosen not to? I wondered, feeling certain that they would have heard about it, especially after Solzhenitsyn was awarded a Nobel Peace Prize for his work in 1970. But my grandparents had narrowly escaped Soviet Russia and the gulags, whereas Solzhenitsyn had not. After years of unsettled travel, including years in China, my grandparents gratefully received refuge and stability in the West. They gained the freedom to raise their families, go to church, and run small businesses to feed and clothe themselves, and to service their new communities. They no longer needed to fear tyranny, slavery, or murder so they never discussed it with their grandchildren.

Did they shelter me from my history? Or did they shut themselves off from it? I asked myself. But history is not patient and it is too late for me to ask them the many questions I now have.

I thought back to my interview with the Senior Official. I had thought he was crazy to insist that his daughter go and watch the CCP's slaughter. I'm sure my father would have covered my eyes and blocked my ears.

But why? I wondered.

"There is always this fallacious belief: 'It would not be the same here.' "

The CCP Official wanted to show his daughter the truth and to teach her how to survive in a society they seemed condemned to live in. Whereas my father had arrived in a free country as a teenager and saw no benefit of sharing any of his dark days of terror with his children. And perhaps, since neither the crimes of the CCP upon the Chinese people, nor the crimes of the Soviets upon the Russians have ever been tried and condemned, communism remains an ever present danger that many, like my family, prefer to face only through faith and prayer.

Solzhenitsyn wrote a warning to us that no country is immune to the poisons of communism:

> "There is always this fallacious belief: 'It would not be the same here; here such things are impossible.' Alas, all the evil of the twentieth century is possible everywhere on earth."

I made a note for myself and for my own children: The lessons from a long history are still available to us in the Free World, but we must be humble students and be willing to learn them before it is too late.

CHAPTER 12

The Wedge

"I was the Chief and Party Secretary of the Justice Bureau in my city, the Chief and Party Secretary of my city's Prison Management Bureau, the Chief and Party Secretary of the Re-education Through Labor Bureau, a Committee Member for the Central Commission for Discipline Inspection, a Committee Member of my city's Political and Legal Affairs Commission . . ."

This man had held these positions in Shenyang, the capital of Liaoning Province, and the largest city in China's northeast with a population of over 8 million people.

I felt sorry to reduce this official's long list of high ranking titles that he had worked so hard to earn down to a single title of Former Chinese Labor Camp Director, which is how he is credited in our documentary, *Finding Courage*. That title was needed for brevity in the context of the film's narrative. But he was far more than that.

His black hair and black shirt were as black as the hanging fabric background we had placed behind him. It made his every hand and facial movement all the more expressive. He said he was glad to accept my interview, but he kept wringing his hands. I wasn't sure if it was because they were still cold from the frigid weather outside or if the many cameras and lights pointing at him made him nervous. His visa status was also being scrutinized by the authorities of his new country at that time and he hinted he was worried about being mislabeled an accomplice to the crimes of the CCP.

> **He didn't allow himself to smile. He kept his eyes and his demeanor wide open, as if he were holding his arms outstretched, willing to be searched and probed and proven that he really had nothing to hide.**

"China's dictatorship machines, like the Public Security Bureau (PSB) and the Justice Bureau, have a dual function," he explained, describing two departments he had worked for in China. "They are like double-edged swords. With one side they protect by arresting murderers, rapists, and so on. But with the other side, when the regime wants to kill people, you have to kill people. It is an anti-human function."

Anti-human? I wondered if that was a term he had developed, or picked up after leaving China.

He paused. I noticed he often paused throughout the interview. He knew that I was receiving translation through a small earbud in my right ear, so he kept waiting to make sure the translator had caught up with his words. I nodded at him to continue. I didn't want him to break his concentration as he spoke—that was the point of having simultaneous translation so he couldn't see or hear anything coming in from another room to another source— the earpiece that was soundless to him. But this former high-ranking PSB Official paid particular attention to the details of everyone in the room—a trait that had allowed him to survive for decades in the CCP. If he had lost any of the quick wits that had allowed him to survive for decades in the CCP, he didn't show it.

He didn't allow himself to smile. He kept his eyes and his demeanor wide open, as if he were holding his arms outstretched, willing to be searched and probed and proven that he really had nothing to hide. While he kept his outer guard down for the entire interview, his inner guard was always on high alert.

He continually checked with the second translator—who sat in the room with us and translated my English questions into Chinese for him—if he had correctly understood the question I was asking before he answered. And after he answered, he would check again that he had given the information I was looking for.

Although he wasn't quite old enough to be my grandfather, I imagined that he was, and he readily obliged when I asked him to treat me as a young person who wanted to learn from her elders.

"Eventually I understood." He said, explaining that it was only after he came out of China that he finally had access to conduct his own research into the CCP's criminal history. In China, he had read between the lines of the CCP media reports on the Tiananmen Massacre, and he had been wise enough to gather a sense of the truth at the time. That had driven the first wedge between his personal values and the values of the Party that he loved. But it was only after another decade, by reading and watching eyewitness accounts, that he learned the depth and breadth of the CCP's brutality against the innocent students.

Three words was all he could say to describe his awakening. A gut-wrenching pain was almost audible as he lowered and shook his head, as if trying to shake the agony of the truth from his mind. "Disappointed. Very disappointed." He said.

My Western mind had many questions, but it was likely that none of them were the right ones.

Was he more disappointed in himself for not recognizing the truth earlier, or for ignoring the signs that might have taken him to the truth? Or was his devastation purely from learning that his beloved Party-mother that had bred and reared him, had cunningly, and cold-bloodedly pummelled his younger brethren to death while he slept, and then still smiled at him again in the morning as if all was good and all was right?

I didn't ask him those questions. Like many Chinese we interviewed—officials or not—the awakening to the truth of that betrayal was never easy to accept and was hard to recount. And sometimes, Western concepts or misconceptions seem to only add salt to the wounds.

Anti-human wasn't a term this PSB Official learned from his own research or life learning, although his personal experience had proven it to be an accurate description for what he had been a part of. It was the West that had put that term onto him, and it made him uncomfortable.

"Even though I don't think I did anything anti-human," he continued, "I was deemed to have worked in an anti-human department. The Canadian government deemed me a high level official of the CCP's anti-human departments. It was only then that I knew I had worked in an anti-human department."

"I decided that at least I am not going to be an accomplice."

He told a story that described the fatal wedge that had been hammered hard and deep between himself and his beloved Party. It was this wedge that drove a terrible fear into him and drove him out of his homeland. But it was not a fear of what the Party might do to him physically. It was a fear of what the Party would do to his mind—what he would become if he stayed on the Party path.

"It was a conflict of values," he said at the only point during the interview where both his outer guard and inner guard had fallen down. "I had developed my own opinions about the CCP. But of course I didn't say those things out loud," he emphasized. I imagined he shuddered at the thought of the consequences of speaking against the Party. But he didn't flinch.

"For a long time I wanted to make changes from within, I wanted to push forward and promote progress within

Guangsheng Han, former PSB Official.

the system. Later on I realized I was just a tiny ant. I absolutely couldn't change anything."

He paused longer. A mixture of guilt and grief were upon his face, but he kept his chin high and his eyes wide. His face was the most open at that very moment of all the officials we had ever met. He gulped silently, but I saw it. He opened his mouth and left it open for many moments, as if it wouldn't close by itself. He inhaled and exhaled slowly, as if to disguise his heavy breaths. But his reaction was unmistakable.

He swallowed before recalling that final defining moment of leaving the Walking Dead.

"Because I had no way to change anything, I decided that at least I am not going to be an accomplice, so I chose a different path," his voice cracked ever so slightly and he swallowed again, flushing away any drops of fluid that might form a tear in his eye. "I chose to leave," he concluded.

He looked at me for a few seconds, his head gently nodding.

His choice had eventually become clear. If he stayed in China he would join the ranks of the Walking Dead. He would betray his conscience, participate directly in the anti-human functions of his departments, and forgo his soul. His alternative was to leave everything he knew and loved, and seek refuge with his Party's enemy—the West. There he would be scorned by the Party-led Chinese diaspora as an "anti-Chinese traitor" and be interrogated by the authorities who would question his motives, his sincerity, his loyalties. And he would be dependent on translators he didn't know to present his truth for him in the West.

"Policemen are not stewards on an airplane. Policemen are violent machines."

He wasn't stationed in Beijing at the time of the 1989 massacre and therefore wasn't directly part of the PSB forces that carried out the action. Although he had seen through the Party's lies on the television, he remained a good Party member, following the Party's discipline for himself and enforcing it among his lower-ranking cadres.

"You need to know what policemen are," he once told some students who complained to him about his police officers beating their fellow students in the street. "Policemen are not stewards on an airplane," he said to them sternly. "Policemen are violent machines."

That was a fact he knew only too well. And as the representative of his city's PSB, he sent the students away and did nothing to reprimand the officers. He had no need to.

Ten years later, he was directed to participate in the CCP's next assault on a new targeted group of citizens. He was immediately disturbed.

"It was in 1999 when I served as Chief of the PSB. That was when the crackdown on Falun Gong began. At first, it was mostly executed by the PSB and they detained Falun Gong practitioners in detention centers. Later on it became too big, so they were detained in labor camps."

"The deputy leading the PSB and Justice bureaus came and gave me the order to detain Falun Gong. I refused. I told him that labor camps are for people who committed minor misdemeanors, not for Falun Gong."

"That deputy became furious and told me: 'You have to follow the order. If there are any *political consequences*, I will handle it.' "

"Political consequences" is a communist euphemism, a catch-all phrase that means getting into trouble with the Party. It can be for anyone for anything—for following the rules and for not following the rules—but the consequences were most heavy for Party members whose lives and livelihoods depend entirely on the Party and its fickle mood swings.

At that time, this PSB Official took a great risk. He broke a CCP constitutional rule—he was not subordinate to his superior. Well, kind of. But it wasn't as clear cut as that. Because of the CCP's excessive bureaucracy, officials are required to follow both vertical and horizontal chains of command.

He explained:

"Both the PSB and the Justice Bureau are under dual leadership, which means they have two leaders. One is leadership from the system, vertical leadership. For example, for public security there are public security bureaus, then public security departments, and then police stations. Systematic, vertical leadership. In terms of actual business, we receive more leadership in this direction, vertically."

I appreciated his geometric description. It helped to disentangle the volley of names, departments, bureaus, and offices that he was reeling off.

"The other kind of leadership is horizontal," he continued. "For example, a city police station or city Justice Bureau has to accept the leadership of the city's municipal CCP Committee and city Municipal Government."

This horizontal leadership structure is the parasitic parallel Party structure that attaches to, but rules over, every level of social existence. It claims to be horizontal, but that is also a euphemism. The horizontal CCP position is always one step over and above any parallel position.

So, in order to avoid locking up Falun Gong practitioners in his city's correctional institutions (correctional institutions in China is also a euphemism for slave labor camps, prisons, reeducation centers), the Official took a horizontal sidestep, followed by a vertical jump, and found another superior he could talk to so that he could avoid the central order.

"I called the Chief of the Liaoning [provincial level] Department of Justice," he explained. "I said to him: The city told us to detain Falun Gong. I think this is wrong. Falun Gong are not criminals."

"At first he said: 'I agree. We cannot detain them.' But not long after that, it was implemented down the entire system in a unified manner. Starting at the central authorities, they established a special agency to handle it all, called the 6-10 Office. It was out of my hands. I could not refuse anymore. I had to open up a labor camp to detain Falun Gong."

The 6-10 Office is a Party name.[15] It has no obvious euphemistic meaning. At face value, it has no obvious meaning at all, which gives it a benign outer skin that is curious but forgettable to anyone who has no direct relation to it. The general Chinese citizen may never hear of the 6-10 Office, but every CCP member knows its exact meaning and purpose.

The PSB Official explained the CCP's safe choice in the office's numerical title:

"It was not easy to find a name for this office," he said. "If it was called the 'Falun Gong Crackdown Office' it sounds unjustifiable. So it went by a codename based on the date it was established: June 10, so, 6-10."

I knew of the 6-10 Office as a gestapo-like authority. I envisioned mechanically stern and firm German SS officers in olive green uniforms striking fear into every Jewish person in Europe in every WWII movie I'd ever seen. But 6-10 officers don't have their own special uniforms. 6-10 doesn't need them because 6-10 is not distinct from any uniform-wearing CCP member. It is over and above all uniform wearers and has access to them all—from police officers to military personnel—across the entire nation.

"What kind of resources does the 6-10 Office deploy? All the resources," the PSB Official said, with a heavy emphasis on "all." "Including deploying all the dictatorship departments like Public Security and the Justice Bureau—powerful departments. 6-10 can deploy all the resources, anything at all that it needs."

The Secret Agent who worked at a city-level 6-10 Office for five years outlined the pervasive nature of the 6-10 structure:

"From the Central Political and Legal Affairs Commission of the CCP down to the lowest level of counties, villages and township, they all established a 6-10 Office. The public security authorities, which includes the Public Security Bureau, the prosecutor's office, and the courts, also established their own 6-10 Offices. The 6-10 Office is considered an organ department of the public security authorities and a department of the government."

That meant the 6-10 Offices had leadership both vertically and horizontally.

Like the Gestapo, the 6-10 Office was also a bureaucratic and geometric maze of police at all levels of public security that overlapped with security and justice departments and wielded immense power and fear over the people.

"The CCP must have thought that it could suppress Falun Gong practitioners within a short period of time and make Chinese people forget Falun Gong, like they did with June 4 [1989 Tiananmen Massacre]. But it did not succeed."

"It is a top-down structure. But don't just look at the 6-10 Offices at the top. The branches below them are gigantic," elaborated the 6-10 Officer as he described the operations in his city of Tianjin, which were mirrored in every city across the entire country.

"There were sixteen regions and districts which all had Public Security Bureaus, which all had 6-10 Offices. There is a police station below each of them, and the police would help 6-10 handle certain things, such as gathering specific intelligence information. Later on, as 6-10 expanded, it merged into the Domestic Security Bureau. Its functions were also expanded and it was given the additional task of carrying out overseas intelligence work."

"Why did 6-10 expand?" the 6-10 Officer asked me.

I was getting used to being asked rhetorical questions from officials, which pre-empted my own questions. I didn't know if it was a Chinese cultural thing or a CCP cultural thing. Either way, it was emphatic and helpful, and I rarely had an answer.

"Why did 6-10 expand? Because the CCP must have thought that it could suppress Falun Gong practitioners within a short period of time and make Chinese people forget Falun Gong, like they did with June 4 [1989 Tiananmen Massacre]. But it did not succeed. So in 2003, there was the so-called 6-26 meeting. Zhou Yongkang was the Chief of the Central PSB. He organized and held the national 6-10 meeting at Tianjin City's Taida Hotel. It was then that the Domestic Security Bureau was established. Its responsibilities and operations are similar to the national security agency. It is required to extend antennas overseas."

I liked the translator's use of the term "antennas." It was an apt description of the extension of the CCP's tentacles into foreign countries to return intelligence information to the motherland. (I also liked it because it reminded me of the comparison between the CCP and a colony of parasitic social ants.)

While the CCP repeatedly blared that no country should meddle in another's domestic affairs, it was sending CCP agents into foreign countries for the purpose of further persecuting its own people and probing deeply into the personal lives of foreign citizens.

"One piece of intelligence information can earn you $260,000, so the money is a huge temptation for overseas Chinese people."

"They were everywhere: Oceania, Asia, North America, Europe, all had them. Each city and each province had them," the Officer continued. He was in charge of Oceania and Asia.

"When I was in China I thought this was all very normal. Because in order for the CCP to continue its dictatorship, it will do whatever it can to extend its antennae into other countries to prevent, disrupt, or stop communications between dissidents outside China and those inside China. Internet, emails, phone tapping—they will control you with whatever is necessary to maintain its one party dictatorship."

The Officer used the word "were" because he was describing his time in China, but the 6-10 Office still exists and continues its operations today.

"Do these 6-10 agents operate via the Chinese embassies and consulates?" I asked him.

"No. These secret forces have nothing to do with the Chinese consulates. They do not belong to the Chinese consulates, they belong to the Domestic Security Bureau of the Public Security Bureaus," he stated plainly. "These people are directly under the control of the 6-10 Office that manages them. Our involvement with the secret forces was to uniformly manage the secret forces sent overseas by the 6-10 Office. To collect uniformly, and then uniformly send the collected information to each city's 6-10 Office."

"Special agents are sent overseas by the CCP, and through work relationships, or when some overseas Chinese return to China and build a working relationship with the CCP through relatives or friends, then, using money as a temptation or threats of law infringement against them, they get their help. If they refuse, it will have a long-lasting negative effect on their ability to enter China, including their business in China, or even just if they want to go to a nightclub. It will have a life-long effect."

"One piece of intelligence information can earn you $260,000, so the money is a huge temptation for overseas Chinese people."

With those types of tempting payments available, I wondered how many foreigners had completely sold themselves and willingly become full-time CCP agents in their own countries.

"There are three levels of the CCP-deployed overseas secret forces," continued the 6-10 Officer. "The highest level is Special Informant. The second is Ears & Eyes. The third is Work Relationships. These three levels were named: Three Year Plan."

I did like the sound of the secret forces titles. They were much cooler (and probably far more accurate) than any spy titles in all the *James Bond* films I've watched. But the glitz starts to wear thin when you realize the spies aren't acting just so you can enjoy them with your popcorn.

> **I found many parallels between the operations and culture of the CCP and other communist parties. But I didn't find any connections between CCP culture and Chinese culture.**

The cool titles were likely to have been pirated from the vast array of spy labels given to secret informants by KGB secret operatives under the former Soviet Union, or the KGB's successor, the SVR (Foreign Intelligence Service) of the Russian Federation. Their operations may entertain us when the news gives us a spin on the occasional story the spy agencies want the public to know about. But in reality, their covert operations primarily revolve around achieving their long-term goal of eliminating their main target— American independence.

The CCP and the KGB/SVR still share the same long-term target. "Target" used to be called "enemy," but with the fall of the Berlin Wall, and the renaming of the KGB to the SVR and the FSB (Federal Security Service) (the KGB was never actually dismantled), "target" became the euphemism in their operations.[16] It's quite possible that this same thinking is why the CCP changed the name of its "Propaganda" Department to the "Publicity" Department.

I found many parallels between the operations and culture of the CCP and other communist parties. But I didn't find any connections between CCP culture and Chinese culture. Being a foreign import to China, the Communist Party positioned itself as the antithesis of all things traditionally Chinese, and the CCP's Cultural Revolution in the '60s broke any remaining roots the Chinese people had with their ancient ancestors. After the Cultural Revolution, China's past only existed through careful reframing by the CCP.

When it is of benefit to the CCP's power, the CCP will conjure ancestral images and ancient wisdom and present it to the Chinese people—but that always does, and always must, contain the ideological essence of the CCP. It can never be truly Chinese. The CCP is determined to define all culture that is, or isn't, Chinese. And maintaining the populace's belief in the CCP's official faith, atheism, is a fundamental part of the CCP's grip.

In the words of the CCP's number two idol, Lenin, about the CCP's number one idol, Marx:

"Atheism is a natural and inseparable part of Marxism, of the theory and practice of scientific socialism. Our program necessarily includes the propaganda of atheism."

The issue of culture, and theism versus atheism, is the fundamental conflict between the CCP and Falun Gong. It has pitted one against another in the CCP's longest and most brutal battle on its own soil, which continues today.

Yet Falun Gong's immense popularity and expansion from zero to 100 million practitioners in seven years (according to CCP estimates[17]) made Chinese traditional spirituality a great thing again. Falun Gong repopularized a belief in invisible, heavenly beings, in the image of pre-communist Buddhas, Daos and Gods. It repopularized the old, pre-communist belief that spirituality is beyond the secular human world, which implies that humans can exist without the CCP. It repopularized the individual quest to seek spiritual enlightenment under spiritual guidance that also exists independent of the CCP. An individual quest requires individual thinking, which is a dangerous foe for socialist control, and the ultimate heresy of communist culture.

People practiced Falun Gong whether they were Party members

or not. Political affiliations were not taught or required. In Falun Gong's teachings, individual thinking was encouraged to inspire a practitioner to always strive harder to raise their energy levels and to not compare one practitioner's level against another. These teachings caused a communist knot to unravel in millions of minds. Many of them believed in a sense of the divine again. Some may have even been inspired to remember that China, as a nation, existed for thousands of years before the CCP, and that in a not-too-distant past, Chinese people called China, "The Land of the Divine."

And although Falun Gong taught strict nonviolence, nonaggression, and showed (and has proven) no intent to replace the CCP with its own leadership, 100 million Falun Gong adherents had shifted their communist-formed mindsets in one big step toward traditional Chinese culture. This was particularly dangerous for the CCP, because out of the 100 million people practicing Falun Gong for health, any number of them might have awakened to a personal, inner, spiritual belief that their lives can and will still exist, even if the Party does not.

"I did not have much of an understanding about Falun Gong," said the 6-10 Officer. "At the time, we just understood it was a way for people to get healthier and to do good deeds. They were defined as 'petitioners.' I saw some retired or unemployed people, also some working teachers and professors who went to petition. To us police officers, they were not bandits."

"We just thought the government had made a mistake." ▌

Bandits or not, the orders to destroy them were unquestionable.

"At the police station, we listed all the Falun Gong practitioners and their family members, one by one, from the household registration system," he continued, describing the CCP's family monitoring system that doubles as a type of domestic passport system to restrict citizens' freedom to move between cities. "This is a special method the CCP uses to manage and organize and control Chinese people. Not a single person can escape the household registration system. For example, if a child wants to go to university, apply for a job, and so on, but their parents are Falun Gong practitioners, there will be a very clear note in the register, and the child will receive heavy discrimination."

Despite the enormity and pervasiveness of the crackdown, Falun Gong practitioners continued to petition the CCP to allow them to practice.

"We still had hope in our government. We just thought the government had made a mistake," were the words we heard over and over again, when interviewing regular Chinese citizens who had tried to petition the government to stop the Falun Gong persecution. It took them years to understand the extent of their beloved CCP's intolerance. But by then, the CCP's persecution apparatus had grown and evolved tremendously.

"When we were transferred to the 6-10 Office, everyone thought it would be a temporary job. Nobody thought it would become a department or a long-term job," said the 6-10 Officer. "But Falun Gong is not a political event. It is mainly a religion, so its fundamental ideologies are different from those of dissidents and democracy activists. So, even now, Falun Gong has not disappeared in Mainland China; it hasn't been eliminated."

"I really didn't understand the CCP much before. I really didn't understand communism." said the Chinese Professor. He had been famous in his region, recommended by the CCP Youth League to be a nationally recognized student, and was well on his way to a high-ranking Party position when he got a whiff of the political assassinations that would be on his path. He instead stopped in his tracks and became a professor instead of an official, to the deep dismay of his educators and Party comrades.

"Even after the CCP killed the students in the June 4 Tiananmen Square massacre, I still did not completely lose faith in the CCP. I still thought it can change," he reflected. "It was only after the persecution of Falun Gong began that I truly started to understand the CCP. Why did it suppress Falun Gong? Why did it define Falun Gong as the most dangerous, historically? Why did it deem Falun Gong as its most dangerous enemy?"

To help him process his thinking, he conducted his own study and published a book on the subject called, *The Riddle of All Riddles*.

In our interview, he retold me some of his research findings:

"Chinese people did not have goals, no faith. As soon as Falun Gong came out, many people thought, 'Good!' The national Premier Zhu Rongji even said: 'Practice Falun Gong and you can get healthy. Great! It can save the country a lot of medical bills.' Qiao Shi, (China's then third-most powerful official) stated in his own 1998 research report that Falun Gong is, 'all benefits with no harm for any ethnic group, any nation, or any political party.'"

"A business owner told me secretly she would only hire Falun Gong practitioners, but she wouldn't say it publicly because the CCP was suppressing them. But as long as they were a Falun Gong practitioner she would take them. Why? Because she knew she was getting honest people."

Falun Gong requires its adherents to apply the tenets of "Truth, Compassion, Tolerance" to their thoughts and actions on a daily basis. It teaches that to raise one's energy level, a practitioner has to follow those tenets with sincerity, and not with lip service. That was a core aspect of the first tenet of truth. And Chinese people really took it to heart as best they could, even within the confines of the CCP culture. And as a result, CCP officials and official CCP media reported a leap in social morality due to the practice.

Those official media reports immediately disappeared as soon as the crackdown began. Yet we were able to source many of them from outside of China so that we could include them in our film, *Finding Courage*. They gave a fascinating insight into the genuine public excitement about Falun Gong.

"I remember at the time when Falun Gong was being taught," continued the Professor, "there were many people, hundreds, sometimes thousands of people who attended. With so many people, it's inevitable that someone will lose something, like a wallet or a watch or something. But after listening to the Falun Gong lecture, if something was lost, someone would find it and return it. It happened a lot. But in China, where else do you see this happen? It doesn't! But after people were learning Falun Gong, such good behavior started happening."

He finished his stories and his tone changed to a lament. The Professor had the unique skill of being able to change the emotion on his face and in his voice without changing his stunningly fast tempo, which never skipped a beat.

"The CCP wants to destroy moral standards," he said. "I met some Chinese international students studying medicine in the West. They told me, 'I only know that when I was little they made me sign that Falun Gong is an evil cult.' All elementary and secondary school students had to sign. An entire generation of young people, caused by Jiang Zemin, had to say that Falun Gong is bad."

Good? Bad? I wondered. In comparison to the overly complicated euphemistic communist terms and phrases, the simplistic words of *good* and *bad* were a bit of a shock to my mental system.

We all love an epic story of good versus evil, but that's just in fairy tales and Hollywood, isn't it? Isn't life a lot more complicated than that? I asked myself.

Chinese people had been going to petition with weapons that the CCP saw as powerful and dangerous, but they were merely words on fabric that said, "Falun Gong is Good!" It was the simplest of language in the most complex of worlds. And perhaps that was what made the threat all the more frightening.

"Jiang Zemin jailed good people," said the Chinese Professor about the Chinese dictator who rose to power by advocating for the 1989 Tiananmen massacre and who had pushed the button on the CCP to set the Falun Gong persecution in motion. "He knows they are good people. Other leaders knew too. After Jiang Zemin, none of the other Chinese leaders have publicly said that Falun Gong isn't good, like Jiang Zemin did. Why? Because they are still persecuting, but they know that Falun Gong is good."

Far too many of Jiang Zemin's speeches have been translated into English and published—three large printed volumes in all—and some official documents have been leaked over the years. Jiang first talked about Falun Gong in April 1999 and continued throughout that year. Then, as his persecution failed to have the effect and legacy he had hoped for, the term "Falun Gong" disappeared from his public words and the CCP's propaganda altogether.

"The creation and spread of Falun Gong is a political struggle to gain our position, a fight against our party from domestic and external anti-forces." Jiang had written. "Is the Marxist theory of Communists and the materialism and atheism we espouse insufficient to defeat this heresy preached by Falun Gong? If that were true, we would become an extremely big joke."

While no other Chinese group has withstood and pushed back against an internal CCP persecution campaign for so long, the failure of Marxism to defeat Falun Gong has left a yet-to-be-counted death toll, estimated in the millions. And it is certainly no *big joke*.

"The CCP has always easily defeated anyone they label a target. But the CCP has never run into a group like Falun Gong," said the former High-Ranking Official. "I think Falun Gong has truly done something extraordinary by making people who had been kneeling down [to the CCP] to stand up again."

"When Jiang Zemin declared that he will defeat Falun Gong, never did he imagine that twenty years later Falun Gong would now prosper in over 100 countries around the world." His eyes suddenly lit up as he continued:

"Falun Gong's main text *Zhuan Falun* [which had been a year-on-year national bestseller before Jiang banned its publication][18] has been translated into about forty languages and is published in many countries. Two hundred thousand people have filed lawsuits against Jiang Zemin. This is unprecedented. Jiang Zemin really shot himself in the foot."

"My rank was the highest, so they used me as a negative role model for the rest of the country."

This was said by one of the highest-ranking CCP officials we interviewed. He had become a Falun Gong practitioner in 1995. His superior had shown him Jiang Zemin's persecution order in 1999. Soon after that he had written a letter to Jiang Zemin titled: *The Chinese Nation and the Chinese People have Everything to Gain and Nothing to Lose from Falun Dafa (Falun Gong)*. He was expelled from the Party soon after.

"I was the first Party member in China who had his membership expelled for practicing Falun Gong. The first in China." He almost seemed proud of it. "My rank was the highest, so they used me as a negative role model for the rest of the country."

His first of sixteen agonizing years of endless propaganda-watching sessions, constant surveillance, long term work arrest (in a Party apartment designated for his work unit) began in 1999. He was cut off entirely from everything—including friends and family . . . Cut off from everything except for CCP propaganda.

"The propaganda against Falun Gong was nonstop from morning till evening and I was in captivity and completely cut off from the outside world, guarded by armed police twenty-four hours a day. It was hard to even breathe," he recalled. "I had to think very seriously about Falun Gong. Is it right for me to have faith in 'Truth, Compassion, Tolerance?' How should I choose my future path? I was very conflicted."

When he had refused to transform his mind and relinquish his belief in Falun Gong, he was put into a detention center and eventually given a show-trial and forced to serve a prison sentence until 2013. He managed to flee China in 2015.

"I do have regret," he said, breaking momentarily from his plastic outer smile. "I lived in Beijing for some twenty years, but when I left it for good, I was upset and depressed. Why? Because they just wouldn't listen. They just wouldn't listen," he said, shaking his head. He had written countless letters inside prison to CCP members, including Jiang Zemin, in an attempt to reason with them on the persecution, but to no avail. "In the end, I had no choice but to leave the country with that regret."

While it was not easy to track down former CCP officials willing to speak on camera, I knew I had to ensure that our selection presented the widest range of rank, position, age, family background, education, and choice of faith. I wanted to maintain a sense of balance and avoid their stories skewing toward feelings of victimization or antagonism against the CCP. As it turned out, about half of our interviewees had come to practice Falun Gong at different points in time—some before and some after the persecution began. At first that worried me.

Would their stories be overly biased? Would their stories be judged by their belief system rather than on their own experience and merit? I questioned myself.

Kay Rubacek (C) interviews Youqun Wang (L) for *Finding Courage*. Sarah Shao (R) translates.

But as I unraveled each of their experiences, my fear subsided. Each official had a unique story to tell that was true to their life and withstood our cross-referencing and fact-checking processes. Regardless of their faith, almost all of them, especially those who do not practice Falun Gong, had been particularly impacted by the Falun Gong persecution, so much so that for many of them, it had been the final wedge that had made them choose between life among the Walking Dead and freedom in a foreign land. The 6-10 Officer and the PSB Official are two such examples.

"In my jurisdiction, there was a fifteen-year-old girl who was electrocuted with electric batons," said the PSB Official who was also the Labor Camp Director. The young girl imprisoned at one of his labor camps had refused to denounce Falun Gong and received four consecutive hours of torture with electric batons all over her body, including on her genitals and breasts while the PSB Official—the man responsible for overseeing the labor camp she was held in—was out of town.

"After I learned about it, I strictly prohibited it," he said. "I couldn't let them do that. I even transferred the person in charge."

But the pressure on the Official kept compounding.

"There's a correctional institution in Liaoning Province called Masanjia," he said. "It is also in Shenyang City (the PSB Official's city), but it is directly managed by the province. Masanjia became the model institute for transforming Falun Gong practitioners. Its director, a lady by the name of Su Jing, became the model for Falun Gong transformation."

The CCP holds Masanjia as its model re-education institution. It was expanded in 1999 to accommodate Falun Gong practitioners. But for survivors, staff, and undercover investigators, Masanjia is the most evil of China's concentration camps, known particularly for its brutal sexual torture of women.

"It's just a hell on earth," stated former *New York Times* photojournalist Du Bin in a published interview about his newly released (2014) book, *Vaginal Coma*,[19] which reveals the brutal sexual torture of female Falun Gong practitioners and petitioners detained in Masanjia. "This book is to remember the humiliation and tragedy inflicted on those women who carry the task of human reproduction," stated Du, who also released a documentary on the same topic the year prior.

"I'm a human being, I have conscience and humanity. Thus, I recorded those cases one by one, and spoke out about them after I was released," he said in the published interview.

Du's retelling of the victims' accounts is a difficult story to hear, but a necessary truth.

The CCP also found it a difficult story, so it banned any media reports on Masanjia:

> Without exception, do not reuse, report, or comment

on the article about the Masanjia Women's Labor Re-education Camp and related contents.

From a leaked directive from the Central Propaganda Department on April 9, 2013.

A survivor of Masanjia, a lady by the name of Liping Yin, testified before the Congressional-Executive Commission on China in Washington in 2016. She held up Du's book and said: "Three toothbrushes were tied together, and inserted into and stirred up female private parts. I saw with my own eyes a group of men beating an elderly Falun Gong practitioner in the restroom. They forcefully inserted a broken broom stick into her private part."[20]

I wanted to order Du's book for my library, but just the illustration on the cover alone scared me. Dozens of naked women, hand drawn in black ink, stand shoulder to shoulder, heads lowered and hands covering their reproductive organs. Beneath their feet,

Liping Yin holds Du Bin's book, *Vaginal Coma,* while describing her experience at the Masanjia Labor Camp before the Congressional-Executive Commission on China, April 14, 2016. (Source: Epoch Times)

they are standing on a wide platform. They form the bristles on a giant toothbrush against a blood red background.

> **Where the citizens of China have been denied encouragement for innovation in general, the depraved creativity of prison guards and inmates has been greatly rewarded by the CCP.**

The PSB Official described how his labor camp, and all others in Liaoning Province, were required by the CCP to send staff to Masanjia for study and training on how to transform Falun Gong practitioners:

"My subordinate, the Deputy Chief, went there," he said. "After studying from them, he said to me: 'Chief, one word sums up their transformation procedure. Beating.' I told him: 'You cannot learn this. I forbid it. No beating.' "

"*Beating*" is a euphemism for torture.

For a limited window of time, this PSB Official was able to maintain his policy at his institutions. During this period, he received a special delivery from Masanjia.

"There were ten women at Masanjia who never transformed despite how much they were tortured. They were tarnishing the reputation of Masanjia, so they were sent to me," he recalled. "Upon hearing of their arrival I went to visit them one night. I entered one of the cells where two ladies were detained. I talked with them. I asked what kind of abuse they received at Masanjia. They told me many things."

The torture methods and techniques honed and created by the

Guangsheng Han, the former Labor Camp Director and PSB Official, demonstrating how electric batons are used to abuse captives in China.

Guangsheng Han speaks publicly for the first time in August, 2005, after defecting from the CCP in 2001.   (Source: Epoch Times)

CCP during the persecution is astounding and horrifying. Where the citizens of China have been denied encouragement for innovation in general, the depraved creativity of prison guards and inmates has been greatly rewarded by the CCP. What a human being who hasn't lived such torture can bear to read or hear is very limited. Even after reading so many accounts myself, I still struggle to retell them. In our movie, we chose to imply the torture rather than describe it—except when it was necessary to the story—and that was already more than enough.

The PSB Official gave the two women pens and paper and asked them to write an account for him. He then forwarded their accounts to his superior, the director of Liaoning Justice Department.

"Because the Masanjia correctional institution was within his jurisdiction, I forwarded them to him and asked him to look. Do you know what the result was?"

I shook my head.

"He got angry because I found fault with him. After that, it was announced from the top level that funding for our city was cut—because I found fault with him."

"The world of CCP officialdom is very cruel and dark."

The official held out his hands, palms up and stared at me.

His window of grace was over and the pressure to increase Falun Gong transformation rates intensified. And transformation meant terrible torture.

"I entrusted a resignation letter to my friend to pass on to my

Who are China's walking dead?

superior. In the letter I wrote that the world of CCP officialdom is very cruel and dark. I did not want to act against my conscience and I did not want to be a tool of the CCP anymore."

The pointed wedge had broken through and had now entirely separated him from the Party.

And then he left his luxurious position, his rank and titles, and started a new life in the West as a delivery driver—and most importantly as a "human being" who was no longer treated as "a high-paid slave and lackey."

CHAPTER 13
Turning Points

"Why do these lights make my eyes water?" questioned the former 6-10 Officer and Secret Agent abruptly, interrupting the interview and pointing to the bright photography lights a few feet above his head. He glared at the translator and then at me. He was not happy. "Why are they making my eyes water?" he repeated curtly.

Our crew immediately began adjusting the lights. They were not our normal choice of lights. We had rented them when we flew into this city just to meet this man, and had limited time to perfect the lighting in the hotel room we booked for the interview.

> **I knew he was acutely aware of how the CCP uses cameras to twist and turn their subjects, but we had no intention of using such CCP propaganda techniques in our interviews. Facts were all we were after.**

I watched him curiously as he tilted his head down and wiped his eyes with his fingers. Then we looked at each other. Years of interrogation and intelligence training had earned him the perfect poker face. He was calm and steady and revealed no emotion in his responses. But for a very brief moment his eyes flashed with suspicion— possibly anger—questioning my motives. For a brief moment, our interviewer-interviewee trust was broken. He questioned if I wanted the lights to make his eyes water to make him appear emotional on camera. I reassured him that I did not.

Fengjun Hao, "The Secret Agent, 6-10 Officer, and Police Officer."

I'd been told that he wasn't willing to do interviews much these days. It had been ten years since his high-profile defection from the CCP, and he was now busy running his own small business. I had been warned and prepped that he might not turn up for the interview. That had happened the last time my contact had scheduled an interview with him for another media. So I was very grateful that he had come and was still sitting beneath our imperfect lighting.

The light brightness was fixed and I thanked him. I knew he was acutely aware of how the CCP uses cameras to twist and turn their subjects, but we had no intention of using such CCP propaganda techniques in our interviews. Facts were all we were after.

The Officer resumed his poker face and I continued my questioning.

"What made you leave China?" I asked.

"I also talked about this when I first came out," he answered.

From his indirect response I understood he was indicating that he didn't want to go into the details of two key events that had become turning points in his life.

I already knew about these events—they had made a strong impression on me when I heard them in 2005 when he first went public, but I knew we wouldn't include them in our movie, so I didn't press him to repeat them on camera.

> **"The reason I left China was because of the suppression of Falun Gong. What I saw in jails and labor camps when I went to interrogate Falun Gong practitioners shocked me too much.**

I think I sensed his relief but he showed none. His poker face was flawless. But I was sure that these two turning points must have affected him so intensely, so emotionally, that they had at some point not only broken his poker face—they had also broken him away from the Walking Dead.

Instead, he gave a three-sentence summary of these two life-changing events:

"The reason I left China was because of the suppression of Falun Gong. What I saw in jails and labor camps when I went to interrogate Falun Gong practitioners shocked me too much. Also some filming of Falun Gong practitioners by CCTV when they created some false propaganda harmed me personally, but it also enlightened me."

After watching a preview of our movie, *Finding Courage*, a movie reviewer said to me, "I want to know that 6-10 Officer's story. I want to know what he saw. What happened to him?"

I told the reviewer his story and they were enthralled.

There is only so much you can put into the story of one single movie, but in this book of essays exploring the lives of CCP officials, I felt it more appropriate to retell the story as the Officer wanted it told. I have included an excerpt from a 2005 public testimony he wrote himself (originally in Chinese), aptly titled *In His Own Words*[21]:

My Heart Sank to the Bottom Witnessing the Miserable Experience of an Innocent Mother and Daughter

In the beginning of 2002, the authorities started arresting people involved in the "103 Case". In one day, seventy-nine Falun Gong practitioners were arrested, and another two escaped. One of the escaped practitioners was a thirteen year-old girl named Xu Ziao. This girl's mother, Sun Ti, was arrested and little Xu hence became homeless at the age of thirteen.

One night in February 2002, I received a call asking me to go back to work and accompany a Falun Gong practitioner to see a doctor. I rushed to work and drove with a female officer to the prison of the Nankai Branch of Tianjin Public Security Bureau. When we arrived at the prison located at Erwei Road, Nankai District, I saw Sun Ti sitting on a table in an interrogation room. Sun's eyes were so swollen because of the beating.

I regretted that I didn't stop this from happening.

The police who interrogated Sun was Mr. Mu Ruili, captain of the 2nd division of the 6-10 Office of the Bureau of State Security. Mu was holding a steel rod (0.6 inches in diameter) with its screw thread stained with blood. There was a high-voltage electric baton sitting on the table.

As we entered the room, we asked Mu to leave. Sun burst into tears and was going to show us the injuries. I volunteered to leave the room since she was a woman. Sun stopped me and showed me her back. I was terribly shocked. Almost her entire back turned black and there were two cuts about eight inches long with blood coming out.

After a while, Zhao Yuezeng, the assistant director of the Bureau of State Security and the director of the 6-10 Office, came. To my surprise, Zhao ordered me not to mention this to anyone and asked me and the female officer to take Sun to the infirmary of the prison. For the next thirty days, we had to apply medicine to Sun.

Almost every day I heard Sun ask about her daughter's whereabouts and tell us how Falun Gong practitioners are good people. My heart was shattered. I knew Falun Gong practitioners are good people and I cared about her daughter even more. A thirteen-year-old girl who lost her parents and couldn't even go to her relatives (all her relatives were monitored), how could she find food and a place to sleep?

I regretted that I didn't stop this from happening. My heart became anxious and heavy and I cried.

I often dreamed about what happened to Sun and Xu and the miserable scene I witnessed, and I lost sleep. I was in total despair about China's future and my future as a police officer.

Later I heard that Sun Ti was sentenced to seven to ten years and I am not sure whether she is alive now or not.

My Sympathy for an Old Scientist Started It All

It was just after the 2004 New Year, in Tianjin State Security Bureau, where I served, that I received a special assignment. Four or five policemen, led by 6-10 Office Chief Shi He, went to Shijiazhuang city in Hebei Province to handle a *special* case. After they had returned, I saw a white-haired, elderly man hanging from handcuffs in the interrogation room. I later learned that he was Jing Zhanyi, a high level official in Hebei Province.

After his interrogation, a reporter from China Central Television came to interview Jing Zhanyi. The plan was to show the world how much this official regretted his involvement with Falun Gong.

I knew in my heart that to fight him is like throwing an egg at a stone, so I kept silent.

I was outside the door that day, while the interview was being carefully conducted. I heard Deputy Director of the State Security Bureau Zhao Yuezeng, tell Jing Zhanyi that they would reduce his sentence if he was willing to recite some lines that they had prepared for him, otherwise he would be charged with treason and face either a life sentence or execution by firing squad. The poor old man complied with their requests and went on TV to criticize Falun Gong with their words. Afterward, he was sentenced to seven years in prison.

The reporter saw me as she was leaving the interview and asked me for my comment, probably wanting to gather some supporting statements. But to her disappointment I said to her, "Aren't these lies?" I walked away leaving her standing there, shocked.

My comment to that reporter brought me enormous trouble.

Two days after the incident, Deputy Director Zhao Yuezeng came to me and asked what I had meant by "lies." Without mincing my words, I asked him, "Why did you threaten Jing Zhanyi?" He pounded the table and claimed that I was revolting. I knew in my heart that to fight him is like throwing an egg at a stone, so I kept silent. He said that I should think the matter through and write a formal self-criticism statement before returning to work.

I was thus kept in solitary confinement in a cell at Tianjin Public Security Bureau 7th Division, where there are solitary confinement cells specifically for policemen. The moment I walked into the cell I was in total despair. That was the first and only time I have been locked up in a cell. The ten square meter cell has no windows. A light hangs from the ceiling by a cord and stays on 24 hours a day; the toilet in the corner emits a constant foul stench. February was extremely cold in Tianjin, but the cell had no heating.

I lived for nearly a month in these conditions. When I walked out of the cell, my ears and hands had been damaged by the freezing temperatures and my hands were swollen like steamed buns, while my ears constantly emitted pus.

During those thirty days, I wasn't even once allowed to call my family. I was tormented mentally and physically by those people to the brink of collapse. Even then, I did not say or write one word of repentance. Finally one day I was released without being given any reason. Later I learned that they were trying to keep the incident low-key, fearing that I might expose their torture of Falun Gong practitioners and other scandals.

After my release I was moved to the mailroom, delivering newspapers and mail and doing various chores, until I fled abroad. My fiancée suffered greatly while I was in solitary confinement. She sensed that something was wrong, but when she, my mother, and my brother called the office looking for me they told her that I was on a business trip. I was heartbroken when I heard this. They are so deceitful that they would even lie to the family of their own officers! What would they not do? Where is justice?

CHAPTER 14

Chameleon Skin

To hide, to attract, or to repel, Mother Nature infused many animals with the ability to change their outer appearance as a survival mechanism. Some, like the squid and the octopus, change the color of their skin by gathering and spreading specific color pigments that exist within their skin cells. But a chameleon's ability to change its outer appearance is unique.

Contrary to popular belief, a chameleon doesn't change its actual color to blend in with its surroundings—it just changes the appearance of color.

In a 2015 scientific study,[22] researchers found that chameleons have two layers of skin. The chameleon's outer layer of skin contains grids of tiny nanocrystals that expand and contract, and change the structure of the skin cells according to the animal's mood. The nanocrystals in the skin change the way light reflects off the chameleon and changes the color that our eyes see. And the mirage works. Before our very eyes—sometimes in as little as five seconds—the chameleon changes the appearance of its outer skin. Not only to blend into its surroundings, but also to reflect its emotions and its inner state of being.

Of course, we're talking physical skins here, so this is only a surface-level analogy—and I'm certainly no biologist. But with decades of practice and experimentation, the CCP's flesh has grown upon Soviet bones. Its muscle tone has toughened and its outer crust has hardened and leathered. And with the skill of a chameleon, the CCP has continually morphed its second layer of skin to communicate through an evolving array of euphemisms that dazzle its captives and deflect them from its bloodshed. This skin is an essential aspect of the CCP culture.

"Party culture is not a fixed model. Party culture is actually changing," explained the Chinese Professor who is particularly well-versed in CCP cultural studies. "Today the CCP says this is bad; tomorrow it can say it is good. It flips. It negates itself. It does not come from a position of truth. It does not have truth. It does not have morals."

> **A method may be legal or illegal, help people or harm people, be honest or dishonest—it doesn't matter. As long as the method achieves the goal, the method is "good."**

Former CCP dictator, Deng Xiaoping encouraged the distortion of any fixed sense of morality via his now-famous saying that has sunk deep into CCP culture:

> "It doesn't matter whether it's a black cat or a white cat; if it catches mice, it's a good cat."

The meaning of this phrase is that it doesn't matter what method is used, as long as the desired result is achieved, then the method is good. In other words, a method may be legal or illegal, help people or harm people, be honest or dishonest—it doesn't matter. As long as the method achieves the goal, the method is "good." This phrase says a lot about the concepts of morality and ethics of the CCP. Something that may have been considered wrong or bad or even evil according to Chinese culture, can now be considered good under the CCP's culture.

And it doesn't only relate to methods used to achieve a goal. It also explains and attempts to excuse the CCP's changing policies and attitude toward groups or individuals.

For example, one year the CCP may say that intellectuals are good, but the next year the CCP may say they are bad. So, today the black cat is rewarded but tomorrow the cat may be punished. A cat may even change the color of its coat, and if that achieves the CCP's goals, then that's just fine too. Anything is justified, even evil can be called good, as long as it gets the job done.

Older Party members, like the PSB Officials we interviewed, still bear coats made of the CCP's old leather. "The CCP's philosophy is class struggle," said one PSB Official of today's CCP. His words were from the old CCP language.

"The CCP wants to instigate class struggle and class hatred," he continued. "Although a society's survival relies on cooperation between different classes, the CCP wants a relationship of mutual struggle, mutual murder, and mutual hatred."

"Class hatred" is a dated term from old-school communist language. Class hatred and class struggle are no longer common CCP phrases. For regular Chinese educated in CCP culture, they are more like terms from a fog-covered past that one is taught to ignore. The old phrases draw an invisible line in history between the always-present, always-correct CCP of today, and the hard-line CCP tactics of the sometimes-slightly-imperfect Mao Zedong.

For CCP members, these old terms are from a time when the CCP's skin was still thin—when the CCP exposed too much bone.

While the driving theories of the CCP haven't changed, some younger officials—those born between the time of the thickening of skin—have the clarity to compare and articulate the change of CCP language over time.

"Struggles need an enemy. Only when everyone continues to focus their attention on opposing an enemy can the CCP secure its power"

"Marx divided our society into different classes: the lower working class (proletariat); and the upper wealthy class (bourgeois)," explained the High-Ranking Official. "But in reality, society is much more complex than that. People have many different occupations and different social levels exist from top to bottom."

Like all the other officials we talked to, he did not agree with Marx's or Lenin's theories anymore, although he had so done for much of his life. As a good CCP member, he had studied them all and even memorized some of them.

"During the time of Lenin, Stalin, and Mao," he continued, "the lower class struggled against the upper class. But by the time of Deng Xiaoping and Jiang Zemin, they made a slight change to the language. They said, 'The CCP struggles against its *enemy forces.*' All those who hold a different point of view, or an opposing view, are seen as *enemy forces.*"

Enemy is a choice word for our times.

"To ensure its power is secure from these enemy forces," continued the High-Ranking Official, "the CCP is constantly on the defense and taking measures to suppress and clamp down on them."

"The CCP needs people to have an enemy to keep fighting, to always struggle. Struggles need an enemy. Only when everyone continues to focus their attention on opposing an enemy can the CCP secure its power."

Struggles need an enemy. . . . Of course, I thought.

While the name of the target has changed over time, the action required against the enemy target has never changed: *Struggle*.

Like a good many Chinese words, "struggle" encompasses more in contextual meaning in Chinese than it does in English. In Chinese the word is *dou zheng*, which is often translated as the rather impotent word, struggle. The Chinese meaning includes an emphasis on violence, fighting, and war. And all our interviewees had difficulty providing a definition that would be correctly understood in the West.

"The essence of the CCP is to struggle," stated the Army Colonel. His speech was clear, but his face betrayed a complex thought process, as he searched his mental vocabulary for words to express the concept to me.

"To struggle is absolute, unconditional. If there is no reason to struggle, then you make up reasons. To struggle is to attack and bring down the target. There's no right or wrong or evil or justice or good or bad. It's just to struggle and keep on struggling. In the West, there's no such thing. In the West, if something is wrong, then it's just wrong."

The Colonel's eyes darted around the room, unsatisfied with his own answer. From our first interaction he had come across as a perfectionist. He was extremely cautious in choosing his words. He didn't want to be mistaken or misrepresented.

"How can I explain this?" he asked himself. He shifted in his chair, turned his head from side to side, all the while still avoiding eye contact.

The Colonel was the only Chinese person in the room. There was no translator in the room either. Besides myself and my Caucasian co-producer who was also operating the camera, no one else was visible. Our Caucasian camera assistant was sitting out of his sight behind a low wall, ready to quickly adjust a light or change a battery if needed.

On a table next to me was a cellphone with an open line to our only translator for the interview, who was sitting in another room. I could press the MUTE / UNMUTE button to allow the translator to speak in Chinese to the Colonel when she wasn't speaking into the other microphone that transmitted quietly into the bud in my ear. But to reach

Baigen Li, "The Army Colonel."

the phone, the Colonel would have had to stand up from his interview chair, or worse, he would have to ask me. And since we weren't yet making eye contact, that didn't seem likely. So I just waited.

Tiny grey dust particles swirled between the bright camera lights and black screen behind the Colonel. He sat awkwardly, seemingly out of a sense of obligation.

Like most officials we interviewed, he had no desire to become a public figure, or to see his face in a movie. He didn't understand why a Westerner would ask the questions I did, let alone what use his answers would be to anyone. But he had agreed to the interview nonetheless. I knew—but he knew even better than me—that it is the lifelong CCP officials who understand the CCP and its policies the best. No expert or scholar or victim can match their experience or insight.

> **Struggle seemed such a tame translation for the term that had stopped the beating hearts of millions of people and brought so many millions more to their knees.**

I watched him as he struggled to find the words to express himself. This was a struggle that I knew. It was uncomfortable, but harmless, and certainly not fatal. It was a struggle with an inner conflict or moral dilemma—rather than a struggle in a physical scuffle or tug of war. Struggle seemed such a tame translation for the term that had stopped the beating hearts of millions of people and brought so many millions more to their knees.

"Struggle is something unique to the Communist Party," he finally concluded with certainty.

"The CCP is about hatred, extremes, and violence, isn't it?" he asked me.

Like all the other officials, he stated these unalterable facts and truths, and then asked me to agree. In CCP culture, this is how officials are trained to speak: You should only speak words with certainty if and when you are completely sure the listener will agree.

These officials all expected me to agree with their statements, to reassure them that they were saying the words I wanted to hear. But we were on Western turf and the integrity of our journalism was at stake. I wanted only to understand—not to absorb—the CCP culture, so I reserved my right to make no comment and give no assurances.

However, there are always exceptions to the rule.

In contrast, when I was interviewing the Chinese Professor who had written numerous articles about CCP culture, he barrelled his answers out at me as if CCP authorities would be at our door at any minute—as if both our lives depended upon him imparting as much knowledge as he humanly could into every single minute before our time was up.

"There are two fundamental characteristics of the CCP's philosophy," he said.

"There are a thousand things in Marx's ideologies, but one phrase sums them all up: Rebellion is justified; rebellion is struggle. It means: If you have a position, I am going to overthrow you."

"One: All people are animals. You are an animal. Thus, according to the principle of 'survival of the fittest,' the weak are prey for the strong. And because animals act according to instinct, they don't have a sense of morality, so the CCP culture does not have any constraints. It doesn't need to have a sense of what is right or wrong."

"Two: Marx and Lenin are the guiding ideologies of the CCP. There are a thousand things in Marx's ideologies, but one phrase sums them all up: Rebellion is justified; rebellion is struggle. It means: If you have a position, I am going to overthrow you. This is its core mode of operation."

He gave an example:

"The CCP likes to say: 'Soldiers who do not want to be generals are not good soldiers.' They use this sentence to educate every person."

"What does that actually mean?" I asked him.

"Everyone should want to be the leader; everyone should want to be the boss. So nobody is ever content with their position. For example, if I'm a farmer, then I don't want to be a farmer, I want to be a landlord, so I have to fight landlords until they collapse. If you have a better scientific invention or technology than me, then you must be put into a labor camp and gotten rid of. So there is always fighting. It puts the whole society in turmoil."

The CCP's "struggle" term has come a long way since Marx and

Engels began popularizing it. Today's Chinese struggle doesn't bear the "Chinese characteristics" that the CCP claims. But it does bear "CCP characteristics." And they have stretched and burst out of the vintage skin of old-time class struggles.

The Chinese Professor gave a modern business example:

"The CCP says that doing business is competition, and competition is war, or struggle—it still brings in war and struggle. So what mentality do people have these days? 'As long as I can make money, I don't care about the methods I use.' The CCP develops these thoughts in you."

A modern military example of the new and expanded CCP-struggle concept can be found in the 1999 CCP war manual, *Unrestricted Warfare,* written by two CCP army Colonels[23]:

> "The first rule of unrestricted warfare is that there are no rules, with nothing forbidden."

> "We acknowledge that the new principles of war are no longer 'using armed force to compel the enemy to submit to one's will,' but rather are 'using all means, including armed force or non-armed force, military and nonmilitary, and lethal and nonlethal means to compel the enemy to accept one's interests.' "

The former Judge had a more nuanced comparison of "struggle" and "competition."

"Struggle only happens in dictatorial and totalitarian countries, but we have another term called competition. Competition takes place in a fair and open playing field, where opposing parties showcase their strength or their policies in order for the public to make a judgement. Like, 'I support you or I support him.' That's the nature of competition. But when struggle occurs, competition is not allowed to take place. To struggle is to brutally attack the group of people opposing you, to even wipe them out. That way there is no one left who will say no to you."

The Senior Official, who had survived the most CCP struggle campaigns, described how one particular struggle hurt him the deepest. He had been forced to change his skin, which tore him apart from the inside during the process. It was an experience that had changed his very being—one from which he would never recover and that had become part of his culture. It was invisibly being passed down to his children and grandchildren without them ever really knowing what it is themselves.

He hadn't only been forced to wear the skin of the Party, like most CCP officials, he had been forced to represent it and become it. He had not only been forced to believe the illogical and the impossible—as if believing that 2+2=5—but he had had to force others to think the same way.

"When I joined the Party we all thought the Communist Party was so wonderful in every way," the Senior Official recounted. "It was so incredible, the best in the world, so we joined with great earnestness. My classmates and I were all determined to fight for the communist ideal, we saw it as the greatest ideal of mankind."

"In 1956, the CCP faced a difficult situation. Communism worldwide had collapsed as a result of Khrushchev denouncing Stalin, so China had no choice but to stand its own ground and lead communism worldwide. Zhou Enlai later visited some countries that had abandoned communism and concluded that they had alienated the masses, so Mao and Zhou felt it was necessary to improve the relationship between the communists and the masses and they launched the Rectification Movement. They said it would be 'wonderful in every way.' But as the Rectification Movement began, the Anti-Rightist Movement also began."

"*Movement.*" I noticed that most of our Chinese translators used this term when translating the names of the CCP's organized destruction-fests.

In English, a movement can be defined as:

> *a series of actions or activities intended or tending toward a particular end (dictionary.com).*

A few translators chose instead the term "campaign," which can be defined as:

> *a systematic course of aggressive activities for some specific purpose (dictionary.com).*

I found neither term sufficient, but chose "campaign" as the term to use in our film because I believe it is closer to the truth. I added both *campaign* and *movement* into my list of CCP cultural euphemisms.

"I will give you an example," continued the Senior Official. "I was in the third year of college. There were more than 100 classmates in my major and we were divided into three classes. We had identified about a dozen rightists, almost twenty rightists. Not only that, we had identified many more who were 'right-inclined' people, meaning their thoughts leaned toward the right. I was the youngest in my year—all of my classmates who had been identified as rightists had taught me how wonderful the Party is and had helped me to join the Party, but all of a sudden they had been labeled rightists. They included active members of the CCP, the CCP Youth League, and members of the school CCP Committee. They included elderly people who had joined the revolution in 1937. All of them had been identified as counterrevolutionary and rightists. And I was told to criticize them. Just days ago, they had been my dear teachers, but all of a sudden, I had to stand on a podium and condemn them. I couldn't make sense of it at all."

"I actively read all the notices and posters [by the CCP about the campaign] but I still couldn't make sense of why these people suddenly became enemies. But I had no choice but to announce them as enemies and I had to condemn them and I was told to run the 'struggle sessions' against them. In my heart I couldn't bring myself to do it. But I had to. If I were to refuse, they would label me an enemy as well and I would be criticized and struggled against. I began to have insomnia. I just couldn't figure out the reasons behind such madness. For five or six years I couldn't sleep. I had a splitting headache day and night. I became very ill and my health just collapsed."

> "Ever since those movements I knew that the only people who could have survived the movements were either those who sold their souls or fools. No one else could have survived. Chinese people as a whole couldn't find a way out."

"A classmate of mine studied physics at Beijing University. At the time, only the most brilliant students studied physics—the brightest students. His class had a total of seventeen students, among whom, eleven were identified as rightists. They were merely twenty-year-old kids. Out of seventeen kids, eleven were labeled rightists. What kind of society was this? I was very heartbroken after the movement. None of these bright people could make it out of this movement in one piece."

"If you tried to survive the movement, people would label you as a rightist and do away with you. Only certain kinds of people could survive the movement: fools and idiots who didn't understand anything and who didn't care for anything. They were the only ones who could survive intact. The other type of people were those who were very smart but their hearts were corrupt. They betrayed their friends and families, they betrayed their conscience, and all kinds of wicked things. Their souls were very much tainted. These two types of people were the only ones who could survive the movement. So how could this nation have any hope? How could the Chinese people have any hope? What was the point of living?"

"Ever since those movements I knew that the only people who could have survived the movements were either those who sold their souls or fools. No one else could have survived. Chinese people as a whole couldn't find a way out. Back then we didn't see the CCP for what it was, like we do today. We only felt very frustrated because we couldn't find a way out. We didn't know what to do."

"And what happened to you?" I asked, wondering which of those two groups of people he classified himself into.

"And what happened to me?" His eyes widened. "I was promoted to the post of Political Counselor!" He rolled his eyes and laughed.

"What's a Political Counselor?" he asked me, knowing I wouldn't have the answer.

"You know of Hu Jintao, don't you?" I nodded. Hu Jintao was the least memorable Chinese dictator squeezed between his puppeteer and previous dictator, Jiang Zemin, and his successor and current Chinese dictator, Xi Jinping.

"Hu Juntao was a political counselor while he was at Tsinghua University. He was six years younger than me. It's the equivalent to being a cadre [leader]," he explained, illustrating how high a level he had been pushed to for destroying his teachers, friends, and classmates. "And later, what did they ask me to do? They asked me to persecute rightists!"

He continued with obvious indignation:

"Those rightists really suffered. My classmates who were thrown into prison met with miserable fates. One of them was in prison and had to be reformed. He had been imprisoned for ten years and had been working very hard on himself to reform. In prison, a group of three people determined how well each person had reformed himself, and among the three was the head of the workers' propaganda team, who was also the head of the prison. One time they were determining which prisoner could be released and the head of the propaganda team stated: 'A dog would never change its habit of eating feces, therefore a rightist could never reform himself. How can a rightist truly reform himself? How can a dog change its old habits?' "

"So this person, my former classmate, basically had a nervous breakdown. His mental state collapsed completely. He began to eat feces and drink urine in prison. Later he died in prison."

He shrugged his shoulders. I'm sure he could have talked about that one struggle campaign for days on end, but he moved on.

"You have no idea how many times we have been on the brink of death."

"Why do we say the CCP is a force to be reckoned with? Because the CCP knows how to terrorize and suppress in such a way where no one is spared. As soon as you disobey in the slightest you are doomed."

"What came next?" he asked. "There was the Great Leap Forward. This movement diverted everyone's frustrations and resentment into conquering nature and surpassing Great Britain and the United States within five years—to advance toward communism on a fast track. We all pledged to fulfill the realization of communism even if we had to give twenty years of our lives. The Great Leap Forward distracted us from the miseries we had felt from the previous movements. We lived on empty hope."

He threw his head back and laughed. This time not at me—he was deep within his own memory.

After some time he looked at me squarely. "You have no idea how many times we have been on the brink of death." His voice trailed off. I waited.

"Your only way out was to be a slave who obeyed completely and willingly and who didn't have any thoughts of your own. If you expressed yourself you would be doomed. But you were still alive, and you either had to give in and betray your conscience or you could hide in fear, or remain completely silent."

He had remained silent for decades. Looking like a fool had been safer than letting on that he had a mind of his own.

"But we ourselves were in that system . . . We just didn't want this type of thing to happen to us."

Another Official recounted a story from a later CCP campaign:

"I had a classmate, he was the son of provincial-level officials. He was just a teenager and he said one sentence, 'Socialism is not good' and they shot him dead." That official preferred not to discuss how he himself had managed to survive campaign after campaign, while rising up in his CCP rank.

Another Official talked indirectly about how he had survived:

"We lived through the struggles. We knew about the CCP's extremes and hatred. We knew the CCP doesn't follow normal reasoning in its actions and that it goes to extremes in whatever it does, that it will become hostile and turn against good people unpredictably. But we ourselves were in that system, we weren't that clear on it, we didn't have a deep understanding. We just didn't want this type of thing to happen to us."

Chinese people know that the CCP is always watching. The gigantic and all-pervasive big-brother policing system—the Public Security Bureau (PSB)—has always been, and still is the backbone of the CCP's citizen control mechanism, called Domestic Security. Domestic security and public security are both euphemisms for enforcing compliance with the regime.

The CCP spends about twenty percent more on policing its own people than it does on its military defenses against foreign enemies.[24]

"In China, there are political police officers, criminal police officers, patrol police officers, household registration police officers . . . There are many more detailed ranks of police officers and they each have their own privileges, like receiving settlement money for resolving particular cases, embezzlement and bribery, and the power to provide local illegal groups with an umbrella of protection. Other privileges are basic, like for the lower levels of the police force, you get free meals, get into clubs and other places for free. In some cases, you can give someone money and a criminal will be released; businesses give you gifts, and so on. As long as you have a bit of power or a title of some sort, you more or less have access to these privileges." This was said by the former CCP Police Officer and Secret Agent who observed how vastly different China's law enforcement system is from policing in the West.

The CCP's surveillance state has grown well beyond George Orwell's prophetic dystopia in *1984*.

The Xinjiang region—where an entire ethnic group of Uyghur Muslims have been taken hostage by the CCP and are being decultured, imprisoned, and organ harvested—is now arguably the most surveilled location on the planet.

A 2019 technology report by IT company Comparitech,[25] found that eight of the ten most surveilled cities in the world are in China, and up to 626 million surveillance cameras are in use across the country. Named *Sharp Eyes* by the CCP, after the infamous Cultural Revolution slogan that forced citizens to spy on their neighbors (*The People Have Sharp Eyes*), the camera network boasts the ability to recognize the face (even with a face mask), body temperature, and gait (walking style) of citizens—even if they just take a few steps outside.

Artificial intelligence is being used to process and analyze gigantic amounts of citizen data that the CCP has collected with military precision, using high-tech techniques such as DNA and biometric sampling and multi-angle camera surveillance systems. City dwellers are required to use their phones and phone apps for pretty much every aspect of daily living—from purchasing goods, to paying bills, and entering stores—and the CCP requires access to all phone and internet data, and all Chinese companies and foreign companies doing business in China must comply and deliver the data.

As always, whether it be under the guise of socialism, communism, or any other -ism, this surveillance and public control is under the euphemism of "For the Public Good." As if the more tightly wrapped in the cloak of the CCP, the "better" the public will be.

"In Zhongnanhai, as soon as you enter, there is a big sign that reads: 'Serve the People,' said the Army Colonel. "So people assume that the CCP *serves the people.*"

Zhongnanhai is the headquarters of the CCP in China's capital of Beijing. In the large compound, top CCP officials carry out their administrative duties. Since the Tiananmen massacre it has mostly been closed off to the general public.

A large, impressive entrance at the southern end of the compound is flanked by two giant banners—huge white Chinese characters scream out against a bright red background: 'Long live the great Communist Party of China! and Long live the invincible Mao Zedong Thought!' Between the two larger-than-life banners, two uniformed officers stand guard on either side of the main central

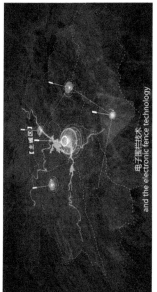

Examples of human surveillance technology already in action in China, and monitored by the CCP's Public Security Bureau.
(Screenshots from video advertisement for Megvii Face++ Intelligence Public Security Solution, 2019)

banner, which says: 'Serve the People' in gold print on red. These golden words are said to be in the handwriting of Mao. They are the official slogan of the CCP and are famous in word and sight throughout China.

"The CCP has a lot of superficial things that it says and does," said the Army Colonel, talking about the CCP as if it were an entity in itself. "The saying, 'Serve the People' sounds really nice, really euphemistic. It makes people think the CCP is worth following, worth making efforts for. I received this kind of education as a soldier. But beneath this beautiful phrase there is a lot of hypocrisy, cunning, and darkness."

On China's Big Brother internet, netizens have shown contempt for the CCP's guiding phrase and turned 'Serve the People' into a parody. By adding one Chinese character at the end, 'Serve the People,' becomes: 'Serve the Renminbi.' Renminbi is the official currency of China.

Of course such phrases are censored by the CCP because they are true. Such phrases reveal the inner skin of the CCP.

Some regular Chinese citizens still have their natural creativity to come up with such a pun, and some still search for and value concepts such as truth. But this is a dividing line between regular Chinese citizens and CCP officials. A CCP official wouldn't dare to even think about such things.

The realm of CCP officialdom is not within Big Brother's internet wall. CCP officials cannot and do not vent their woes online or in public. They are not allowed creative freedom or wit to make light of their master and his policies. They have taken the oath of loyalty to the CCP above all else. They are considered Party elites, not regular citizens of China, and may reap the power and financial benefits, but they are forever captive and forever beholden to the CCP.

Where Orwell's *1984* social hierarchy runs down from the

omnipresent Big Brother to the Inner Party elites, to the Outer Party members, and then to the Proles (Proletariats), the CCP has maintained a similar structure since its socialist inception.

Using Orwell's prophecy as a comparison, the CCP is Big Brother, CCP officials are the Inner Party members, CCP members are the Outer Party members, and the masses—the general public—are the Proles. The hierarchies and rules within each Party level become more and more strict, and more and more opaque to all levels below as they reach closer and closer to the revered inner circle of the everlasting Big Brother.

> **"No matter if you are a big or small official you have guaranteed wages, you have power over others, and many other benefits because the power can be exchanged for gain."**

In a sense, CCP officials are the skin of the regime. They, and other CCP members face the masses. They present the words and slogans of the regime. Their necks, their limbs and mouths are moved by Big Brother. They cover the rotting flesh formed by decades of upper Party leadership formed over old, sinister bones.

"The CCP has controlled all this for a long time already," said the former Propaganda Official with remorse. "I don't feel proud of working in the Propaganda Department, but in society people certainly do look up to people in that type of position. They see it as a superior position because you have power. No matter if you are a big or small official you have guaranteed wages, you have power over others, and many other benefits because the power can be exchanged for gain."

As the Propaganda Official spoke more and more, his speech

had become more relaxed, but the look of discomfort on his face hadn't changed. I had thought that he didn't like being filmed, but as he continued, I realized my questioning had awoken competing layers of guilt, remorse, and regret.

"I thought about quitting my job," he said, "but I've spent half my life doing this. If I quit I'll lose everything. A few decades of working records would be completely wiped out."

The conflict between one's conscience, the need to earn a living, and the social pressure to remain a CCP official had, for a long time, grated painfully in the minds of most of these insiders.

"If you are a judge," said the former Judge, "others see you as an extraordinary person. You can benefit your family, relatives, and friends—they would all be so proud of you. If they were to run into some kind of trouble, you are in a position to help them."

"Chinese bureaucracy is in a very abnormal or morbid state," he continued. "Because of control and directives from the Party, you have no way to make use of your talent and capabilities. There are all kinds of rules and disciplines that restrict what you do, and dictate what you should and shouldn't do. You have no degree of freedom. You cannot do what you want to do. You cannot avoid doing what you don't want to do."

"Because you are a judge in China's courts, you have no way of avoiding it. You have to do it. So what you do is against your will, and sometimes even against your conscience. I'm not sure if you understood that."

I nodded my head. This concept I did understand.

To the horror of his friends and family, the Judge had quit his post and had begun to take cases as an independent human rights lawyer inside the country with the world's worst human rights record. His legal practice didn't last long and within a few years he fled China as a last resort to stay out of prison and protect his family. But he had left China with a clear conscience and with his sanity intact.

> **They can't lead a normal life like ordinary people. Their minds are twisted and morbid, and they live constantly under enormous stress.**

He explained what would have been his fate if he had remained a CCP judge:

"A few days ago I read an article, which said that over the past several years more than eighty CCP officials committed suicide: some hung themselves, some shot themselves, and some jumped off buildings. There have been many cases. This number was only the publicly released figures. I believe there have been many, many more suicide cases of CCP officials."

"Why would they kill themselves? Because their consciences are in a state of conflict. They can't lead a normal life like ordinary people. Their minds are twisted and morbid, and they live constantly under enormous stress. In the end, suicide was their only way out. At least I was able to quit and keep myself sane and sound, both physically and mentally. To be frank, this was not easy to do. You need to be very strong-willed to do that because you have to be in that environment every day. In Chinese we say: You go along with the bad example of others. It means you become just like the rest of them—as bad, morbid, and distorted as the rest of them."

"What I feel most proud about is that I didn't end up like one of them. It's possible that if I hadn't quit and continued to work as a judge, I would have become just like them. That would have been horrifying."

It was rather disturbing to me how many Chinese citizens we

interviewed had considered or attempted suicide, or knew someone else who had. One interviewee, a dissident (not an official), had jumped out of a four-storey window onto a concrete platform to escape another round of torture by CCP authorities. Rather than a suicide attempt, it seemed more like a frantic, spur-of-the-moment decision made when he had been left alone for a tiny moment in a room with an open window. Either way, he was extremely lucky to survive the fall. And as soon as he recovered enough to drag his newly crippled leg behind him, he was sent to prison and tortured some more.

In Orwell's *1984*, two Outer Party members, Winston and Julia, look out a window at a woman, a Prole, on the street below. They see the ordinary woman and her class of ordinary citizens as the only hope for a future society of "conscious beings," who would "stay alive against all the odds . . . passing on from body to body the vitality, which the Party did not share and could not kill."

Orwell wrote:

> You were the dead; theirs was the future. But you could share in that future if you kept alive the mind as they kept alive the body, and passed on the secret doctrine that two plus two make four.
>
> "We are the dead," he said.
>
> "We are the dead," echoed Julia dutifully.
>
> "You are the dead," said an iron voice behind them.

As in *1984*, within the Outer Party ranks of the CCP, the iron voice is always behind—or perhaps above—every Party member, ensuring that the Party's skin turns and reflects the colors it requires to project to the masses. The morality and conscience of Party members must be willing to die for the Party. Physical death is the least painful.

As in *1984*, CCP officials are the bearers of the Party's culture. They are required to be masters of the euphemistic language of "double-think" to survive. Lying is institutionalized. Corruption is the welcomed opiate. And morality is constantly redefined at the Party's whim, to such an extent that it no longer bears any fixed meaning at all.

Unlike in *1984*, the CCP has learned to add more color and flair to its outer skin, and gold and glamor to lure in the willing. CCP apologists are often dazzled by its sheen and—knowingly or unknowingly—become accomplices to the bitter and bloody crimes of the CCP.

CHAPTER 15

Lives of Grass

Cutting grass. The sharp, hard rotary blade of a lawn mower, spinning at 200 mph, sucks the grass blades upward in a continual air circulation, raising them up straight and tall toward a metal sun, then slices them cleanly and precisely at a height established by a great big hand, and in a split second, cuts them all down to size with speed and ease. The grass that remains is left to rot or is airlifted into a bag for easy dumping.

Thousands of blades of grass are cut for every minute of mowing. On a single summer morning, my husband possibly mowed down a million blades.

"The CCP kills people as if cutting grass," said the former PSB Official.

I later found a more literal translation of the phrase he used:

"The CCP kills people like scything flax."

To *scythe out a life* seems a more communist-appropriate term.

A scythe looks very similar to the communist's symbolic sickle. A layman may easily confuse one for the other. A sickle is used for a wide range of agricultural work, while a scythe is used almost exclusively for cutting grass, wheat, or other flax-like plants. Both the sickle and the scythe have a sharp curved metal cutting blade and usually a wooden handle.

Some say the Grim Reaper carries a sickle. Some say he carries a scythe. Many say his tool is for the purpose of harvesting or reaping human souls into the afterlife. Is it just coincidence the Grim Reaper's tool of choice is the same as that of the Communist Party?

"The CCP treats our lives like grass," said another Official, who also used a different phrase, with a similar meaning:

"The CCP kills people like swatting flies."

The communist penchant for murder is immortalized in the Chinese saying: *sha ren ru ma*, which means that many lives are killed and the lives were devoid of any value or meaning to the murderer. Google Translate converts the phrase to simply: Murderous.

"Killing quotas . . . you had to kill 1%—1.5% of the population."

Following the Marxist way, communist dictators have always strived to utilize the most advanced scientific methods and technology available for killing in each historical time period.

The PSB Official described the top mathematical approach available seventy years ago, which the CCP used to decide which citizens would be killed in the 1950s:

"Killing quotas," said the Official. "For example, in Shanghai you had to kill between 1% and 1.5% of the population. Or it could be 0.1% to 0.15% of the population, depending on the city. This quota was personally ordered by Mao Zedong."

"At that time, Shanghai had a population of six million people, so a lot had to be killed. But when Shanghai started the campaign, not enough people were killed, so the central authorities came and criticized Shanghai authorities, and then the major media criticized Shanghai, saying they did a bad job. Shanghai had to act quickly. Who should be killed? They organized arrests and many innocent people died."

"Think about it," he asked me, "how can you arrest people based on a percentage of the population?"

I shook my head and frowned.

"The communist doctrine is based on killing—killing to scare people, to make fear, and keep their rule."

The former Secret Agent and 6-10 Officer didn't flinch when it came to talking about killing:

"It was after getting into the National Security Agency and after joining 6-10, from a political point of view, it [the role of a CCP agent] truly became a killing machine of the CCP, to help them suppress dissent."

"That's their way," said the former Diplomat. "The communist doctrine is based on killing—killing to scare people, to make fear, and keep their rule."

The Chinese Professor philosophized:

"We judge someone as good or bad according to whether they are helping or harming society. If a person does serious harm to society, they would be in jail according to law."

I agreed that was an expected, civil norm, regardless of one's moral position.

Magnitude of genocides between 1955 and 2014

The shown magnitude of deaths from genocides is a non-linear measure – see the source tab further details.

No data   0   1   2   3   4   5

Source: Political Instability Task Force (PITF) State Failure Problem Set, 1955-2014 (Death Magnitude)   OurWorldInData.org/genocides/ • CC BY
Note: The death magnitude scale used is non-linear, for more information please consult the OWID page or PITF codebook.

The map here shows the magnitude of the total genocide or politicide deaths between 1955–2014 as recorded by the Political Instability Task Force. (Note that data for Yugoslavia had been omitted from the map.) (Source: Max Roser and Mohamed Nagdy (2013) – "Genocides." Published online at OurWorldInData.org[26]

"In the past, the CCP killed eighty million people. That seems more serious than what Hitler did in World War II, but actually this loss is small."

I wondered if I heard him correctly. Killing eighty million human beings is like wiping out the entire population of Germany!

It would be easy to blame the millions of deaths on Mao Zedong if the regime had changed after his death. But it didn't, so the legacy of the biggest murderer of all time stands with the CCP, which still worships and advocates Mao's "Thought" nationwide, and continues to drive murderous campaigns to this day. Add to the CCP's death toll the murders by Stalin and Hitler and other communist or socialist dictators who looked to Marx as their liberator, and Marx and his communist theories become ground zero for the most deadly serial killing ever seen.

Why was the Professor saying that the death of eighty million people is "small"?

"The most serious factor," he explained, "is that the CCP made people's thoughts disappear, made their thoughts of morality disappear. It could possibly make a billion or more people into wolf-like CCP people. This is the most evil aspect of the CCP. Its poison goes very, very deep."

I was aware he was jumping between fact, experience, and opinion, but he spoke so fast, it was better to let him theorize than disrupt his lightning speed presentation, and then sort the fact from opinion later.

"The CCP's evil surpasses that of the Nazis," he continued. "Nazis kill other people, they don't kill their own family. But the CCP doesn't only kill other people, they also kill their own people, their relatives, even their parents. Parents and children become enemies, spouses become enemies, siblings become enemies."

One of the CCP's most devastating campaigns, which doesn't

usually have its numbers included in the CCP death count, is the One-Child Policy. It's known as "China's One-Child Policy," but that's not even a euphemism. It's an outright lie. It was the *CCP's One-Child Policy* and it killed at least 400 million lives, both inside and outside the womb: forced abortions; forced steralizations; mothers forced to kill their newborn babies before the authorities punished the entire family; fathers forced to abandon their newborns on the street to prevent their wives from killing the child and themselves—in the desperate hope that someone else would help the baby live.

Like the CCP's insane sparrow-cide two decades earlier, this mass infanticide has never been seen anywhere else in history.

Many Chinese echo the CCP's words and say that the One-Child Policy was the only way for China to manage its expanding population. Even though the 36-year campaign wrought immeasurable suffering and uncountable killing, the CCP's way is "never wrong"—it is the "only way" and it is "always right." That's what the CCP culture teaches and that's what its students repeat.

The High-Ranking Official disagreed with the CCP and its apologists on this. He argued that the CCP's killing policies are the direct result of the CCP being a fanatical extremist group.

"Since its inception," he explained, "the CCP aimed to completely break away from all traditions. This is an extreme ideology. The result of such an ideology is an extremist political party."

He argued that the CCP didn't have to impose the One-Child Policy, but that the policy is merely another example of its extremist behavior.

"Back in the 1950s," he explained, "a well-known demography expert named Ma Yin-Chu warned of China's rising population problem and advised that each family have only two or three children. But Mao Zedong didn't listen and instead families had at least four or five children. This is what it means to go to extremes—at first there is a complete lack of the concept of birth control, and as a result, the population explodes. Then suddenly, you are only allowed to have one child."

Many Chinese had used the term "extreme" when describing CCP actions and policies, but this example gave me the most vivid visual clarity. Today, giant billboards advertising abortions are seen throughout China. After generations of forced abortions, women no longer have to be forced to have an abortion. It is now a standard part of CCP culture.

"Almost all of us women in China have had to do it," a Chinese business woman in her 60s had whispered to me during an informal discussion about the culture in China today. She directed me to typical advertisements in China for abortion clinics and I was shocked by what I saw.

Today on bus stops, buildings, and on flyers, glamorous young Chinese women smile and lie luxuriously in strapless gowns and in romantic settings, among flowers and jewels. Chinese slogans flutter around them:

"Bye bye pain, hello happiness"

"Painless as a dream"

"If you love her, give her the best"

"Painless, safe, gentle to the womb"

"Relax in being a woman"

"Relax for three minutes"

"Terminate your pregnancy in three minutes"

"Abortion—painless and carefree"

Abortion advertisement on the Changsha Tianlun Women's Hospital website offering "Painless Abortion Bundle Price for 480 RMB" using "She's advanced abortion technology." (Source: Changsha Tianlun Women's Hospital[27])

Without the English translation of these Chinese advertisements, by the imagery alone, I guessed they were for romantic getaways, cosmetic surgery procedures, or relaxing day spas.

How wrong I was.

I realized that I could no longer look at the CCP's killing campaigns independently as I had been, placing them on a timeline, one

> **"In the past the CCP didn't have much technology to kill, so they just dragged people out and beat them to death. And that was it. But now, the CCP can sell your organs—the things in your body it can make money from."**

after another, contrasting dictators and technology. No—the campaigns can't be separated or viewed as merely past or present. They are all inextricably linked. Each campaign overlaps and winds and twists upon a long line of fierce barbed wire within the CCP's iron loom. They form a warped tapestry that binds blood and bone, and heart and soul over China to maintain the CCP's singular goal of total and ultimate control.

"Killing people is not difficult for the CCP," the Professor said in a disturbingly nonchalant manner. "In the past the CCP didn't have much technology to kill, so they just dragged people out and beat them to death. And that was it. But now, the CCP can sell your organs—the things in your body it can make money from. So it jails you, draws your blood, and tests the health of your organs."

This procedure is called forced organ harvesting—not by the CCP who punishes anyone who talks about such a thing—but by independent investigators who have researched and compiled the evidence of this heinous crime.

Forced organ harvesting is a term free of CCP euphemism. It is a clinical term for a clinical procedure with disastrous implications for humankind. It is an honest term coined by honest people.

> "Thousands of innocents have been killed to order having the physical integrity of their beings—their bodies—cut open while still alive for their kidneys, livers, hearts, lungs, cornea, and skin to be removed and turned into commodities for sale."

"Doctors killed those innocent people simply because they pursued truthfulness, compassion, and forbearance, and lived lives of healthy exercise and meditation that was seen as dangerous to the interests and objectives of the totalitarian state of the People's Republic of China."

These statements were given in the *Final Judgment* of the Independent People's Tribunal into Forced Organ Harvesting from Prisoners of Conscience in China on June 2019,[28] after twelve months of reviewing thousands of pages of evidence, and countless hours of witness and expert testimony.

This People's Tribunual, called the China Tribunal, was led by one of the world's leading experts on genocide and crimes against humanity, Sir Geoffrey Nice, Q.C., who also led the prosecution of Slobodan Milošević, former president of Serbia, at the U.N.'s International Criminal Tribunal for the former Yugoslavia.

In a packed London room of lawyers, human rights advocates, academia, politicians, and others—many of whom had traveled from around the world to hear the tribunal's final conclusions—Sir Geoffrey Nice read the judgment with solemnity and a refined British accent:

"It gives the Tribunal no pleasure to reach this conclusion to which it was driven by evidence and the application of reason and logic together with its appraisal of witnesses who gave evidence.

The conclusion shows that very many people have died indescribably hideous deaths for no reason, that more may suffer in similar ways and that all of us live on a planet where extreme wickedness may be found in the power of those, for the time being, running a country with one of the oldest civilizations known to modern man which, ideally, we should be able to respect and from which we should be able to learn."

The China Tribunal, led by Sir Geoffrey Nice, Q.C. (inset), presented its final judgment in June 2019 in London. It concluded that the CCP has been harvesting organs from living, innocent, prisoners of conscience for over a decade.

The CCP found their "final solution" to their failed Falun Gong persecution campaign and turned it into a multibillion-dollar operation that shows no sign of stopping.

And as the CCP has been depleting their main organ pool— hundreds of thousands of Falun Gong practitioners—they have found another source of living human organs to sell in the bodies of the Uyghur people of Xinjiang.

Investigative researcher and journalist Ethan Gutmann visited the region in 2019 to speak to witnesses. He estimates that around 25,000 Uyghers are currently being killed for the sale of their organs annually.[29]

This crime is almost too evil to comprehend.

The China Tribunal placed the CCP's forced organ harvesting alongside the world's most hideous crimes against humanity:

"...victim for victim and death for death, the gassing of the Jews by the Nazis, the massacre by the Khmer Rouge or the butchery to death of the Rwanda Tutsis may not be worse than cutting out the hearts, other organs and the very souls of living, blameless, harmless, peaceable people."

It is easier to lay the blame on a dead figurehead than to face the strange reality that the most prolific murderers are subordinate to the same entity: the Communist Party.

Research who is history's biggest killers and you'll find Mao Zedong at the top of the list, followed at a distance by Joseph Stalin. It is easier to lay the blame on a dead figurehead than to face the strange reality that the most prolific murderers are subordinate to the same entity: the Communist Party.

Dictator after dictator, by sickle or scalpel, the killing under the CCP has never ceased. It continues right now, today, as we in the Free World inhale and exhale.

The word to describe the Nazi's mass killing of the Jews didn't exist until the heinous crime was discovered and a word was needed to describe it—the Holocaust. While in some parts of Europe, the biblical Hebrew word *Sho'ah*, meaning catastrophe, is preferred, Holocaust is the most widely used term.

For those who have learned about it, the mere mention of the term immediately evokes a magnitude of suffering. It conjures freakish imagery of naked emaciated bodies with heads so gaunt that their eyes bulge from their sockets. Bodies, barely recognizable as human beings, standing against each other, as if to prevent each other from being blown over by a mere breeze. Bodies, discarded in mass uncovered graves.

According to Britannica, the term Holocaust is "derived from the Greek word *holokauston*, a translation of the Hebrew word *'olah*, meaning a burnt sacrifice offered whole to God." The images I remember are of bodies in camps, but the name refers to the images we don't see—the burning of these bodies, whole, in crematoriums or open fires.

In recent decades, the CCP has put more emphasis on burning the bodies of its victims—either in whole or in parts. Burning—cremation—is the CCP's standard procedure carried out on the involuntary "donor's" remains after all sellable organs have been cut out. These organs are then sewn into a living human who paid money to the CCP hospital, doctor, organ broker, hotel, airline, etc., and whose payment will inadvertently go to the many Western companies who supply the CCP with the technology and drugs they use to carry out organ transplantations in China.

> **There is yet to be a term coined—without euphemism—that represents the CCP's vile criminal and senseless destruction of countless human lives by human hands under the guise of a desolate and desperate political system.**

Prior to its entry to the World Trade Organization in 2001, the CCP worried less about the scrutiny of foreign observers. So the bodies of its victims could be dealt with any which way. But now that the CCP requires international acceptance to fuel its constitutional desire for wealth, and while it continues to vehemently block any third-party investigation into its crimes, it cannot afford to have images of its victims escape to the West as they have in the past. Burning the bodies leaves no evidence, no recognizable remains, and no imagery that can be meme'd and made viral inside or outside of the CCP's internet walls.

"How can they do this?" the Professor asked me before immediately answering himself. "Because the CCP deems human beings as things, as animals. Humans are supposed to produce resources. You are a resource, an animal. Animals let people kill them. Members within the CCP all know this situation."

There is yet to be a term coined—without euphemism—that represents the CCP's vile criminal and senseless destruction of countless human lives by human hands under the guise of a desolate and desperate political system. But I believe that one day such a term will be named.

An old Zen proverb reads:

> "Sitting quietly, doing nothing, spring comes and the grass grows by itself."

It was very strange to witness how common it is for the Chinese people to talk about their lives under the CCP as helpless blades of grass, ready at any moment for the Grim Reaper to come with a sickle for his harvest of souls.

But it was even stranger to come to understand that many citizens, who have been raised and bred by the CCP, no longer believe that grass can—as it once did—actually grow by itself.

CHAPTER 16
Beans and Bulbs

"When you are in prison it is almost impossible to commit suicide. They won't let you. You can't die in there," said Max. He was fourteen when he was imprisoned and required to do slave labor at a Chinese prison factory.

"Metal, glass, shoe laces, belt, glasses, ring, watch, lightbulb— anything that doesn't dissolve—they won't let it anywhere near you. Someone would cut themselves with anything sharp and blood would spurt out and then they'd spend one day at the prison hospital. That would be one day of treatment, one day off from prison labor. That was considered a good day."

Max wasn't a former regime insider, but now in his 20s and so much younger than our other interviewees, I wanted to see how his experience differed from those of typically older survivors of slave labor in China.

Max opened a bag of dry, uncooked soybeans that he'd bought from a Californian grocery store and rolled them all out on the dining table where we were interviewing him. Against the red tablecloth, I could see brown, oval spots on the cream-colored beans.

"At first I thought the beans were for us to eat." He laughed to himself. "Then a prisoner told me these are for us to sort."

He removed his glasses and put his nose close enough to the beans that he might have snorted one up a nostril if he'd breathed in hard enough.

As in prison, he didn't wear gloves. He used the fingers of both his bare hands to roll the beans in small circles. Sometimes he used his palms. He picked up a bean that was darker than the others and held it up to show me. "See, this one is blackish."

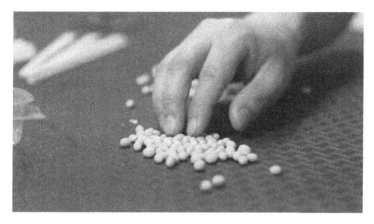

Max Ji Xiaoxin was fourteen years old when he was imprisoned and forced to perform slave labor daily—such as sorting piles of beans—because he and his parents had tried to appeal to the Chinese authorities.

He kept circling through the beans, then held up another one.

"Like this, see? It's cracked. It's not good."

One of his prison jobs—unpaid and involuntary—was separating soybeans into good ones and bad ones. He did this every day for ten hours a day. He was told the best beans were exported overseas to America.

"I never saw anyone wash their hands beforehand and the environment we worked in was very dirty. Some people have skin diseases. It's really disgusting." His head was down, staring at the beans.

"What do you think about when you see these things now?" I asked him.

He didn't answer. I waited.

"When you see this stuff, you think about when you got arrested. I feel a bit emotional being in contact with this stuff." He kept his head down and rolled the beans around and around.

> **"At the police station, the police would scare me by saying: 'We will find ways to kill your dad . . . For you, we will cut you up into pieces and throw you into the sewer.' "**

"Anyway . . ." he composed himself. "It reminds me of when I was young, crying every day while laboring. Because I was young I always cried." He looked at the beans again. "Afraid," he said.

Max didn't think of himself as young anymore. He had been separated from his parents in the prison and his father was later left for dead by the police at his home and soon died. Max's mother had been arrested and brutally tortured in police custody more than twenty times, so she left home to avoid implicating her sons with her peaceful protests for freedom in China. Max and his older brother slept in the frigid northern winters of China huddled on their apartment floor with no heating and little food. Max wasn't allowed to attend school. He was regularly searched and taken for questioning at the local police station.

"At the police station, the police would scare me by saying: 'We will find ways to kill your dad.' Then one officer added: 'Don't worry. For you, we will cut you up into pieces and throw you into the sewer.'"

His experience changed his perspective on law in China.

"I was still young at that time, so I used to believe in the law in China, but I learned that there is no real law in China. They can do whatever they want."

"Why were you arrested?" I asked. "The time when you were put into prison." I had to clarify because he had been detained so many times. "Detention" is essentially a euphemism for arrest. There are formal differences between them, according to the CCP, but for the arrested or the detained, there is little difference.

"I was going to Beijing with my parents to appeal to the authorities," said Max quietly. "On the way, police officers stopped us and asked if we practiced Falun Gong. We said yes. The police took us into custody. They handcuffed me to a flagpole in the front yard of the police building. I was kept there for the whole day in the hot sun."

Humiliating citizens publicly is a common tactic the CCP uses to scare other citizens into captive submission.

"After that, they took off all my clothes and I put on a prison uniform. And they shaved off all my hair!" He seemed most upset about his hair, which I found out later was connected to the trauma of being publicly humiliated again—this time in the classroom—when he tried to go back to school and his prison haircut was still obvious.

"And they took my glasses away too. I have a very high myopia so I couldn't see a thing."

"Is that short-sightedness or near-sightedness?" I asked.

"Near-sightedness. Without glasses, everything looks blurry," he explained. "For those who don't understand what it looks like, you can use a camera and set it to a 2.8 aperture. That's about it, the blurry background effect."

He knew cameras better than I did, but now I understood why he had put his nose so close to the beans to be able to distinguish the good from the bad.

"There was barbed wire on all the barriers and armed guards against all the walls. When the big iron gate was shut, it went 'bang' and I found myself inside and bald. Just like a criminal prisoner. There were many bad prisoners inside who committed crimes like murder, robbery, and rape. There were freezing days when I had to wash in cold water. Other prisoners were treated the same way. I wasn't anyone special. Many days passed. Without a calendar, I couldn't count the number of days and they all faded into oblivion."

> **"Some people broke the lightbulbs previously and swallowed the glass. At this awful place, people would rather hurt themselves like that than stay in there."**

He was looking at the beans lying on the table in front of him.

"We sorted beans from morning until night. When you finish sorting, your vision is really messed up. Everywhere looks yellowish. At night they didn't turn the lights off. The ceiling was very, very high up and the lightbulbs were very bright and there was a steel mesh over the ceiling beneath the lightbulbs."

I wasn't seeing the connection between the lightbulbs, the beans, and his blurry, yellow vision.

"With that kind of really strong, bright light above you, it's hard to fall asleep," he explained. "Sometimes my eyes would open a little bit when I was sleeping and the bright light would startle me. And then during the daytime my eyes were very red. When I cried it was very painful. The light was so strong, my eyes couldn't handle it."

Then he made the connection for me:

"So one day, I asked a prisoner why the lights were so high up and so bright, and covered with the steel mesh. Could we ask them to change it? That's when they told me that some people broke the lightbulbs previously and swallowed the glass. At this awful place, people would rather hurt themselves like that than stay in there. It was a very awful place."

The PSB Official, who was a former provincial director of China's prison and labor camp administration, explained the situation more flatly than Max did:

"China has a policy called Labor Reform. Either in prison or in a correctional institution, one has to perform labor. Since prisons are considered a more standard place of detention, they commonly have factories as well. They're all like that. The prisoners must labor."

"Labor reform" is another communist euphemism. Forced labor

or slave labor are more accurate, honest terms.

Forced labor is the same euphemism used to justify Stalin's gulags and Nazi concentration camps. Yet while those camps have since closed, China's nationwide slave labor network has only expanded and become more entrenched. It goes by many names depending on the type of facility—prisons, labor camps, black prisons, detention centers, brainwashing centers, reeducation centers. In recent years many have been euphemistically relabeled as drug rehabilitation centers so as to "expose less bone" to any noisy Western critics. But regardless of the name, the communist slave labor system has remained the backbone of the CCP's economy— cheap and open for business.

"So Chinese people are aware of slave labor and labor camps in China?"

The former Labor Camp Director and PSB Official seemed surprised that I would need to ask such an obvious question.

Of course they are! In my mind that was what his expression implied.

"For example," he continued. "There's a very common pair of shoes that Chinese people wear. They have a rubber sole. We have a specific name for them. They're called Liberation Shoes. These shoes are all made in prisons. Everyone knows."

The former Labor Camp Director gave me a brief history:

"China's labor camp system came into existence soon after the CCP seized power. At that time there were five groups of people: landlords, rich peasants, anti-revolutionist, bad factors, rightists— their crimes were not severe enough to warrant execution, and there were a huge number of them. So the CCP decided to detain them collectively—to let them work, and reeducate them through labor. Over time, those five groups no longer existed, so new groups came in: drug abusers, prostitutes, thieves, and thugs. In

Liberation Shoes (Source: Yurouguan, iStock by Getty Images)

1999, Falun Gong practitioners were added."

> ## "Ordinary people are just struggling for survival . . . They don't know they have rights. No one ever told them that they have rights."

He spoke so matter of factly, without disdain or disgust. The people of China have long been forced to see slave labor as an "open secret," part of the "dark side" of the nation—one that is best left alone so it never gets close to oneself.

"We knew about those things," said the former A-list celebrity CCP artist. "We knew that many people in China lived a very harsh life, but you ignored them, and forgot about them. We always tried to find excuses for the regime. We were brainwashed to think like that."

The Senior Official explained the sentiment of the general public:

"Chinese people, after having experienced decades of political persecution, they intuitively avoid any kind of trouble. The CCP prohibits you from speaking out, so if you break your silence, you are asking for trouble, and you are asking to be arrested. So people think: why would I risk myself to speak out?"

The CCP Journalist nailed it for me when explaining why Chinese people don't complain about the fact that their system and economy depends on slavery:

"Ordinary people are just struggling for survival. They don't have time to pay attention or they simply just don't know. 'I have human rights? I have rights?' They don't know they have rights. No one ever told them that they have rights."

To be free from slavery is a basic right that I take for granted growing up in the West. Yet under communist regimes, basic rights are stripped from those whom the regime believes are unworthy. And after seventy years of painful socialist rule, the Chinese people don't know what human rights are and thus either work to exploit the slave system to make money, or pretend it doesn't exist so that they won't have to suffer it themselves.

Former political prisoners described to us a huge variety of different jobs they were forced to do as slaves, including folding pages for books which were then taken to a book factory for binding, wrapping individual pairs of wooden chopsticks with narrow strips of paper, cutting fabric for men's underwear, hand painting tiny figurines . . .

"Where does the business for these prison factories come from?" asked the Labor Camp Director. "Some examples are factories that export souvenirs or things like Christmas trees. Christmas trees sold in North America are mostly all made in China. These exporters want to reduce the cost of production so they use prison labor. The cost is very low."

I made a note to ensure I searched harder to find the country of origin on products that I purchase. I have long avoided "Made in China" products, but big online retailers like Amazon.com don't require suppliers to include the country of origin of their products.

The extent of the normalization of China's slavery system really only hit me later, after our film crew received secret undercover footage of the exterior of a women's labor camp and its surroundings in China's Jilin City.

This is what we saw in the footage:

> The rear and side sections of a tall red brick wall that spanned the perimeter of the labor camp were topped with large coils of shiny barbed wire. The upper part of a boxy Soviet-style building was visible in the distance behind the wall. Off-white in color, the labor camp building had simple windows and looked completely harmless.
>
> The moving car from which the hidden camera was secretly filming passed two normal-looking white vans parked on the road next to the camp. Both vans were plastered with Chinese advertisements.
>
> Along the camp's perimeter fence hung a large banner that covered the full height of the wall and was about three times as wide as it was tall. The brightly colored banner was advertising to sellers to come and sell their goods at a local market.
>
> The car turned the corner onto a busy six-lane highway, still staying close to the labor camp fence and filming through an open passenger window. Construction noises were clanging loudly, cars and trucks and motorbikes could be heard revving past, a car horn beeped, and a bicycle bell twanged.

I had to remind myself that I was looking at the exterior of a

Chinese labor camp where one of the characters in our movie had been brutally enslaved, then tortured and murdered.

The camera kept rolling:

> Near the labor camp gates was a large bus stop with aluminum bench seats and two large commercial advertising panels. Both panels displayed the same poster that showed a smiling middle-aged man holding his arms out toward a big, spikey grey-brown blob that was larger than the man's head and torso combined. The man and the blob were against a watery blue background.
>
> The words in the Chinese advertisement read: "Real living sea cucumbers, a Changchun special. Eat a live sea cucumber a day. It's very nutritious for the body."
>
> The car drove slowly past the bus stop, past a tall tree, and to the camp's front gate, which closed as the car approached.

Yes. This was outside the gates of a Chinese labor camp in the middle of a big city.

Advertisements for sea cucumbers are on display at the bus stop outside of the Jilin Women's Labor Camp, which was renamed to the Jilin Drug Rehabilitation Center.

I tried to imagine the Auschwitz concentration camp buildings with advertisements for sauerkraut and bratwurst sausages on its borders, but I couldn't. It is just too absurd.

The camera then captured the front of the camp—from the other side of the highway—looking directly at the camp's main entrance:

> The camp's main building has four floors, three of which jut out high above its surrounding fence. On the left side of the camp gate a giant red billboard reaches up to the third floor of the camp building. In yellow numbers and Chinese characters against a vivid red background, the billboard is advertising retail spaces that will soon be available in a nearby shopping area.

> The camera stayed in position as vehicles of all sorts passed to and fro along the highway in front of the labor camp and its unmissable billboard. It was a cloudless day under a dull blue sky. A lady holding an umbrella for sun protection crossed the highway with two companions and headed toward the bus stop, instinctively steering clear of the gate of the camp . . .

"You can't show that footage in the movie," a colleague said to me after watching it. "That doesn't look scary at all. The audience won't believe that place is a Chinese labor camp."

He was right. It looked like a regular building on any busy city street. We simple Westerners have been trained by Hollywood to expect the visuals of a dark and sinister building, shrouded in secrecy and protected by heavily armed guards.

I tried to imagine the Auschwitz concentration camp buildings with advertisements for sauerkraut and bratwurst sausages on its borders, but I couldn't. It is just too absurd.

Yet, despite the absurdity of the camp's exterior, we had gathered a large body of evidence of the abuse and slavery that took place in the interior of that particular camp. We had eyewitness testimony from former inmates and secretly filmed admissions from prison guards and the current labor camp director that proved torture and death were common. We had photo evidence of products regularly made in slave labor conditions at that camp, which were then exported overseas. We even had photo and video evidence of a woman who was killed at the camp as a result of such abuse.

We found an old photograph of the labor camp taken twenty years earlier. The red brick fence was missing and what is now a highway was just a road. But the camp buildings have hardly changed.

I showed the old photograph to a former inmate at that camp—a small woman in her late 60s. She was one of four female survivors that we interviewed from that camp. Besides being tortured with electric batons there on a regular basis, she was also frequently tied up into excruciating, inhuman physical positions for days on end. In between the torture sessions she was treated as a slave and did all kinds of manual labor.

The woman pointed at the old camp photograph and said:

"When I first entered the labor camp, the building looked quite old. It was just a building on a deserted land with a few houses for feeding inmates. Inside the labor camp, it is very dirty. The walls are all black, and the building was very old."

"We were ordered to work for them [the camp guards]," she continued. "They told us to get rid of those trees and weeds around the camp. We did this every day, for months—from morning until night. We chopped down trees and removed stumps, then we dug ditches, and put in lawns for them. Then they told us to plant

Jilin Provincial Women's Labor Camp taken in the early 2000s.
(Source: Minghui.org)

The Jilin Women's Labor camp in 2015, now simply renamed to the "Jilin Drug Rehabilitation Center."

grapes for them to make the camp look nicer. When you look at it from outside now it looks quite nice, but no one knows that we did all this."

I compared the two photos of the camp side by side.

The labor camp facilities and practices have hardly changed, but the CCP has built up the city around it. But like much of China's cities, the exterior outer layer has been given a costly new coat to give the impression that the CCP has changed its ways. Like many correctional facilities in China, this labor camp had been given the new name: Drug Rehabilitation Center. But, as we found out during interviews with directors of CCP labor camps, the CCP's anti-human system that runs the facilities hasn't changed. And they are just as deadly as ever.

Having labor camps and prisons so close to the lives of Chinese people is another social control mechanism of the CCP to keep an ever-present sense of fear among the people.

Chinese citizens are aware of the "two skins" of the prison system. The exterior layers make the facility appear legal and legitimate, but beneath the outer layer of skin, the citizens know what's there and they know to keep their distance. Having labor camps and prisons so close to the lives of Chinese people is another social control mechanism of the CCP to keep an ever-present sense of fear among the people. Every citizen knows intuitively that it only takes one wrong move to be sent to a camp.

"The Public Security Bureau alone has the final say over whether or not a person will be stripped of their freedom and sent to a labor camp," explained the former Labor Camp Director and PSB Official.

He outlined the PSB's procedures:

"First a police station or a department within the PSB decides to arrest you. Then they establish a case against you and report your case to the city's Office of Labor and Reeducation Committee, the director of which is also the Vice-Mayor of the PSB. The Office approves the case and says you get three years in a labor camp. So, the legality and legitimacy of your case are single-handedly determined by the PSB."

Communists and socialists like to simplify law and order. Checks and balances are seen as impediments to their efforts.

In his book *Toward Soviet America* (1932),[30] American communist leader, William Z. Foster explained the type of court system a socialist strives for:

> "The Soviet court system will be simple, speedy and direct. The judges, chosen by the corresponding Soviets, will be responsible to them. The Supreme Court . . . will be purely juridical (administrative) and entirely under the control of the Central Executive Committee. The pest of lawyers will be abolished."

Under a socialist central government, slaves are quickly and easily found, formed, and utilized throughout the system without any moral concern or restraint. And as long as there is demand for cheap slave-made products, the system has no reason to change.

CHAPTER 17
Ad Break #2

2016 CHINESE COMMUNIST PARTY PUBLIC
SERVICE ANNOUNCEMENT[31]

Dawn over the ocean.

A keyboard plays a gentle, major chord arpeggio.

The camera pans downward to reveal more dark sand. The back of a man's head appears in silhouette, very close to the camera in the center of the screen.

A tall orange flame billows out of a shadowy cauldron on the sand between the man and the sea.

A deep, raspy male voice asks in Chinese:

Who am I?

What am I?

The man in silhouette, full body, walks on the sand toward the edge of the sea.

Maybe you've never given it much thought.

A lone college student cleans the chalkboard in a large classroom, then switches the lights off to leave.

> I am the last one to leave.

A lone cleaner picks up a broom and begins sweeping the middle of an empty three-lane road lined by green leafed trees.

> I am the first one to start.

A tired surgeon takes off his face mask.

A small group of nurses gesture to each other to be quiet.

The surgeon is sleeping on the floor, sitting against a wall of a hospital hallway.

String instruments join the piano in a long, emotive harmony.

> I am the one who thinks of himself the least.

A police officer stands in the rain directing pedestrians at a busy intersection.

He stands alone in the center of the intersection when there are no more pedestrians.

> I am the one who sticks it out to the end.

A middle-aged man changes a lightbulb with a ladder, while children play and an elderly man watches.

> I am the one who acts fastest.

An older man works on a wharf in the pouring rain. He is thrown a rope, which he winds around a pile to secure a boat. His wiry arms pull hard on the rope.

Rain and sweat dripping over his worn, tanned face, he opens his mouth and lets out a silent roar.

A chorus of "ahhs" join the music.

I am the one who cares for others most.

The music builds with emotional drama as each character traveling home from their duty is played in a montage:

The student walks in the center of a wide empty path lined with rich leafy green trees and lush, manicured shrubs.

The middle-aged man bounds down a narrow corridor between houses with happy, small children at his ankles.

The dock worker rides a bicycle over a bridge, passing large seaboats on the water beneath him.

The weary-looking officer drives his motorbike down an empty tree-lined road.

The surgeon stands in front of an open locker door and removes his head covering.

The cleaner walks along the edge of an empty highway.

The six characters sit together in a neat semi-circle on

the neatly manicured grass on a wide open hillside. Tall green pines and large yellow-leafed trees jut out beyond the hilltop. The characters smile broadly as they gaze directly into the camera, each clasping their bent knees, and with their heels resting toward the center of their circular formation.

The camera slowly zooms out as they hold their passionate smiles.

The voice concludes solemnly:

I am the Communist Party of China

And I will be with you forever.

"What am I? . . . I am the Chinese Communist Party and I will be with you forever." (Screenshot from 2016 CCP Public Service Announcement)

FADE OUT.

A mega creepy shudder pulsed down my spine when I first watched this ad.

The CCP asserts that the people of China cannot be good or virtuous without it.

This brightly colored agitprop would have made Stalin and Mao proud and likely duped countless viewers to be so dazzled by the shining generosity of the Party that they missed the inner meaning. Or perhaps, they already knew and had accepted the inner meaning.

The CCP doesn't merely personify itself. It gives itself physicality. It gives itself human form. It calls itself a "being." It takes credit for every good deed done in the entire country of China. It claims to embody all that is good and of merit in the people of China.

Basically, the CCP asserts that the people of China cannot be good or virtuous without it.

And it kindly reminds all Chinese people to smile, and to believe that this is the best they are ever going to get, and that the CCP will never, ever leave them:

> "I am the Communist Party of China and I will be with you forever."

CHAPTER 18

Bloodlines

The former PSB Official asked me a question for which I had no answer. But I didn't mind. I'd become accustomed to it.

"How can Xi Jinping become the highest leader of China today?" he said, giving me a moment to respond. "Does he possess incredible abilities?"

I could pretty much name all the Chinese dictators from Mao onward, but who put them into power? Advisers? Factional leaders? Family? Wealthy elites? Warlords? I didn't really know. Nor did I know anything about Xi's education or upbringing.

CCP propaganda states[32] that there are seven million CCP officials in China and that they don't need to be voted into power because they are selected and moved up and down in rank according to their "merits." The CCP calls this process Meritocratic Screening, and the decision of one's merits is based on the mood of the CCP.

I think of Xi Jinping as the round-faced dictator offended by being called a lovable, huggable teddy bear. Winnie the Pooh is bad for his hard-line image, so Xi makes Winnie-lovers and taunting meme-makers suffer for drawing a comparison between him and the beloved bear. China's previous dictator, Jiang Zemin, is publicly likened to a pudgy green, and often evil, toad. To my Western female mind, a bear—even a chubby, nonviolent bear— is stronger and more dignified than a toad, so I thought Xi's bear

Artwork by political cartoonist, Badiucao.   (Source: China Digital Times)

fanclub was at least a step up from Jiang's night croakers.

So, does Xi have other "incredible abilities" that brought him to the all-powerful dictator status beside punishing China's teddy meme makers?

"No," the Official explained. "The single most important factor is that he is a *Red Second Generation*. Xi is the son of a senior original CCP founding member. You have to have a very hard-line birth."

I wrote down this new communist term in my notebook: "Red Second Generation." It sounded more like the newest model of a high tech gadget.

"This organization, the CCP, emphasizes your loyalty to it and really emphasizes your origin of birth. In the past if you were a landlord's child or a capitalist's child or an intellectual's child, that was no good. But today, it matters whether you are a *Red Descendent* or not; whether you have the CCP blood or not. The bloodline is like that."

"This organization, the CCP, emphasizes your loyalty to it and really emphasizes your origin of birth . . . The bloodline is like that."

This was coming from a man who had grown up in a family of farmers, but because his mother's family had been previously classed as being from a landlord family he had had to work extraordinarily hard, and undergo heavy personal scrutiny before he was allowed to finally achieve his dream of being accepted into CCP membership.

"Chinese society has an element of feudalism as well as dictatorship," he said. "If you aren't 'born well,' you will face lifelong prejudice."

"Up until today, for the CCP to maintain its power, it cannot share with other people. It cannot change its color."

I was yet to understand the importance of color tone or hue in the ranks of CCP membership.

"I'm very *Red*, you see." said a Chinese businessman who had refused to enter the ranks of CCP officialdom despite his family's high-ranking CCP status.

No, I didn't see.

He explained:

"When my father was a teenager, he joined the revolutionary

army of the CCP, and he retired respectfully from the CCP. That's how I became *Red Color*. I was famous at my school because of my father's background, everybody knew me. I was a Secretary, and *Secretary* became my name wherever I went. That's how people knew me. It's a kind of reputation."

I had been taught a different form of Red Reputation.

As a child, my religiously pious grandmother had warned me about the color red in large amounts on anything from clothes to cars. "Never buy a red car," she repeated. "It's the color of the devil."

I had wondered why the leather ladies dance shoes with lovely square heels that we wore for traditional Russian folk dancing were exempt from the rule and allowed to be a beautiful red color. But those shoes were from pre-Soviet times when Russian women danced in long embroidered tunics and beaded headpieces. That was before the nation was divided into Red Russians (communists) and White Russians (patriots), with the whites being targeted for exile, slave labor, or death.

Red cloth became the symbol of Marxist revolution—a revolution to destroy all that was old, all that was traditional, and all that was inspired by a heavenly faith. The vivid red pigment became synonymous with the spilling of human blood.

In the safety of the Free World, as Russian-born or Russian-descendent girls and women, we always wore a cloth headscarf and a long skirt to enter the *Old Believers'* Russian Orthodox Church every Sunday morning. But the cloth we wore was never red. My grandmother made sure of that.

The Chinese Professor wasn't concerned about the color of the CCP's bloodline. He was concerned about its physicality.

"The CCP refers to itself as a 'lifeform.' It always refers to the 'Party's Lifeform,'" he said without hesitation.

That was not just a foreign concept to me. It was a completely alien concept, as if from another galaxy. And it was also just creepy. But other officials we'd spoken with had also used the same term.

"The lifeform of the CCP has not perished at all, it is still exerting its influence on people," one of them had said with all due seriousness.

I was perplexed to find the concept of the CCP existing as a "lifeform" is a concept that the CCP itself wants to perpetuate.

> ***How do you present words like that to a Western audience who doesn't speak that language?* I asked myself. The easy solution most journalists take is: You just don't. That option was very tempting.**

"If the CCP is a lifeform, then it's easy to understand that this life came for the purpose of destroying human lives," continued the Chinese Professor.

That is easy to understand?!? I was astounded. It was a constant surprise to me to see how far Western reality was from the concepts of the CCP culture.

I looked at the Professor wondering how on earth I could explain something like this "lifeform" concept to anyone else.

The Professor continued:

"Many people within the CCP, including me, did not know what the CCP is, what its true nature is. Only by understanding its inherent nature can you understand why it set up a long-term revolution—all these political movements." He spoke as if he thought I was understanding him.

"Before we didn't know its nature, so we would look back on its killing campaigns and say, 'Ah, this looks like it was a just mistake.' Even me and some of my friends who are old intellectuals would just think that the CCP made a mistake. You're in that kind of environment, so you just don't know."

The term "mistake" came up again and again from both regular Chinese and CCP apologists. They seem to have a miraculous ability to accept the CCP's bloodshed and to excuse it by hiding it in a mental envelope that is filed and forgotten in a dusty pigeonhole in the memory labeled "Mistakes."

The Professor continued his effort to share his awakening with me:

"In order to destroy humankind, the CCP first has to destroy people's minds and culture. Because as long as people have culture, they will be part of a culture and an ethnic group."

"Look at China," he said. "Why are the people there called Chinese people? Because they have Chinese culture. So when this culture no longer exists, they are no longer Chinese people. What kind of people are they? They have taken on a new culture, they have absorbed communist culture. We call it CCP culture or Party culture. It implants in you and tells you how you should be, and then that's what you become."

"It uses lies to support its Party culture and then implants it into people's blood."

If I hadn't been hearing this from such an accomplished academic—with a PhD and two master degrees—an author, and a former CCP model student, I would have squirmed far more at the extremely cultish description of the CCP that he was giving me. Those are the types of phrases and descriptions that immediately sideline victim testimony in the minds of Western journalists and researchers who don't have the time or patience to decode each sentence.

How do you present words like that to a Western audience who doesn't speak that language? I asked myself. The easy solution most journalists take is: You just don't. That option was very tempting.

We didn't include anything like this in our movie. It was out of the question. But as I decoded the Professor's explanations, I was able to look at China's Walking Dead in a completely new light.

In the very first line of the *Communist Manifesto*, Marx wrote:

"A specter is haunting Europe—the specter of communism."

At first I had mistaken a specter for a scepter—a wizard's magic wand or staff. But this is not Harry Potter in Hollywood. This is reality. And Marx is talking about a ghost.

> *Specter: a visible incorporeal spirit, especially one of a terrifying nature; ghost; phantom; apparition, or some object or source of terror or dread (dictionary.com).*

I wondered why I'd been taught Marx's socialist principles at university, but was never encouraged to read his original texts. If I had, someone would have had to explain to me, firstly, what a specter is, and secondly, why Marx believed in ghosts while advocating for materialism and atheism along with the destruction of belief in things that can't be seen with the human eye.

I had previously likened the CCP to a poison, then to a captor or hostage, and later a parasite. But now, from this perspective, the CCP was a demon in possession of a vast nation and all of its people.

Demonic possession doesn't have to be a religious concept. I found this secular definition to be quite fitting:

> *Demonic possession: A condition where the victim can no longer exercise free will (wake-up.org).*

But was Marx wrong in calling communism a demon?

The CCP doesn't seem to think so. They think Marx, like the CCP, is ever-correct.

In 2018, the CCP produced a slick, red-toned, 5-part television series targeting Chinese youths and aptly called it: *Marx Got It Right*.

"For some, Marx is just an image of someone who always has a big beard," says the petite female TV host with a smile. She's talking to an audience of 20-year-olds, doing their best to show enthusiasm as she lectures them through Marx's life and legacy using audio/visual presentations and panel discussions with middle-aged men in suits.

Xi Jinping seems to be retracing his bloodlines all the way back to a bearded non-Chinese European, and reinvigorating the Chinese nation's love for their founding father.

Marx is "the greatest thinker in modern times," said Xi in a broadly televised speech in 2018, spoken to thousands of CCP officials on the 200th anniversary of Marx's birth. "No idea or theory in the history of human thought has produced a broader or deeper impact than Marxism," he said, vowing that Marxism will remain the CCP's—and therefore China's—blinding lighthouse into the future and beyond.

That same year, the CCP sent a larger-than-life bronze statue of Marx to his birthplace in the German city of Trier. The CCP spent a good amount of its annual $10 billion budget for international propaganda efforts[33] on peddling Marx and his

Screenshot from the TV show, "Marx Got it Right."

(Source: China Central Television)

ideology through various mediums.

And in China, more propaganda was on the way: a two-part documentary called *Imperishable Marx*, about the writing of *The Communist Manifesto*, followed by a seven-part celebratory animated series that dramatized Marx into the *Leader* that he never was in his actual lifetime.

I scrolled through the online episodes of *Leader*. Its pastel-colored palette of Japanese-style animation lulled me pleasantly away from the harsh red and black color tones of *Marx Got it Right*. But it was the strangest thing to see Marx and his wife—thoroughly non-Asian, with wide eyes and creamy skin (and looking rather trim, toned, and dapper)—speaking fluent Chinese throughout every European set that they were drawn in.

"We have a saying," one Official had said to me. "The saying is: 'Go see Marx.' It means you will go and see Marx in your afterlife." He chuckled a little. "But you are a descendant of Chinese emperors, why would you end up in the same place as Marx?"

"The CCP educates people to love Marx and Lenin. It teaches that loving Marx and Lenin is loving China, so many Chinese people say that we are the offspring of Marx and Lenin," said the Professor.

> **The matrimony of a dead Marx with a dead Lenin spawning the demon of the CCP . . . is a grotesque union to envision.**

The matrimony of a dead Marx with a dead Lenin spawning the demon of the CCP . . . is a grotesque union to envision—but perhaps it is a singular truth from the CCP about its true nature and hellish origins.

"The lifeform of communism didn't die with Mao, it still exists," said the High-Ranking Official. "The theories, principles, mentality, behaviors, and method of government—everything remains the same as it was. The overall political system has not changed. This political system is controlled utterly by the theories and mentality of the Communist Party."

A penny dropped upon the floor of my Western-bred brain.

The CCP erased 5,000 years of rich Chinese heritage and replaced their entire Chinese ancestry with one big white guy with a big grey beard. Despite the fact that this particular big-bearded guy is responsible for inspiring the slaughter of millions and millions across the globe, he was a white guy. He is not Chinese. It was ludicrous to think the CCP would try to fool the Chinese people into honoring a big-bearded white guy as their beloved ancestor, let alone their savior that would greet them at the other side of this life.

Chinese men can rarely even grow big beards! I thought.

It was like Po the Panda in the *Kungfu Panda* movie being fathered by a duck. He called the duck his dad and treated him as a dad, but of course he wasn't his *real* dad. You just knew that a duck and a duck, or a duck and a panda, or a duck and an anything couldn't produce a purebred panda. It is hilarious character development, but to believe it as truth is insanity.

Another penny clanked and began to spin in my mind as I drew together the perspective from each of the CCP insiders.

The CCP states that "the founding of the nation of China" took place in 1949. That is the year that the CCP took over China and implemented its socialist totalitarianism.

"I don't like to use that term, 'The founding of the nation,' " one Official had said. "The CCP did not found the nation. They took power over the country."

Did China exist before the CCP? I wondered. The CCP says "no," and that question is not allowed to be debated in China even though it is illogical and contradicts thousands of years of existing, documented Chinese history.

Did the CCP form the nation of China? I wondered. The CCP says "yes," and that question is also not allowed to be debated in China even though it is illogical and contradicts thousands of years of existing, documented Chinese history.

> **"To Westerners, the CCP's methods of propaganda must appear rather monotonous, but . . . after a few decades of it, you get used to it."**

"The vast majority of people, they don't care about politics," another Official had said, "but due to long-term brainwashing by the CCP they just believe whatever the CCP says is correct."

"To Westerners, the CCP's methods of propaganda must appear rather monotonous, but in the environment of China, after a few decades of it, you get used to it. From childhood to adulthood, you wouldn't even think to doubt it," another Official had explained.

"As for regular people, nobody studies Marxism or Leninism anymore," said another Official. "But the CCP has continued to drill it into people's psyche since 1949."

"Marx said himself that those who believe in him are nothing more than idealists, and those who support him support slaughtering," said an Official who had studied all of Marx and Lenin's writings.

"The CCP stated that struggling against heaven is endless joy, struggling against earth is endless joy, and struggling against other men is endless joy. That's just their philosophy. But this philosophy actually came from Marx. Marx talked about destroying everything using violence. Marx was a mad man. What could you do about it? The creator of this philosophy was mad to begin with."

The older officials we interviewed had studied Marx's teachings the most thoroughly—Lenin's and Mao's too. The younger the official, the less they needed to know all of Marx's teachings. They were only required to know the specific parts of Marxist theory that the CCP wants them to.

The Chinese Professor, although not quite in the category of a senior official, but getting on in his years, had also studied Marx thoroughly. He said:

"When Marx created his communist theory, his intention was to destroy mankind. He said that he shall stand up amid the ruins of a destroyed world and burst into laughter. This is his goal. If you look at the several dozen volumes of Marxist philosophy, beneath all its decorations, his intentions are right there."

"Not many people completed reading all of Marx's writings after they were translated into Chinese. Not even people who research and study Marxism finish reading them all. The few that do finish reading them see that it's all trash."

I couldn't help but connect the Professor's sentiment to a popular Ronald Regan quote that explains his approach to identifying a communist:

> "How do you tell a communist? Well, it's someone who reads Marx and Lenin. And how do you tell an anti-communist? It's someone who understands Marx and Lenin."

That quote might get a good laugh out of political conservatives, but the "lifeform" of the CCP—as ridiculous as it may seem to Western thinkers on all ends of the political spectrum—is no laughing matter.

I realized that my sidelining these foreign CCP cultural concepts had come from a place of ignorance and close-mindedness—even a hidden sense of Western superiority.

Following the CCP's bloodline from today back to Marx as the originator of not only the CCP, but also of the nation of China and the people of China is an absurd abomination. To take any leader that promotes that as truth seriously (whether they actually believe it or not), is akin to believing that Po the panda burst forth from the loins of a duck.

During the interviews with the CCP insiders I had sometimes chuckled to myself at the phrases and concepts they introduced to me. In a way, I just couldn't take those words seriously. And perhaps, at the time, I didn't want to. I was ready to sideline those aspects and just stick to the concepts that are more familiar and palatable to us Westerners.

But once the pennies began to drop, I realized that my sidelining these foreign CCP cultural concepts had come from a place of ignorance and close-mindedness—even a hidden sense of Western superiority.

I had always taken these CCP insiders themselves seriously, but I hadn't taken everything they said seriously enough to investigate all fronts. This became particularly apparent when I approached writing this chapter. But now, after seriously considering the full scope of the insights from the insiders, I feel somewhat lightened by the knowledge that was revealed to me, and clearer in my perspective on China's Walking Dead.

Without having lived bloody revolution after bloody revolution myself, without having been indoctrinated and bred from birth as a CCP captive, without having been possessed by a bloodthirsty demon hell-bent on animalizing and cannibalizing a nation, I am unwilling to revoke my cultural heritage and ancestry and replace it with anything but the truth. If those important family ties of mine were somehow cut, I believe I would find myself walking towards a zombie-like existence.

Any apology I felt for CCP advocates when originally going into the making of this movie and this book has disappeared. I am unwilling and unobliged to find excuses for the CCP regime and its apologists. And I am aware that this position leaves me wide open to the likely onslaught of "anti-Chinese" sentiment when I publish this book.

And isn't this the ultimate irony in this zombie saga, that anyone who points a finger at the white, non-Chinese, anti-human ancestor of the CCP will be labeled "racist," "anti-China," or "anti-Chinese?"

CHAPTER 19

Of Pigs and Fish

The Chinese Professor looked like he was in pain.

He had concealed any internal distress throughout our interview. But tiny signs—a pursing of his lips, the furrowing of his brow—had betrayed his outer skin and revealed a deep anxiety at a few particular points.

This was one of those points and his visible agony took me aback.

Patrick Ling, PhD, "The Chinese Professor and CCP Model Student."

"The entire country is covered by smog and the water is undrinkable," he said, shaking his head from side to side in such a worry about his motherland that his brow had contorted and formed deep ridges that seemed to want to run both down and across his face.

Isn't he exaggerating? I wondered.

1.6 million Chinese citizens die every year from air pollution-related health issues. That's 4,400 people dead, every single day.

Only in hindsight did I realize how justified his anxiety was.

A 2015 study called *Air Pollution in China*[34] by California-based climate research organization, Berkeley Earth, found that 1.6 million Chinese citizens die every year from air pollution-related health issues. That's 4,400 people dead, every single day. (Note: such studies revealing accurate data of the suffering of Chinese citizens most often comes from researchers who live outside of China and ironically have more access to truthful data sources than those in China who wish to do the same.)

In many areas across China—urban, industrial, rural—levels of hazardous airborne particles known as particulate matter or PM2.5 have often exceeded the acceptable limit more than twenty times. Where the World Health Organization has estimated a safe concentration of PM2.5 is no greater than 25 micrograms per cubic meter, China's Beijing region—where locals discuss and compare their "Beijing coughs"—has often sat around 100 micrograms per cubic meter, and has even reached 900 micrograms per cubic meter on particularly hazy days. However you look at the numbers, it's been well above dangerous levels for a very long time.

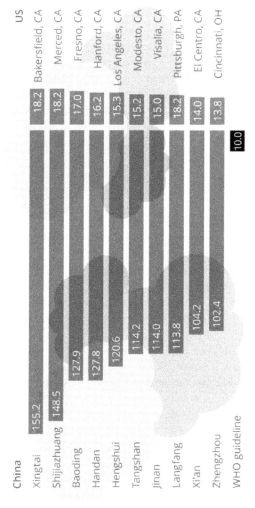

Air Pollution Levels In Perspective: China And The US

Daily average particulate pollution (PM2.5) in the 10 worst Chinese and US cities*

China		US	
Xingtai	155.2	Bakersfield, CA	18.2
Shijiazhuang	148.5	Merced, CA	18.2
Baoding	127.9	Fresno, CA	17.0
Handan	127.8	Hanford, CA	16.2
Hengshui	120.6	Los Angeles, CA	15.3
Tangshan	114.2	Modesto, CA	15.2
Jinan	114.0	Visalia, CA	15.0
Langfang	113.8	Pittsburgh, PA	18.2
Xi'an	104.2	El Centro, CA	14.0
Zhengzhou	102.4	Cincinnati, OH	13.8
WHO guideline			10.0

* Anything over 10 micrograms per cubic meter of PM2.5 considered hazardous to health by WHO

Sources: Washington Post, Chinese Ministry of Environmental
Protection, American Lung Association, WHO

@StatistaCharts

statista

(Source: Statista, 2015)

"Several billion people can't just migrate to another country, can they? So the only option is to wait for death."

"Something that is far more scary than smog and the polluted environment in China is the water," continued the Professor. "I have a friend who works in the environmental sector in Guangzhou. They said very early on that there was already no more clean water in Guangzhou, no clean water to drink. Actually, water in China is almost totally polluted, except for some places in Tibet where there is still clean water. Everywhere else the water is no good."

The discussion of China's physical environment and its degradation revealed the Professor's greatest anxiety:

"Underground water is the ultimate," he continued. "If something disastrous happens, people can pump water from underground, but now some factories directly release toxic water underground. Many large cities' underground water stores are completely polluted. As soon as you pollute it, it won't return to purity for thousands of years or more. The underground water is for mankind's posterity, but the CCP destroyed this."

I'm sure I noticed a slight involuntary shudder run down his neck and shoulders. He kept shaking his head, and continued talking without pause, but now as if he was only talking to himself.

"Chinese people no longer have a backup. Without a backup, several billion people can't just migrate to another country, can they? So the only option is to wait for death."

A billion people waiting for death? It was rather shocking to think about that. And although I tried, it was hard to keep the Professor's discomfort from penetrating me.

The descriptions of China's Walking Dead had come at me from many surprising angles, and this was another unexpected sign post. Of course I knew about the smog. I'm sure I've shared a meme or two about China's buildings that disappear day by day behind dangerously opaque veils of man-made pollution. But without living in it myself, it was easy to forget it or easier to imagine that it was confined only to limited areas or limited times of day. And without being a scientist, deep down in my ignorance I thought that maybe the smog may just one day move along and blow itself away.

But water? Water seeping through the ground, flowing through the rivers, evaporating and then falling from the sky, over crops, into drinking pans, over the children of the next generations. . . .

And the Professor was right. Almost ten years ago it was already reported that 90 percent of China's underground water was polluted and 60 percent was in the extremely polluted category.[35] And since then? According to persecuted Chinese environmentalists, at least "190 million people drink contaminated water,"[36] and contaminated water has bred more than four hundred known "Cancer Villages," where in every other house someone young or old is dying from pollution-caused cancer.

A true assessment of China's environmental pollution today is unavailable. That is a CCP "state secret" and, despite the fact that Chinese people can see, feel, taste, and die from the pollution, the CCP continues to insist on hiding it.

Leaked CCP propaganda directives (translated and published by *China Digital Times*) give a glimpse into how the CCP orders media to hide the truth of China's dire environmental state:

> Regarding the trash dumps in the upper reaches of the Miyun Reservoir, all media coverage is to be conducted in accordance with the information released by the Beijing Municipal Environmental Protection Bureau. Media is not to conduct its own coverage or commentary. From now on, the media is to submit drafts of all reports

involving public opinion to be examined and approved by the Municipal Propaganda Department.

Beijing Municipal Propaganda Department on February 25, 2013.[37]

————————————

Do not republish [coverage] of, comment on, or independently investigate reports of an explosion at a Xinjiang Bagang Steel Structure Co. Ltd. workshop; all websites must delete previous posts.

State Council Information Office (November 11, 2013), regarding a liquid ammonia explosion at a Shanghai refrigeration plant that supposedly killed 15 people and sickened 26 others.[38]

————————————

Regarding lawyers suing the governments of Beijing, Tianjin, and Hebei Province for not fulfilling their pollution management responsibilities, without exception do not report and do not forward online information.

Issued to media departments responsible for Beijing on December 20, 2016.[39]

————————————

All websites find and delete The Paper's article *Peking University Research Team: 260,000 Excess Deaths From PM2.5 in 31 Cities; Highest Rate in Shijiazhuang.*

(February 5, 2017) Original source not published to protect the source of the leak.[40]

"In CCP-controlled media, there are two types of news reports. In one type you get paid to report the news, in the other you get paid to not report the truth."

> ## *"In CCP-controlled media, there are two types of news reports. In one type you get paid to report the news, in the other you get paid to not report the truth."*

This was said by the former CCP Journalist. She had worked for one of the CCP's most pervasive national media platforms. She had taken up the Christian faith and been forced by her workplace to spy on her fellow church goers or lose the livelihood for her and her daughter. Torn between her faith and her ability to survive, she fled to the West where we were able to interview her.

"It's very difficult for journalists in China," she said. "In the eyes of regular citizens, being a journalist is a very good job with a higher income and social respect. For example, I had a lot of opportunities to report specific news stories or reports and receive a lot of money for it, payment from other people, not from my workplace. And if I don't report on certain stories, I can receive a lot of money for covering up the "dark side." Opportunities like this happen very often. In such a system controlled by the CCP, you can really earn a lot of money."

"So the role of the media in these cases is: If you do not expose the business, the business will give you a reward in return. The media receives money from the business or becomes a media partner, or allocates a budget for advertising. In this way, the dark sides don't get reported. The media will say something good about the business or even turn black into white."

"Can you give an example of how they do that—how they turn black into white?" I asked her, knowing that she had smuggled out audio recordings of some of her work meetings at *People's Daily Online*, one of the CCP's largest online platforms.

"In China, under the CCP, the CCP says that the business

has created so many jobs and provided tax revenue for the local government. So that's what gets said in the media. They completely ignore the environmental pollution, the health issues brought by the pollution, the pollution to the soil, and to the underground water. The business will use its connections to please the Propaganda Department, then the Propaganda Department will talk to the heads of the media and tell them how important it is to protect the business, to protect the economy, to save people's jobs. So, in the end, the health of the local people will be ignored, as well as the environment."

"*China Daily Online* has been doing this. *China Daily* is the agent that is utilized most often by the government to control media and speech," she continued. "They will report that the enterprise has imported some environmentally friendly equipment, and all the smoke released is up to standard, etc. because now all the Environmental Protection Offices have real-time online monitoring systems, all of the waste water outlets are attached with monitoring devices, so the office will publish that the waste water released from the business is up to standard. However, in reality, the local residents have complained that the business put pipes underground that direct the waste water directly into the Yangtze River. So the media is committing a crime as a co-conspirator."

The Journalist paused and looked at me. Unlike all the male officials who had asked me questions as a method to get my attention, my agreement, or just out of habit, she actually had a question that she genuinely wanted me to think about:

"Why are a lot of businesses built around the Yangtze River?"

It sounded like a riddle and she was waiting for me to respond.

I immediately thought geographically. The Yangtze is China's longest river. It is a beautiful, cultural icon of China, providing evocative imagery as it runs through picturesque stony gorges, alongside magnificent mountains, under powerful bridges and makes a stunningly circular 180-degree turn from south to north at Yunnan and eventually reaches the East China Sea.

According to the Asian Development Bank, the region surrounding the Yangtze River is "home to 40% of the country's population, it contributes 45% of gross domestic product and holds 36% of the country's water resources. The Yangtze itself is the PRC's longest river, providing drinking water to about 400 million people and accounts for 20% of its total wetland areas."[41]

My time was up and any answer I might have eventually found would have only been a guess at best.

"Why are a lot of businesses built around the Yangtze River?" she asked. "The answer is because it is so handy for them to release their waste water directly into it."

> *"Why are a lot of businesses built around the Yangtze River? . . . because it is so handy for them to release their waste water directly into it."*

Her answer was not what I expected. And I prefer funny riddles.

She maintained the same demeanor, as she had throughout almost the entire interview—serious and unemotional.

I rocked forward gently. With a kind of full body nod I encouraged her to continue.

She said:

"As a journalist I knew some of the business owners whose factories polluted the environment very badly. One of them became a deputy at the National People's Congress."

CCP apologists seem to lay the blame for the poisoning and suffocation of Chinese citizens on massive amounts of inanimate black lumps of earth. "Coal is largely to blame for the degradation of air quality," writes the highly influential U.S.-based globalist think tank, The Council on Foreign Relations, in their 2016 report, *China's Environmental Crisis.*[42]

But some Chinese citizens are coming to understand the real cause.

"Today, factories take care not to pollute during the day, but when I'm fishing at night, I can see them pumping waste into the river," said Ms. Wei Dongying, also known as China's Erin Brockovich, to WorldCrunch media in 2017.[43] "The government is obsessed with economic growth and, meanwhile, we ordinary citizens pay the price." Wei has been arrested numerous times by CCP authorities for trying to file environmental complaints in China.

The CCP's Constitution also supports that notion in action: Wealth at any cost. And since it's a socialist state, wealth and economic development isn't required for all people, only a majority of the people. And the majority are defined by the whim of an elite minority. So the actual human cost is never a real concern for the CCP.

Ordinary Chinese (that's how they call themselves)—the CCP's "masses," the non-CCP members, the non-CCP officials—are supposed to produce and consume and trust the CCP to handle their environment for them. For better or worse, until death does them part.

Former CCP celebrity TV anchor and author, Chai Jing, quit her job after her newborn baby was diagnosed with a benign lung tumor. After her baby's successful recovery, Chai became concerned about the air her child would be breathing in Beijing. She began a self-funded documentary project that was eventually released in 2013 called *Under The Dome*, and which reached 150 million views in China within just a few days.

In *Under The Dome*, Chai recalls how she had interviewed a six-year-old girl in 2004:

> Chai: "Have you ever seen a real star before?"
> Girl: "No, I haven't."
> Chai: "What about blue sky?"
> Girl: "I've seen one that's a little blue."
> Chai: "What about white clouds?"
> Girl: "No, I haven't."

It was only a decade later that Chai made the connection between the little girl who had never seen white clouds and the smogful skies that had been over much of China for too long a time already.

"I was right in the middle of it, but I didn't even realize it."

Chai recalls in her documentary how she had thought it was always just a weather problem:

> "Back then we thought it was just fog. We kept calling it 'fog.' "

> "At that time everyone said the haze was caused by random weather patterns. Hardly anyone took it seriously. It seems like China at that time was immersed in smog, blanketing twenty-five provinces and 600 million people. I was right in the middle of it, but I didn't even realize it."

Chai's documentary is exceptionally well-researched and documented. The active brains behind her pretty face are self-evident as she presents on stage to a captive audience in the documentary—TED-Talk style—in a well-practiced, steady manner, wearing an unassuming white blouse and jeans that fall

Chai Jing speaks in her documentary about the young girl who hadn't seen a blue sky in China. (Source: Still from *Under the Dome* by Chai Jing)

loosely upon her trim figure. But even as a capable, intelligent woman, and a high-profile media figure reporting on China's environment for more than a decade, she had never questioned the status quo.

Even in her position of power and influence, Chai had really believed what "everyone" had been saying about the smog. She parroted the Party line even when she had seen its damage with her very own eyes and felt it with her very nose and throat—even after she'd seen it permanently block the blue sky from that little girl in 2004.

Chai had probably never seen the CCP directives that her editors would have received, requiring the media to censor or distort any negative reports on China's environment. Thus, this intelligent and loyal CCP citizen had believed it was only fog that often blocked the beautiful views from her Beijing city apartment.

Even when Chai's throat bothered her because it was lined with dangerous daily amounts of particulate matter, she didn't worry about it because no one else was worrying about it, and the CCP hadn't told her to worry about it.

Chai says:

> "But the sensation in my throat remained. When I was in Xi'an, I was coughing so badly that I couldn't even sleep, so I cut up a lemon and put it beside my pillow."

The year of her documentary release, the smog brought another airpocalypse that stopped traffic in China's Northeast. China's ordinary people on the CCP's extraordinary Internet island turned the CCP's famous "Serve the People" phrase into "Feed Smog to the People," which, despite heavy censorship, became China's most popular search term of the year.[44]

After watching Chai's documentary, Chinese netizens began to comment online[45]:

> "It's not that I'm afraid of dying, I just don't want to live like this."

> "Shocking, just watching this makes me want to throw up. We don't need China to be #1 in the world, so can we slow down the pace of economic growth just a bit, even slowed down till we are rank 100 or below would be okay. Can we raise pollution management so that it is higher than military build-up? Can we make it so that environmental researchers are better compensated and treated than government cadres? So that we can truly and properly control pollution, restore the environment? This is not only our future or China's future, but also humanity's future."

Under the Dome cleverly only pointed an indirect finger at CCP authorities and it survived on China's internet for three weeks before being removed by censors—likely it was online longer because of Chai's nationwide celebrity status and removing it would bring attention to the CCP. If the film had been made by anyone with less influence it would most likely have been removed immediately.

Leaked directives from the Propaganda Department stated:

> All media must refrain from further promoting *Under the Dome*. Online public opinion [surrounding the documentary] must be regulated. (February 28, 2015)[46]

> Video websites are to delete *Under the Dome*. Take care to control related commentary . . . We reiterate that media personnel must not post content that violates regulations on either personal or official public platforms, or else face severe punishment. (March 6, 2015)[47]

But a discussion among ordinary Chinese about China's environment had started. And of course, the CCP needed to get that under its control.

"Before I came out of China, my main duty was to analyze public opinion and public sentiment," said the former Chinese journalist in the interview with me. "In the Beijing head office, there were about 300 staff using more than 100 computers to monitor online media, printed media, 'independent' media, WeChat, WeiBo Blog and Official Public accounts. Together these have become a mature and industrialized form of media."

"How?" I asked.

"For example, you monitor all public opinion and sentiment of the people and then take the lead in public opinion in a way that the masses are not aware, so they are being fooled."

In the online commenting surrounding Chai Jing's *Under the Dome* documentary, a slew of Chinese netizens began taking the spotlight away from China's environment and the CCP's culpability. It was most likely they had been—knowingly or unknowingly—directed by the CCP's public sentiment analysts to redirect public attention away from the real issue.

Thus, instead of demanding accountability for the environmental damage, they reignited a recent fire that had been flamed when it had become public knowledge that Chai—who has the public persona of a Chinese patriot—had chosen to give birth to her first child in America instead of in China. Many ordinary Chinese chose to overlook the facts about their dire environmental situation in Chai's documentary to instead discredit Chai as a traitor. This change in public opinion and sentiment twisted Chai into an enemy in arms with the CCP's nemesis, America, which suited the CCP to a tee.

"Before an avalanche, not a single snowflake feels they are responsible."

Some clearheaded netizens tried to call out the bluff, but in the end, they could only lament. One said:

> "Seeing most of the [early] popular/upvoted comments arguing over Chai Jing's American nationality and her daughter's tumor, I suddenly feel like China cannot be saved! After watching this, shouldn't people be lamenting that the current situation in China deserves being improved!? Shouldn't it be about thinking of ways to make things as environmentally friendly as possible!? If we don't save ourselves, who should we rely on to save us!? There is already someone [referring to Chai Jing] warning us, yet are we going to continue being preoccupied with making fun of each other and gossip, without change/improvement!?"

Another posted:

> "I saw a comment saying an American should just stay in America and not interfere with China's internal affairs. I want to say, this is f***ing [ridiculous]! That such a comment even has so many upvotes, is truly f***ing [ridiculous]! I feel there is no hope left, and no longer know what to say."

Another netizen summed up the situation in a single pithy proverb:

"Before an avalanche, not a single snowflake feels they are responsible."

A smashing avalanche of the health of an entire nation seems inevitable under the weight of enforced pursuit of national wealth enacted by more than a billion snowflakes.

Now living in safety outside of China, the Professor laid the blame clearly on the CCP:

The term the CCP has chosen to label the man-made smog is "meteorological disaster."

"The CCP labelled the smog in China a 'natural disaster.' Clearly it's caused by the CCP. It destroyed the environment," he said.

"Natural disaster" may have been an incorrect translation.

Natural disaster isn't the actual euphemism the CCP has chosen to describe China's deadly smog. Language is so important for the CCP and the development of CCP culture that they would have chosen the term very carefully.

The term the CCP has chosen to label the man-made smog is "meteorological disaster."

Most English dictionaries have a definition for natural disaster, such as the Merriam-Webster Dictionary that defines it as: "a sudden and terrible event in nature (such as a hurricane, tornado, or flood) that usually results in serious damage and many deaths." But they don't have a definition listing for a meteorological disaster.

Meteorology: a science that deals with the atmosphere and its phenomena and especially with weather and weather forecasting (Merriam-Webster Dictionary).

Therefore, the CCP has classified the suffocating smog over China as a weather-related disaster.

The lack of existing definitions for meteorological disaster makes the CCP's choice even more convenient because they can reform their own definition to suit their own communist dictionary.

In an official CCP statement (2016),[48] Beijing Municipal People's Congress used the standard, obtuse, CCP cultural rhetoric to justify their decision to hold the weather responsible for a man-made problem:

> "Meteorological disasters are closely related to everyone. But our understanding of meteorological disasters is different. Some people think that meteorology is a natural phenomenon, meteorological disasters are natural disasters, and it is a matter of God. Facing the disasters caused by wind, thunder, rain and snow, people can only bear the buck. In fact, this understanding is not very scientific . . . "

> " . . . In fact [*it's ironic they use 'in fact' to preface an untruth*], 'heavy fog' and 'haze' are traditional concepts in meteorology and are weather catastrophes . . . "

> "In summary, we believe that: meteorological disasters are the disasters formed by meteorological factors acting on disaster-bearing bodies in a specific disaster-preventing environment; meteorological disasters include primary, secondary, and derivative disasters; the definition of meteorological disasters is not a simple conceptual problem, but an important issue related to the establishment of government agencies. When this problem is clarified, the management system of meteorological disasters will be

smoother, and the design of the meteorological disaster prevention system will be smoother. This is also a point of understanding gradually formed in the legislation."

These three paragraphs were taken from a document that was nine paragraphs long and spoke mostly about weather theory until "haze" and "smog" were swiftly pulled into the equation toward the end.

Of course, regular Chinese citizens are not going to bother to read these types of documents even if they were able to access them. If they did, they would be unlikely to understand them. For Western minds, understanding and interpreting official CCP dialog is even more difficult and, I must say, terribly tedious and eye-wateringly boring. But to summarize the official stated stance, the CCP says that smog is haze and is therefore a weather problem that is now classified according to three factors:
1. Humidity
2. Visibility
3. Particular Matter (PM2.5)

Therefore, deadly particles in the air caused by the CCP's wealth-over-life-and-living policy that are killing thousands of Chinese citizens every day, are a weather problem that the CCP is working on solving. And "heroically," of course.

I reread George Orwell's book *Animal Farm* to remind myself what Orwell had prophesied about socialism in 1945. And of course, like the CCP, the pigs were forever placing themselves as the leaders and the heroes of all the animals, despite the fact that they created the problems that they were now claiming to be heroically working to solve.

As in *Animal Farm*, the delusions of the pigs' and the CCP's "reality" would be pants-wetting hilarious if only they weren't so damn deathly serious.

Two leaked CCP propaganda directives pierce the porky skin of the CCP's "heroism":

> Regarding the *Beijing Municipal Meteorological Disaster Prevention Statute (Draft)* plans to include smog on a list of meteorological disasters, all media must refrain from comment.
>
> *(December 20, 2016)[49]*
>
> All websites must take care to resolutely delete content which puts the issue of smog on the shoulders of politics, as well as all content and commentary which stir emotions or incite disturbances.
>
> *State Council Information Office (April 7, 2014)[50]*

The former PSB Official voiced his dismay using two sayings in Chinese, which read like awfully gloomy poetry when translated into English:

> "The system is a cesspit; it breeds flies.
> The system is a forest; it breeds tigers."

The former CCP Heart Surgeon spoke in a more direct, almost desperate manner:

"You see in China, the air is toxic, the water is polluted, the crops all have heavy, unregulated and hazardous chemicals and pesticides, and China has reached the point where people lie and cheat each other. There are Chinese videos that teach you how to make fake eggs that you can con people into buying and eating— they look exactly like real eggs. Society in China has reached that extent. There's no hope left. No hope left."

His fake egg reference opened up another dark rabbit hole that I reluctantly jumped into.

Fake eggs sold as real eggs have been bought by unsuspecting consumers throughout China, Asia, India, and maybe elsewhere. Fake rice has been bought by unsuspecting consumers throughout China, India, and likely other countries.

I watched a video of a Chinese man in dark glasses and a face mask teaching me how to make fake chicken eggs at home, using a combination of resin, starch, coagulant, sodium alginate, and pigments for the egg white; then a mix of resin and pigments for the egg yolk, and then paraffin wax, gypsum powder and calcium carbonate for the egg shell. Yeah. It's not really edible, but it won't kill you immediately. And some fake egg makers claim you can earn a decent profit selling them as real ones.

"Earn" doesn't quite feel like the right term. It's true that the fake egg makers spend time and money creating a product and therefore feel justified in receiving money for their eggs, but they sell the fake eggs to unsuspecting customers who think they are buying real chicken eggs.

Scam feels like too light a term for such a deceitful business model.

I watched a family in Hong Kong open and dissect a boiled egg that didn't look quite right among the rest of their dinner food upon the table. After removing the egg shell they found that the egg white had an unusual texture. And to their surprise, the cooked egg yolk bounced upon their plastic table cloth again and again. When they dissected the yolk, its texture looked like modelling plastic—like the type my daughter uses to make play jewelry and figurines. It never dries out and its packaging is clearly marked: DO NOT EAT.

I watched a man in Malaysia dissect a poached egg that had been cooked into a popular school lunch item. His daughter had told him about unusual rubbery eggs that they were now being fed at her elementary school, so he had asked his daughter to buy three egg sandwiches the next day and bring them home for him. The man pulled the egg yolk and egg white apart. The

A video on YouTube demonstrates how to make a fake egg. (Note: the You-Tube user states clearly in the description that this egg is not for eating.)
(Source: Channel SEKI SETO on YouTube[51])

texture and color resembled a cooked chicken egg but it was not quite the same. The man gathered pieces of the egg yolk, rolled them together, and formed a ball that was surprisingly firm. He dropped it on his plastic tablecloth and the yolk kept its ball form and bounced around. He bounced it again and again and asked, "Have you ever seen egg yolk that can do this?!"

I watched a large and elaborate shiny metal machine housed and operating inside a well-lit factory that reminded me of a newspaper printing press. Long, thin strips of a cloudy white substance looked like strings or narrow noodles running downwards and then across spinning metal rods. The strings moved fast and without pause until they were cut into tiny lengths at the very end of the machine run. They fell down upon a growing white pile of man-made grain. A hand reached into the pile and let the fake grains—said to be rice made from plastic—roll around in his palm and down between his fingers.

I watched three Indian men take off the cardboard cover from an aluminum takeout tray. Inside was cooked white rice, still hot and steaming. One man prodded the rice with his fingers as if to check its quality. Then he scooped up a handful of the rice into his palm, and began to turn it in his palm until the heat reduced and he could begin to squeeze it into a ball form. This man had obviously done this before. It took almost a full minute for him to turn and form it, as the other men watched on around their lunchroom table. A round white ball was now in the palm of his hand. He dropped it onto the center of the table and it bounced back, much higher than any of the fake egg yolks had bounced. The other two men took turns passing around their new plastic rice ball toy and bounced it up and down upon the table. I don't imagine they were hungry enough to eat the rest of the plastic rice left in the container.

For decades, under the CCP's rule and within the CCP's warped culture, China has continued to produce an enormous menu of tainted foods. Tainted foods are food products that have had nonfood and chemical substances added to reduce the cost of production and increase the profit for the maker. The health of the consumer seems of little consequence.

> **"If you are a farmer who raises pigs, you definitely won't eat pork because you know how the pigs were raised . . . Similarly, a fish farmer won't eat his own fish. But he eats the pork because he doesn't know the pigs are unsafe to eat."**

The CCP has more recently added a new course to their food menu: Fake Foods.

CCP China's tainted foods and fake foods are not produced for glossy magazine photo shoots or for children's toys. They are produced for human consumption. They are not made out of alternative food ingredients such as one might make an edible sponge cake look like a hamburger. No, these fake foods are made out of inedible nonfood substances that will harm the human body. And the producer is fully aware that the fake food will harm the consumer. The maker has no qualms selling the produce to others, but will certainly not consume it himself.

"In the food chain for example, everyone is harming each other," explained the former Journalist who lived and breathed the corruption under the CCP's environmental policies. " If you are a farmer who raises pigs, you definitely won't eat pork because you know how the pigs were raised. You know the meat contains additives and other substances that speed up the pig's growth but that harms people's health. Similarly, a fish farmer won't eat his own fish. But he eats the pork because he doesn't know the pigs are unsafe to eat."

Ordinary citizens are growing more frustrated at being unable to trust any food source in China. Some have tried to strike, or to petition to ask the CCP to act and protect their food supplies.

The CCP knows these practices are taking place and it has acted. It has continued to censor and distort the facts so that Chinese citizens will continue to be unable to trust their food sources:

> With regard to the issue of the flow of rice (contaminated with heavy metal) from Hunan to Nanyue, report in strict accordance with information from authoritative bureaus. Do not sensationalize the story, make it prominent, or lure people to it. We reiterate that the media may not investigate or comment on strikes, sit-ins, petitions, or similar activities without prior authorization.

> *From a leaked directive from the Guangdong Propaganda Department (February 27, 2013)*[52]

The CCP continues to control media reports to prevent Chinese citizens from knowing the dangerous truth about their food sources. In this example, the CCP orders media to not report about the efforts of a high-profile academic trying to raise public awareness:

> No locale or website may investigate, report, or republish [information] concerning Henan School of Finance and Economics professor Shi Pu's sit-in at Zijingshan because of issues with pork in Tongxu county.
>
> *From a leaked directive from the State Council Information Office (March 15, 2012)[53]*

When food poisoning or other serious incidents occur, the CCP responds by providing the media the official "news" they are allowed to report. For example:

> Report and republish official wire copy of the food poisoning incident at Xiandong High School.

Professor Shi Pu of Henan University of Economics and Law staged a one-man sit-in on March 15, 2012 in Zhengzhou's busy Zijingshan Square. The words on his headband read: "Hunger strike in protest. No food safety. Entire government derelict."

(Source: China Digital Times)

From a leaked directive from the Lianyuan Municipal Party Committee Propaganda Department, Hunan (June 27, 2013)[54]

And the CCP doesn't hesitate to blatantly order media to "focus on fraudulent and false reporting." For example:

On the cafeteria issue at Chengdu Number 7 Experimental School, tomorrow's press conference and today's public opinion guidance should focus on fraudulent and false reporting.

From a leaked directive from the Chengdu Online Propaganda Department (March 14, 2019)[55]

In other words, this particular CCP propaganda directive orders media to lie and prevent the public from knowing the truth. In this cafeteria incident, media were ordered to not to report the truth about moldy meat and seafood that had been knowingly fed to unsuspecting school children, who became very ill from eating it.

Besides giving media orders on how they must behave, the CCP also speaks directly to the public via prominent CCP media mouthpieces, such as *Xinhua* and *People's Daily*. For example, after another food scandal in 2013, where rice sold to consumers was found to be laced with the toxic heavy metal carcinogen, cadmium, the CCP only responded after there was a loud public outcry. To help minimize the *negative* (truthful) news, the CCP offered some general advice to help consumers deal with dangerous food sources:

"Experts recommend that people should not consume food and drink from one particular region for long, instead they should diversify to lower the risk."[56]

That advice is written in CCP language, which only Chinese citizens familiar with CCP culture would recognize. They would know that those words signal that tainted foods are everywhere. Buying local is no longer safe and no help is in sight.

It is hard to comprehend how any person or people of authority can be so careless toward their subjects' health and safety, that they would rather their subjects ignorantly eat poisonous food than tell them the truth that might save their lives.

But not all Chinese citizens are ignorant to the truth.

Another former CCP surgeon explained to me how many regular Chinese citizens have trained themselves to decode Chinese media and grasp hints of the truth among the lies. He said:

"We know that in the media in China there is not one sentence that is true. So we developed a way to read the newspaper. We read between the lines, then we can still pick up the news. For example, if the media says that in one province there is harvesting of rice, then we will know: Ah, okay, there is a problem with rice in that province. . . ."

That sounded ridiculous to me but it demonstrated to me how Chinese citizens have been well-trained to either swallow the CCP's twists of truth or to enter a labyrinthine mindset to distinguish the factual grains from the plastic bites.

Now, feeling sickened by fake eggs and plastic rice, I made a mental note for myself that I can no longer trust any food or food ingredients coming from China. Although I consciously stopped buying food from China years ago, it was more so because I didn't want my money to go into the pockets of such a disastrous regime or to support slave labor. And every now and then I would still buy a packet of chestnuts that I knew were from China. I just couldn't find them from any other country and I just love the thick, soft texture, the taste, the satisfaction. I always bought the chestnuts with the USDA Organic label and familiar Western-style packaging so I not only believed they were safe for me to eat, I even believed that they were good for me.

HOW TO MAKE FAKE BEEF FROM PORK:

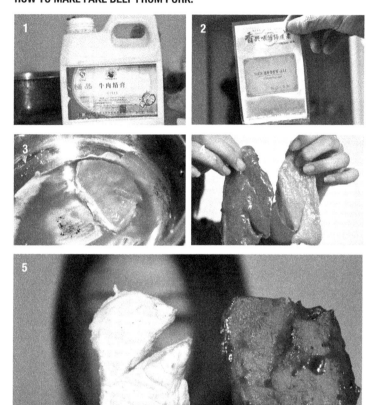

Step 1: Use highest grade beef extract.
Step 2: Use a glazing agent to remove the pork flavor. This small bag will do 50kg of pork.
Step 3: Marinate the pork in a saucer.
Step 4: Pork with beef extract applied (L), pork without beef extract (R)
Step 5: Voila! After two hours of cooking. Real pork (L), fake beef (R).

(Source: Hainan News, 2011)

But again, I was *so* wrong.

Any food grown or raised in China could be deadly.

It turns out that USDA organic standards don't have any requirements for measuring heavy metal contamination, synthetic chemicals, or even polluted irrigation water in certified organic food. The USDA Organic label refers only to the *process* of how the food is grown or produced, but the food itself can be full of mercury, lead, cadmium, arsenic, aluminum, and still proudly bear the "Organic" label. And any food grown or raised in China could be deadly.

The following table lists some of the tainted and fake foods made in China. Be warned, you may lose your appetite reading these:

Food	Contaminants
Rice	Laced with metal cadmium. Fake grains made from industrial synthetic resin. Old rice may be chemically treated and coated with paraffin to make it look healthy. This type of rice has been widely dubbed "Poison Rice" in China. The fragrant and expensive Wuchang Rice from the Wuchang region in China is known to have little to no actual Wuchang Rice in it, but is sprayed with a fragrance that matches the popular Wuchang Rice scent.
Cooking oil	Made by "recycling" leftover oil from restaurants and home cooking, often containing carcinogens or dangerous chemicals. It is widely known as "ditch oil" or "gutter oil" and is cooking oil "refined" from leftover food. In 2011, CCP authorities revealed that up to one tenth of cooking oil used in China might actually be ditch oil.[57]

Baby milk formula	Laced with melamine to replace protein. The first public scandal was in 2008 after six babies died from drinking baby milk formula made by the Chinese company, Sanlu. Hundreds of other babies were hospitalized. Numerous other baby milk and dairy scandals have occurred since the Sanlu scandal.
Table salt	Replaced with or laced with industrial salt that contain hazardous metals such as lead, arsenic or mercury.
Bottled drinking water	Containing E. coli bacteria and harmful fungi.
Pickled vegetables	Inedible industrial salt used for pickling.
White pepper	Faked from plain white flour.
Soy Sauce	Made with cheap amino acids created from processing human hair, gathered from hair salons and hospitals.
Flour	Tainted by adding whitening and other carcinogenic chemicals.[58]
Vinegar	Tainted by mixing water with acetate or diluting vinegar acid with water or other liquids, causing concentrations of heavy metals.[59]

Tofu	Sewage, slop and iron sulfate to increase production and appearance. Faked with a combination of flour, monosodium glutamate, pigment, and ice. Using the carcinogenic bleaching agent, rongalite.[60]
Rice noodles	Tainted with moldy grains normally used for animal feed, and mixed with carcinogenic additives like sulfur dioxide. This was widespread in one particular city where almost 50 factories were found to be producing 1.1 million pounds of tainted rice noodles per day.[62]
Lamb	Faked by adding chemicals to meat from rats, minks, and foxes.[61]
Beef	Faked by chemically altering cheap pork with a carcinogenic "beef extract" and then glazed.
Fish	Turbot and tilapia are known to be the most highly contaminated by China's fish farmers using dangerous levels of carcinogenic pesticides, herbicides, and fungicides to increase fish growth.
Shrimp	Injected with gelatin for extra weight and to stay plump.

Chicken, duck, pork, and beef	Faked with rat meat.[62]
Animal blood products	Faked using formaldehyde or inedible dye and materials used for printing mixed with one animal blood to fake another type of animal blood.[63]
Liquor	Tainted or faked with industrial ethanol with water and other harmful liquids.
Pork buns	Tainted with chemically softened cardboard added to the bun filling to substitute for meat content.
Walnuts	Nut meat replaced with concrete inside real walnut shells. The extra weight of the concrete also increases the selling price of the fake nuts.
Green peas	Replaced with soy beans, snow peas, green color, and sodium metabisulfite.
Mushrooms, garlic, leek, seaweed, other vegetables, and fruits	Tainted by pesticide contamination and the use of chemicals, including bleach, that may cause neural disruptions, cancer etc. to stimulate growth.

And the list goes on and on and on.

Like the thugs and CCP officials who have had no restraint on their creativity to invent new torture methods to reeducate citizens who do not follow Party beliefs, Chinese entrepreneurs have been given free rein to try new and innovative ways to counterfeit food items and incredients to reduce costs and increase profit.

The phenomena has even become a popular CCP cultural saying:

"Shut up and get real rich."

The phrase is bred of the same course language of dusty Maoist slogans, but modernized with, as the CCP would say, "Chinese characteristics." And like all the bitsy paragraphs and phrases in Mao's little red book, this saying is decontextualized, dehumanized, and demoralized. It justifies turning a blind eye to the pain and suffering of others in pursuit of the CCP's drive for wealth.

"It's impossible to have a very successful business in China and be independent from the CCP," explained the Chinese Businessman who owns factories in China and imports goods from his factories to the West.

"I'll give you two examples," he said. "When I started my export business in China, I wanted to attend the biggest fair in China, but I couldn't get a booth. So I contacted my friend who had a good relationship with some officials. He could get the booth at a really cheap price and then sold the space to me. By selling it to me he made more than my business made in a whole year. So when you start a business in China, you need to have relationships to 'get there,' you know."

"The second example: One of my suppliers is my good friend. He was very young and a very good person. He never took his customers to karaoke and saunas like most people (Note: those activities are known as an expected form of bribery in China today.) He wanted a very professional standard for his business."

"His business was doing very well. He spent the profits from his factory to buy more land and build more factories, but after buying the land the local officials wouldn't allow him to clear the land. The local official said to him: 'Let us help you build the new factory for you. You pay us and we'll build them.' My friend refused. He told me: 'The officials don't care about quality, they only care about money. They get into the project and pay their own people to build without quality control.' "

It is so common in China that CCP officials intentionally cut costs and corners on building construction leading to terribly made buildings that they (of course) have created a CCP cultural saying for it: Tofu Building.*64* Tofu is a soft, flimsy, cheese-like food made of curdled soybean. Whether you buy it soft or firm, you are never buying tofu for stability.

The Businessman continued:

"After my friend refused to pay the officials under the table, his competitors kept growing and began taking customers and orders away from his business. Eventually, after three years, he decided he had to change. He gave the officials a few million dollars and told them: 'Don't tell me what you are going to do with this money, I just need to start my new factory.' He was upset and frustrated. He hated the corruption at the time. But a year later he had completely changed. He said to me: 'Friend, it's so fast and efficient! If I insist on doing things my way, I'll lose all competitive power. I'll be finished. But now, if I pay just a bit more, then I can make the money back.' "

The Businessman was disappointed. He had seen these sorts of things happen continually over the past few decades. No matter the industry, it has become virtually impossible to do business honestly and without corruption in China.

"In order to get what they want, many people do illegal things in the legal name of 'being flexible.' "

"Where there's power, there's corruption. That is an open secret. In Chinese we say corruption is an 'unspoken fact.' " This was said by the former CCP Judge in China's criminal court system, who knew many judges that accepted bribes.

"They were judges themselves who'd worked in that position for decades but they ended up being criminals," he said. "But it's not just the Chinese courts and judges who are susceptible to bribery and end up being criminals, many Chinese government branches and administrative offices are fraught with corruption."

"There is a nice-sounding term called 'being flexible,' " explained the Army Colonel. "In order to get what they want, many people do illegal things in the legal name of 'being flexible.' I always wondered if 'being flexible' is good or not, whether it protects or breaks the law or not."

The Colonel hadn't been free in China to discuss such a thought-provoking question with anyone. A CCP official cannot ask such things.

"I had some understanding why more and more laws were being created but the cases of people doing bad things or double-crossing each other were endless to deal with and just kept getting worse," he continued.

But he had a rather large incentive not to question the system when he had the opportunity to leave officialdom and enter China's business market.

"All I could see was profit," he said.

A satirical poem was published on China's Internet around June 2012 about CCP officials. It was so widely searched for by Chinese netizens that the CCP blocked each individual line of the first two stanzas from Weibo search results. The poem got the attention of *China Digital Times* that published an English translation of it—complete with English rhyme—in September 2014:

NO POETIC LICENSE

The people have money—you steal,
The people have women—you rape,
The people have homes—you tear down,
The people have words—you delete!

The people have woes—you perform,
The people are wronged—you lock up,
The people have issues—you reject,
The people have doubts—you edit!

The people's property—you take,
The people's suffering—you flee,
The people's pregnancies—you abort,
The people's food stalls—you flip!

The people curse you as bastards,
But you call yourselves officials.[65]

Although many Chinese citizens are awakening to the extreme damage done to their environment, and their humanity, they often point the finger at the CCP's scapegoat-of-last-resort: Official Corruption.

Almost any problem in China can be lumped onto any CCP official at any time, labeled "corruption," followed by a show trial, and then finished with a heavy prison sentence. It happens so often that officials lose sleep knowing it could be them next if they haven't toadied up close enough to a higher official who will give them "protection."

"Honest people cannot get promoted in the Propaganda Department," said the Propaganda Official. On asking other officials, the same seemed to be true in most, if not all CCP departments.

"You have to seek 'refuge' with different bosses to be your patron, only then can you be lifted up in rank," continued the Propaganda Official. "For a person with integrity who thinks, 'I'll just do my work well and just rely on that,' you won't get promoted for sure."

"The CCP uses all the people around you to create intense pressure and mental stress. If you haven't lived in that environment, it's hard to understand daily life in that environment."

When the CCP blames official corruption for the people's woes, the public buys it. The officials who get the blame may not have done the actual crime they are charged with, but they know that taking the fall for the CCP is the price they pay for the perks of officialdom, and that the only way to escape the firing line is to be more corrupt than those around you.

However, the CCP generally prefers to blame the weather or anything else before it has to blame one of its officials, because admitting that there is a problem with CCP officialdom is admitting there is a problem with Party discipline, which is very close to touching on the root of the problem—the CCP.

I looked at the Chinese Professor sitting between me and the black screen behind him. He was still talking and talking and talking:

"Many Chinese buy houses now and have money. They think 'Life is good now because we have money.' But they don't know that the CCP actually harms them. It doesn't matter how much money you have, your life is done for. Can you live in the cities? Even the water is undrinkable. So what is the use of all that wealth?"

I let the Professor talk for a long time. My mind was wandering now and I knew I would come back to the fully transcribed and translated text of his interview at a later point.

How can a nation become so bereft of human values and care for their fellow man that they would knowingly and continually—for decades—pollute the air they all breathe, the water they all drink, and the food they all eat, in the name of profit?

The CCP won't say that that behavior is wrong, because it is the CCP who created the behavior. The CCP encourages it and perpetuates it.

The CCP seems ever more determined to enforce its constitutional rule of profit above all else, including human life.

CHAPTER 20

Socialist Diplomacy

The former Chinese Diplomat spoke to me in reasonable English. He had aged since our brief encounter in 2005 after his very public defection from the CCP to Australian freedom. Like most Chinese, his taut, thick skin and careful eyes made him look younger than his actual years.

Yonglin Chen, "The Diplomat," shows secret documents that reveal the extent of CCP espionage in Australia to the press in 2005.

(Source: Clearharmony.net)

Although he barely remembered me, I had followed every step of his high-profile defection very closely. I had monitored every media report and quietly fact-checked each one against intel I gathered through journalists, Chinese diaspora, and a friend who was close to his family. I watched how the facts around his personal life, professional life, and present danger were expanded and contracted according to each media's choice of interpretation.

Some Western media presented the genuine concern about the danger that he and his family would face if they were refused asylum and were sent back to China. Other media scuffled with each other for trivial crumbs of his personal life that they twisted and turned into mountains that were no longer recognizable in the context of his actual reality. Some media appeared to intentionally muddy the waters of truth instead of investigating the possible golden nuggets of CCP state secrets that the Diplomat had taken with him from the Chinese Diplomatic Mission before his escape, and was willing to reveal only to trusted eyes.

Late one night I visited a safe house in a middle-class Sydney suburb where the former diplomat was seated among a small huddle of Chinese diaspora. His face was a deep shade of fear—the type of fear that reaches from head to toe and from skin to bone. His bespectacled eyes, rimmed by dark, sleep-deprived skin scanned me with distrust as I entered the room behind my Chinese friend, who became part of the huddle. The Diplomat's larger-than-life public persona, which he had gained from courageously announcing his defection at a press conference just a week or two earlier, and then had bravely faced the swarms of national and international media who wanted blood, had now shrunk behind closed doors. His stature looked almost frail, his youthful face tired and worn. Via a limited whisper of English translation from my friend, I was able to understand the two greatest worries weighing on him:

1. Who can be trusted?

2. Is it safer to stay silent or to continue to speak out until the question of asylum was decided?

Everyone in the room that night knew that there were three lives immediately on the line—the Diplomat, his wife, and his young daughter. We also knew that everyone in China that the Diplomat knew and loved were already in the line of fire. The huddle around the Diplomat could have easily had fears for their own safety and the safety of their families, but most of them were Chinese dissidents who already knew and faced that danger daily. Many of them had personally received discrimination, threats, and property damage instigated by CCP thugs, who had reported their work to the Diplomat at his previous workplace in the Chinese Consulate.

> *All Chinese dissident groups, both inside and outside of China, are targeted and infiltrated by CCP agents. The Diplomat knew this because he had been required to help instigate this in Australia.*

Who could be trusted? Their suspicions didn't pertain to the media. Everyone in the room knew that many news organizations had become merely the mouthpieces for whoever provided them the most persuasive and profitable argument, and that the CCP had a direct line to most newsrooms in the country.

Those suspicions were actually about everyone in the huddle, and everyone who wanted to be in the huddle.

It was through this experience that I came to learn that the real tactics of CCP diplomacy are not carried out through meetings and bureaucracy, but through espionage, via a careful and vast web of spies, agents, and disinformation. Learned from the Soviets and Sinicized by the CCP, this is socialist diplomacy, and it was designed to divide and conquer from within.

All Chinese dissident groups, both inside and outside of China, are targeted and infiltrated by CCP agents. The Diplomat knew this because he had been required to help instigate this in Australia. Motivated by the promise of power and money or the threat of personal pain and suffering, the CCP agents used CCP struggle tactics to sow lies, foment hatred, create enemies among friends, and distrust between families, until the agents could themselves obtain a leadership position within the group's hierarchy. They would sabotage and destroy the reputations of the group's most influential leaders and carefully and clandestinely undermine the group's mission until its members lost hope in their original mission and reduced or disbanded their activities against the CCP.

The Chinese democracy movement in Australia was the clearest victim of the CCP's espionage that I saw. Over the decades since the 1989 massacre in Beijing, Chinese diaspora around the world had tried to band together and continue the efforts of their slaughtered brethren to push for a democratic change in the regime that would allow them to return to their beloved homeland as free human beings. But their efforts were constantly thwarted, their strength constantly split into ever smaller factions, their most emotive leaders were denounced and lost favor, and members had to choose between tiny pockets of dissidents instead of being able to join a growing, strong body that would one day have had the power to move a mountain.

The CCP struggled to conquer the spiritually based Falun Gong group from within because of the lack of membership or hierarchy between practitioners, as well as the group's requirement of not allowing donations and its strict moral code that holds the principle of truth in the highest regard. But that didn't stop the CCP from trying terribly hard.

Since 2005, I had kept my ears open to more stories about the CCP's attempts to infiltrate Falun Gong. One CCP insider we interviewed for our movie, and who was born into a CCP-respected Red Family, but who had turned away from politics, reluctantly told me how he was being pressured to be an agent for the CCP's red diplomacy. It wasn't a one-time spy offer. The CCP had been working on him for many years now and it was wearing him down. He was an Australian-Chinese businessman, so I called him the Businessman for short.

"My business turnover was nearly 40 million at the time. If I had stayed in China I think my business would have been really huge.

I had a lot of property and a lot of opportunities, but now I don't have to worry about losing my life," he said, describing part of what he had left behind when he fled China after the persecution of Falun Gong began.

"When they started persecuting Falun Gong in China, I didn't feel safe," he said. "The police came to my company to research, to try to find some evidence. I had done everything correctly but I still didn't feel safe in China."

Even though the Businessman had lived and worked overseas for well over a decade, he still used the CCP euphemisms he'd grown up with—only now he used them in broken English.

By saying that the police came to "research" for "evidence," he meant that the authorities had come to search for anything they could use to incriminate him to justify his arrest. Any breach of any CCP rule or regulation would have been enough. Even though the persecution was well underway, there were still no actual laws against being a Falun Gong practitioner, so the authorities sometimes had to find other "crimes" to bring in people they knew who practiced.

The Businessman knew that the authorities would be back for him later and they would likely bring their own "evidence" next time.

"What really confused me was that one month prior, the CCP had said that the Chinese government wasn't persecuting Falun Gong and had never done anything to them. They said that anyone who follows the law won't have any problem. Then one month later suddenly Falun Gong was given a bad label, so I knew another movement had come in, so I left China," he said.

He and his wife found safety and freedom in Australia, but he was unwilling to cut his ties to his family in China, and that was what the CCP needed in order to target him to become an agent for them.

> **"The police threatened my elderly mother in China. They told her that if I didn't cooperate with them, they would not let me visit China again and they would stop my brothers from being able to travel overseas by taking their passports away. The police knew that would harm my business."**

"After I became an Australian citizen, I went back to China and I was approached through friends of my father. I was told they wanted to introduce some business to me, so I agreed. When I met them, they told me they were police."

"That changed the whole situation. I felt a bit scared and told them that I don't want to get involved in any politics. I just want to do business with business people. They asked me to work for them. They wanted me to spy on Falun Gong practitioners overseas and provide the police with information about them. I refused again and again. Finally, they said, 'Our department is into making friends, but if you don't want to work with us, then I have to move you to another department. And they use force."

I assumed the CCP meant they would use force on him personally, but the CCP knew it could hurt him a lot harder if it inflicted pain indirectly.

"The police threatened my elderly mother in China," he continued. "They told her that if I didn't cooperate with them, they would not let me visit China again and they would stop my brothers from being able to travel overseas by taking their passports away. The police knew that would harm my business. That's what they wanted to do, they wanted to damage my business."

The CCP did take away his brothers' passports so they could no longer travel.

"The police told my family, 'See, your son is so selfish. Why doesn't he support you? If he worked for us you'd be okay. You should tell him to work with us.'"

Michael Lee, "The Businessman."

It wasn't just his family who couldn't understand why he wouldn't work with the CCP. His fellow Chinese businessmen also couldn't understand his refusal.

"This is a really tricky situation," he said trying to explain in his limited English. "I have a lot of friends in China who are big businessmen, and they don't believe the CCP is persecuting me like this. They say to me, '*You* must have done something wrong, otherwise they [the CCP] wouldn't do this to you."

"Business people are so focused and busy with their businesses. They are just focused on getting rich, and the Chinese media has blocked out any reporting on Falun Gong. The internet in China blocks any mention of it, so they don't know what is happening in China, and they don't want to get into trouble listening to you talk about anything the CCP doesn't allow to be talked about."

The CCP continued to keep constant pressure on both the businessman overseas and on his family in China. It waited for an opportune moment to blackmail him into being their agent.

"A few years later, my brothers and I had set up a new factory in China," he said. He had worked with his brothers from Australia as an importer of the goods from their factory. "With the new factory, the police found an excuse to arrest my brother and close down our factory. They did this to force me to work for them."

The businessman was visibly upset. I now understood why he had been so hesitant to talk with me. I had originally wanted to include some of his testimony in our movie, *Finding Courage*. But after hearing his whole story, and knowing how much his family is suffering right now, I didn't want to put any additional stress on any of them and removed his footage from the film.

> **From the Tibetan people and the Xinjiang Uyghur Muslims, to the pro-democracy student protestors of Hong Kong, and freedom-loving Taiwanese, their bravery to refuse to cooperate with the CCP shows true heroism.**

At the time of our interview, his brother was still in prison. All because he, an Australian citizen, had refused to work as a spy for the CCP. But the most difficult aspect for him was not his brother's suffering—although that was visibly very distressing for him too—but the fact that his family couldn't understand who was to blame.

"I know that by refusing to work with the police, it will hurt my business and my life, especially my family in China. I didn't want this to happen. I tried to help them. The most difficult thing for me is that they don't understand this. The most difficult thing is that the CCP has successfully managed to make Chinese people fight against each other, blame each other, not blame the CCP. My parents and my brothers, I really want them to understand that this is because of the persecution from the CCP. But they still say to me, '*You* must have done something wrong, otherwise the CCP wouldn't have hurt us so much.'"

This man's whole family suffered because he had unwillingly become a cog in the CCP's diplomatic apparatus that is programmed to pursue its enemies at all cost, but he was refusing to be spun on the axle of the regime. Of course, there are many more who give in to the regime than those who don't, but he is not the only one to refuse.

There are brave men and women from every ethnic, spiritual, political, and geographical group that the CCP has labeled an enemy. From the Tibetan people and the Xinjiang Uyghur Muslims, to the pro-democracy student protestors of Hong Kong, and freedom-loving Taiwanese, their bravery to refuse to cooperate with the CCP shows true heroism.

"Chinese diplomacy is a continuation of domestic policy," said the Diplomat. "So for the Chinese regime, the priority of diplomacy is to serve its politics, to maintain its rule in China. That's the main purpose. So in a Chinese Embassy or Consulate, the political official usually has a higher rank and will be promoted quickly, like me." He had worked first in the Chinese Embassy in Fiji and later in the Chinese Consulate in Sydney.

"The most important thing is that the CCP wants to build up an image in China to look like a good government. So international recognition—the CCP's image overseas—is very important."

I was trying to follow his logic. *If the CCP wants to look good inside China, hasn't it already done that? Hasn't it already captured and forcefully convinced its captives? Why is international recognition and overseas perception so vital?*

The Diplomat continued:

"In the 1990s, just after the Tiananmen Massacre, the Chinese regime didn't care much about opposition voices from overseas because they are overseas, far away," he explained. "But now, with globalization, the world is very small, so the CCP has realized that overseas voices can pass to the Mainland and have a big influence, so they need to control the situation. That's why the overseas job is important."

"Overseas job" is a brutish term for my Westernized concept of foreign diplomacy. But in this context—where diplomacy means you can (and should) hire thugs to slash tires and smash home windows to squelch dissident voices, using government funds—it seems appropriate.

"A political diplomat's responsibility is to control the overseas Chinese community and to target opposition groups, to deal with Chinese in exile or Chinese living overseas in democracies, and to scare them so that they don't say much. It means to reduce their voice, to reduce foreign influence in China. That's important," said the Diplomat.

Communism may advocate for fair play, but it never practices it.

Besides brute force, there are many other methods the CCP uses to mute its critics on foreign soil.

"In the beginning, China didn't have much money, but since the 1990s China became richer and richer," he continued. A great amount of China's economic growth can be attributed to CCP-controlled China being allowed to join the World Trade Organization. And after almost twenty years of membership it still smirks and shirks the WTO rules—so much so that the WTO is thinking to rewrite the rules for the CCP instead of making the CCP play fair.

Communism may advocate for fair play, but it never practices it.

"So for example," the Diplomat explained, "the CCP set up a fund for Chinese ambassadors—an Ambassadorial Cash Fund, which can be used at the will of the Ambassador, who can use the cash anywhere: to bribe officials, give money to anyone he likes, to control the local Chinese community, Chinese students. This money increased every year. They have lots of extra money for this."

"If you look around the world, China established a system called the Peaceful Reunification Council (or Association) for China in every country. These are front organizations. Whenever anything happens, they will use these local overseas organizations to serve China's political purpose, to serve the CCP for spying and infiltration. That organization is the main one. It is run by the Peaceful Reunification of China. The overseas organizations are like its branches around the world and the representatives of these groups are officials of China but they register here as a local community group. They are the arms of the regime."

The Diplomat gave more examples:

"In every country, in every university, there is a Chinese Student and Scholars Association. They don't even bother to vary the name because they need to be unified under one leadership—the communist regime. The organization is sponsored and set up by the Chinese government and Chinese companies."

"Another organization is the Confucius Institute. That was suddenly developed all around the world, in every country, because it establishes a connection to mainstream society, to politicians, and is convenient for collecting information in the name of 'building up friendship.' A lot of foreign politicians' children were sent to China to give them a free scholarship. That's a bribe. There are a lot of them in Australia, the United States, and many other countries."

He still had more examples:

"The CCP now successfully controls the Chinese media, the majority of Chinese overseas media."

He continued to list off other goals such as "gaining intelligence" from Western countries, and "stealing technology."

"There is no limit," he said.

"No limit" was a term I'd heard too often now from CCP officials, and I didn't like how it was used in the CCP context of no rules, no laws, no repercussions, no depths too low, no method too sinister, no torture too vile. But for them, "no limit" is the norm. It has been drummed into the heads of CCP officials and they have to mindlessly carry out the pain-inflicting implications on others.

Yonglin Chen calls the CCP a "wolf in sheep's clothing" during his testimony before the Subcommittee on Africa, Global Human Rights and International Operations in the U.S. Congress on July 21, 2005.

(Source: Epoch Times)

I used to think in an upward direction whenever I heard the phrase "no limit." To me it meant reaching for the stars, beating personal bests, doing the impossible once, and then aiming for the impossible again. It never implied hurting, hating, or destroying others to achieve a goal that would then only hurt, hate, and destroy others further.

Having no limit, no bottom line, to me, is like an absolute opposite of the traditional Ten Commandments of the Bible that I was taught as a kid—to not lie, steal, or kill. Or an absolute opposite to the Judeo-Christian Golden Rule of: Do unto others as you would have them do unto you.

The "no limit" downward law of the CCP was closer to the antithesis of the Bible's rules taught by early 1900s occultist or satanist Aleister Crowley, who still influences popular culture today with his maxim: Do what thou wilt shall be the whole of the law.

The term "no limit" is tainted for me now. Instead of thinking upward and reaching for the stars, I think downward into the dark depths of a bottomless abyss of anti-human depravity.

And part of that "no limit" was that all this CCP depravity was primarily directed at Chinese people overseas, to influence Chinese people in the Mainland.

> **"Chinese people are taught to think that America is China's enemy, but that is just CCP propaganda. The CCP's actual enemy is the opposition groups of the CCP."**

On the surface, the CCP seems to want to defeat its foreign enemies and take over the world, but by its actions, it wants the world to assist in maintaining the CCP's stronghold over its captives—China and the Chinese people. (World domination seems to be lower on its priority list.) And the CCP constantly uses foreigners and foreign powers to validate its own legitimacy as the ruler of China and maintain its control domestically.

"Chinese people are taught to think that America is China's enemy, but that is just CCP propaganda," confirmed the Diplomat. "The CCP's actual enemy is the opposition groups of the CCP."

Oh, the lengths the CCP will go to keep power and its captives! I thought.

Back in 2005, on that night when I sat at the back of the huddle of Chinese dissidents who surrounded the newest and most influential dissident of them all, they had already decided who they could trust: a small network of contacts connected to the people in the room. There was always a risk that a spy may come (or be) among them—and they would stay vigilant—but they put their hearts and their missions to stop the crimes of the CCP first.

But they still had another pressing problem to solve: Was it safer for the Diplomat to stay silent or for him to continue to speak out until the question of his asylum status was decided by the Australian government?

There was serious debate, but in hushed voices. If he speaks out, the media may twist his words and damage his asylum chances. If he doesn't speak out, the CCP will get into the ears of the media and tell any twisted tale that suits them. If he speaks out and doesn't get asylum, he'll be persecuted more harshly in China. And if he stays silent, he'll still be persecuted in China.

There were no dice to roll, no chances to be taken. Long into the night they discussed, and all were tired. But they finally came to a hesitant but unanimous conclusion: The louder his voice, the safer he'll be.

Their decision that night made a stronger impact on my psyche than the dark depths of the CCP's limitless inhumanity. And I've repeated their decision as my own mantra many times since, whenever someone has asked me whether I feared for my safety because I have publicly spoken out against the communist regime.

I would often say: The louder I am, the safer I'll be. And over time, that has been proven to be correct.

The CCP preys upon the fearful, and skirts around the brave and the honest. And so it was, after a painful waiting period, the Diplomat and his family received asylum and safety in Australia. The next time I saw him, he was on television and he looked refreshed and renewed.

We interviewed him for our movie for well over two hours and were fascinated by his insights. During a break I suggested that he write a memoir of his experiences. He smiled and thought about it, but made no commitment. And at the end of his interview, as he stood up from his chair and straightened his jacket, he said casually:

"You'll probably only use a few seconds of my interview for your movie, because it is boring, and my English is not good."

I tried to express how interesting his experience really is, but he didn't seem to believe me. And I believe his response was more than simply Asian modesty or diplomatic training.

Most of the officials made similar comments—with sincerity— at some point during our discussions. They really didn't see the value of their own experiences for a Chinese audience, and certainly not for a Western audience. They lamented their inability to speak English well or to understand Western society. Even when I explained to them the significance of their testimony and how useful it will be in helping people to understand the CCP system, they couldn't imagine it. They saw me as an idealist and they didn't want to encourage any of my seemingly false hopes. Nevertheless, they still gave their trust and testimony.

It was clear that none of them had high expectations that their words would do much good. But I sensed a tiny glimmer of hope that, one day, something good may come of their bitter experiences.

With or without their hope, I am truly grateful for their trust.

CHAPTER 21

In Their Words

"There is no future for the Chinese as long as the communist regime is there."

"Many Western scholars argue that China isn't a communist country anymore," said the former CCP Diplomat. "But people should see that these Communist Party leaders, the dictators, the communist regime, is still there. Although not many people truly believe in communism, they have been brainwashed into the evil communist way of seeing things. The communist culture is there and it's anti-human."

I knew that many CCP apologists would never agree with his statement, but that didn't make this official's truth any less truthful.

Communist. Brainwashing. Evil. Anti-human. CCP apologists would refuse to recognize these terms or sideline them as extreme, fanatical, or religious. It could also be because it is not in their financial interests to study the truth behind the words. Or it could be because they follow a Marxist-based morality that instantly propels scorn upon those who would hint at the credibility of a pre-Marxist, faith-based morality—a morality that allows for civil discussion of good and evil, and invisible but tangible interdimensional phenomena.

The irony is that more and more research shows that the upper echelons of Marxist faith groups do believe in the immaterial and the interdimensional, but it is not in their interests to share that with their "useful idiots" or the plebs of the "masses," who they think should remain as ignorant and materialistic as possible.

"There is no future for the Chinese as long as the communist regime is there," the Diplomat continued. "They are sucking blood from the future generations."

The CCP-parasite comparison still makes my skin crawl, but the Diplomat wasn't referring to mythical metaphors. He really did experience literally having his future generations' blood sucked.

He told this story:

"When my daughter was born in Beijing, the hospital gave us the wrong advice, which caused my wife to suffer a lot during birth and our newborn contracted pneumonia and had to receive treatment for two weeks. Then they took blood from our baby. They said it was to test for a genetic disease, but they never gave us test results. I later found out they stole my baby's blood and sold it. My baby had a fever every two weeks for a long time."

The available criminal stories of fetus and infant abuse, of infanticide, of the sale of fetuses and baby body parts under the CCP in China are too horrific to include in the scope of this book.

"I didn't see any hope for China. And I don't want my child to be brainwashed like other Chinese people," he said.

I nodded in sympathy. I felt grateful my children had the good fortune to grow up under blue skies, surrounded by clean water, limitless access to libraries and limited internet access—because I set the limits for them myself.

"Did you see the little girl named She Yeye in Canton?" the Diplomat asked me.

"I think so."

I knew what he was talking about. I remembered watching an awful viral video taken by a security camera in China of a toddler who'd been hit by a car and then lay in the street gutter for a long time while people continuously passed by without helping her. It was obvious she was badly hurt or dying, but they intentionally looked the other way and left the scene quickly.

"Eighteen people, including drivers, pretended they didn't see the girl," he continued. "They even walked around her. They didn't want to help her or tell others. It was an old lady, a cleaner, who eventually helped her."

I had always hoped that the little girl's tragedy had been a random case, an anomaly, an isolated incident.

"This is a very typical case," he said, shaking his head. "There are thousands, maybe millions, of these cases."

"People now think: 'If I help you, you will hurt me.' "

He gave a personal example:

"One of my friends in middle school had a serious fall one day. She fell to the ground in front of a shopping mall. She couldn't get up by herself, but nobody would help her. Why? Because in China there are so many cases where the victim of a supposed 'accident' will blackmail you and make a trap to force you to pay them money."

I had heard of this before too, but like many people, including many Chinese citizens, I had pushed it aside as an isolated incident, an abnormality, not a norm.

Another interviewee, the former CCP Journalist, confirmed these incidents are now standard CCP cultural behavior:

"These cases have become an ironic joke in China," she said.

She then gave a personal example that hurt her deeply:

"An elderly person had fallen down in the street, so I helped them up and helped take them to the hospital. When we got there the elderly person turned around and blamed me for knocking them down and demanded I pay their hospital bills."

The impact the incident had on her was common to all others we spoke to.

"People now think: 'If I help you, you will hurt me.' Once you get hurt you become afraid of being hurt again," she said before emphasizing, "there are too many cases like this," she said.

The Professor was even more emphatic:

"Oh, it's quite common!" he exclaimed. "Some people think that this behavior came out of those earlier struggles, like the Cultural Revolution, and that made people bad, and then these people grew old. But contrary to that, younger people who didn't experience the Cultural Revolution, they don't seem to have the basic instinct to help an elderly person either. So the situation in China . . . it's a very scary thing. Many people no longer have basic moral principles."

"We see this stuff all the time," he continued, waving his hands as if to emphasize the banality and commonality of it all now. "An old person gets on a bus and demands you give him your seat. If you don't, he'll beat you." He shrugged his shoulders. This was a new normal.

I heard these stories again and again but I had to confirm, because there are Chinese citizens who always claim that those types of horrible incidents are the "dark side" of China, and that they are always "isolated cases," never widespread trends or culture.

But basic research confirmed that this disturbing behavior is widespread across the CCP nation, and that it is CCP apologists who label them "isolated incidents." The more thorough research that I insisted on doing only confirmed it further.

The Professor continued:

"There was a child sitting on a bus seat because they had a stomach ache, but an older person still dragged them off the bus and took their seat. That's what it's like. Older people don't have morals and they educate the younger people in the same way. People don't feel it's unnatural when they are educated to do bad things. Why? Because they are educated with lies."

"If you start a fight with or bully an elderly person, you curse and steal from him, people around you will see that it's a bad thing, right? But the CCP spins it so that the elderly person is the bad guy and deserves the beating. They'll add a bunch of false crimes and then the CCP becomes the hero and the elderly person deserves to die. The CCP has done this again and again."

"Once you go through the CCP's brainwashing, then it is very difficult for you to see what is real. You cannot see real things. You don't believe in truth, you cannot understand truth."

Every interviewee had thoughts to share and stories to tell about the modern behavior widespread across China that has been born of the twisted CCP culture. As I went through their interview transcripts, I pieced them together into a paper edit form. I would have loved to have them say their own words on screen in a documentary, but without context, I felt their words alone would appear too bizarre to a regular viewer. Yet in the context of this book—now nearing the the end of their interviews—their stories and phrases, worries and wisdom blur together in my mind and form a verbal montage of truth and tragedy:

"In order to pursue money, the people in China have become very cruel. Even if they don't want to be cruel, society is cruel, so they have to be cruel."

"When I was in Beijing, there was a 20-story building, it had an anti-burglar fence on the first floor and an alarm on the third floor, and on the top floor. One of my relatives lived on the seventh floor, and they thought they would be safe on the seventh floor, but a burglar climbed up and broke in. They were lucky. Nowadays, they kill people first and then take their time to search the house. That's the reality of China now."

"This is what the CCP created under its regime. It crumbled society's morals and ethics, made individuals and society have no bottom line. This is the result of the regime."

"If you ask why so many Chinese want to migrate overseas, it's because China is not safe. They feel insecure, unsafe. Not just because of society, but because of the environment, the pollution, the culture. They earn money, save money, put even up to a million dollars in the bank, but they still feel unsafe, because one day they might have to have an operation and lose it all, not just on health care but in having to pay off officials for the surgery."

"Those who truly know the CCP's evils are the CCP members, officials, including military officials and generals. So why do they transfer massive wealth outside of China? Why do they send their children and families to live overseas? They know the CCP has no future."

"The high-ranking officials in China know everything. They know China is hopeless. That's why they emigrate overseas, transfer their money out of China. They send their wife and their kids overseas. But poor people, the low classes of society, they have no hope."

"My friend, a businessman in Guangzhou told me as soon as he gets back to his city he feels like he is living among wolves. He is afraid to carry cash. He tells me his true feelings when he visits me in the West. He says, 'I feel like I am living among wolves.' "

"There is no environment for human beings to live a normal life anymore. No matter how the CCP pretends and makes things sound beautiful, no matter what kind of strategies it uses, after all these decades, normal people can't survive in that environment. This is something I have come to a deep understanding of."

"In the past, Confucius taught that kindness and honesty are good and that people should care about each other. But in China now, there are no such values anymore because the communist doctrine has brainwashed people to tell lies. It's become natural, so most Chinese are used to this very twisted life. They think abnormally, not like a normal person."

"It's very hard to understand Chinese people, because Chinese people have been brainwashed generation after generation since 1949. And now, because of the twisted economic growth, Chinese people are more like Nazi Germans—very nationalistic and patriotic. The textbooks have nothing about the evils of communism, nothing about the massacres. No one repents, no one says it is wrong. Scholars are stopped from publishing any articles about the Cultural Revolution, about the mistakes of the CCP. So lots of Chinese people still think killing is nothing. Killing millions of people . . . they feel indifferent about their neighbors, they don't care about other people. They don't care much about human rights, about each other. They have been brainwashed to be abnormal people. If you look at individual Chinese, you don't see it, but if you look at the whole country, it's very different from the Western world. China is a strange monster's world. It's not normal."

"With the advancements in science and technology, the younger generations should be the future hope of the country. If they know our history, they can set a clear direction for the future. However, sadly, the younger generations know nothing about the past. Even many adults in China have no means to find the true history or even the true situation in China today."

"In 1989, students protested against official corruption. They were angry and took to the streets. Now after 1989, more officials have become corrupt, no one protests, people find it reasonable. And after graduating, many young people want to join the Communist Party and be a part of the corruption team so they can earn more money. They think: 'The Communist Party is so good and developed our economy. Why are you against the Communist Party?' Everything has been reversed. It's not normal."

Normal. Abnormal. Normal. Abnormal. The words circled in my head. Again and again I heard them say it. I understood the context of what they meant, but I had to ask. I needed to hear them say it themselves.

"What is normal?" I questioned.

"In the West here, I often see Westerners greet people with a smile and say hello on the street, but in China, nobody will do this."

I heard that sentiment over and over again from officials, CCP members, and regular Chinese citizens who had visited or moved to the West—no one in China will willingly greet each other on a street. If you try to do it, you will receive a look of scorn, suspicion, or a closed door.

"For Westerners who live in the environment of the West, you are all very lucky. In a Western society you can still see love and care between each other and you can sense people's feeling of responsibility toward the society. I can still see it."

"A normal person, like in this [Western] country, they are sympathetic, generally care about others and care about themselves and how their lives affect others. But in China, no. In China, people generally care about themselves, their own lives, their own fate, only about money, they don't care about others, they don't care about their neighbors. That's because the regime's propaganda and education brainwashed them to make everything about money, to turn people into being materialistic. To turn them from a human being into an animal."

"China is not a normal country. From the way people think to the way people act, everything is distorted and abnormal. For thousands of years, people in China and other parts of the world believed in and revered gods. For thousands of years, Chinese traditional culture honored the principle of, 'Heaven and man living as one in harmony.' It was never about 'struggle, struggle, struggle.' "

"It's not a human society. It's killing and slaughtering each other and surveilling each other. When you are in that environment and have already become like that, you are used to it. They are used to fighting every day. If they don't fight, they don't feel good."

"You don't have the right to faith, the right to speech, the right to know. For a long period of time we didn't even have the right to think. You wouldn't dare to just ponder things freely in your own mind. The life of the Chinese people is too bitter and miserable."

"A lot of Chinese people, after years of living under the CCP's rule, are extremely afraid. They have become slaves to their own fear."

"China is like an apple. Rotten from the core, completely rotten. Only the peel is red but everything inside is rotten."

> *I had to remind myself that these testimonies are not from regular Chinese citizens, many of whom would scream, "Traitor!" at any Chinese who even thought of leaving their beloved CCP for another land, let alone air "state secrets"—the dirty deeds—of the regime publicly.*

I had to remind myself that these testimonies are not from regular Chinese citizens, many of whom would scream, *"Traitor!"* at any Chinese who even thought of leaving their beloved CCP for another land, let alone air "state secrets"—the dirty deeds—of the regime publicly.

One Official had said:

"The majority of the masses are ignorant of the truth of the CCP's rule, because the CCP has put up the Great Fire Wall between China and the outside world and imposes strict media control domestically. All newspapers and media have become . . . you are only left with one voice. Different opinions are banned, so the average person in China today does not have a very good idea of the way in which the CCP rules the country."

Another had put it more bluntly:

"The CCP tries to make Chinese people have no personal opinion, no brain, to make them incapable of thinking. So, whether the Communist Party is good or bad, they don't even know, they don't even think about it."

But of course there are many Chinese citizens who have awakened to, are trying to, or are beginning to learn the truth of their history and culture—this is the CCP's greatest fear—but these citizens do not have the means to change it.

"Today we are seeing the awakening of some intellectuals and lawyers in China. They have come to recognize the CCP for what it truly is and are doing what they can to oppose the system. But the CCP clamps down on them brutally," said another.

"You can see how the CCP is now. It is teaching people that human rights lawyers 'must be put into prison' without proper reason. The CCP is worried that these lawyers will become morality leaders, build up a good image, get out of the CCP's control, and then replace the regime."

There are also many CCP apologists who defend the CCP system.

"In the Chinese government there are many intellectuals that we call *quan ru zhi shi fen zi*, which is translated as 'Dog Intellectual.'" This was said by the Diplomat who studied hard and studied well as an intellectual himself in China's college system prior to joining CCP officialdom. But using the term "dog" for human beings made me almost as uncomfortable as using the term, Walking Dead.

The surface meanings are awful, but it is time for me to get over that. With context these labels can be understood.

"In China, dogs are looked down upon as mean and low class. If a master asks the dog to bite or bark at anyone, the dog will do it. It will do all the dirty work. That's what we mean by Dog Intellectual. In China, there are millions of them. They are brainwashed, they have no basic human values, they just want money and they serve the regime. They are very intelligent and are the main support of the regime. As long as the regime can keep paying them, they can earn more money and enjoy the privileges of serving the regime."

The High-Ranking Official said:

"The stakeholders under the rule of the CCP praise it because this group of people is reaping the largest share of the benefits. They have the largest slice of the cake."

I considered Westernizing his phrase to "piece of the pie," because I like pie and because the phrase is more common and would thus be easier to read. But then I remembered the Chinese official who called the bulldozed, crushed, and massacred student body parts on Tiananmen Square "pie." So, I decided to stick with "slice of the cake" instead. Right or wrong, everyone likes cake.

The Official continued:

"Others defending the system are some intellectuals who have been able to gain fame and money and intend to get ahead in the system. Who are intellectuals? Intellectuals [well-educated thinking people] are people who carry on the culture, inherit the culture, and advocate and promote the culture. They are the ones who carry forward the traditional culture and promote it."

I'd never really thought about that before. But he was right. The teachers, the academics, the philosophers, the writers, the reviewers—they synthesize and they critique, they present and they preach. Their assumptions and their advocacy becomes our culture. They share our lives and they mold our children. For better or for worse.

I was now thinking about the education system in the West and its cultural takeover by Marxists decades ago, which has widely succeeded in squashing or demonizing any non-Marxist voices with extreme hatred and precision.

But the official brought me back to China. And I was glad. China is still the best example of the bread we have to eat if Marxism continues to sour our system here.

"Almost without exception," continued the High-Ranking Official, "all of China's intellectuals were persecuted by the CCP. As a result we see a cultural fault line in China. The Cultural Revolution especially—from 1966-1976—created a fault line in the continuum of traditional Chinese culture. Five thousand years of China's traditional culture came to a violent halt. The harm done has been enormous."

The Propaganda Official also had an opinion:

"Before the Cultural Revolution, Chinese people still had traditional concepts of their culture, but after the Cultural Revolution your whole being became empty, with no faith in anything, so the only things that people have faith in now are material things and money."

Some people don't have a problem with the CCP's money worship. But the Propaganda Official pulled out his punchline:

"And all the material things in China all belong to the CCP, so you have to follow the CCP."

"People have become *liu shen wu zhu*," the Professor said.

The translator struggled to translate the term and then needed time to explain it. They gave me a few definitions to help me understand:

> *The six divinities—the senses and organs—are without ownership.*

> *Without conscience, perplexed; without direction, distracted; one's soul is not in one's body.*

I understood it as another description of China's Walking Dead.

The Professor continued:

"China is a very scary place now because its own culture—the Chinese culture—is no more."

"According to traditional Chinese culture, we call China, *Zhong Guo*. It means 'Land of the Divine.' All the ancient books basically talk about stories of the divine, about divine principles. They are very profound. So from this perspective, if human beings evolved from animals, then that throws this history away entirely and stops people from coming into contact with our real human culture. When people break away from our ancestors and our own divinities, they become *liu shen wu zhu* and believe they are animals."

"When people do not have faith, they are like walking zombies, as if their spirits are without guardians."

"Faith? Ideals? Aspirations? People have forsaken such things," the High-Ranking Official said. "This is really a terrifying generation. People nowadays are only after two things: money and power."

"The CCP has ruled China for 70 years and over those years it has destroyed people's faith in the divine. People no longer believe the CCP's stuff either. So in reality, Chinese people do not have any kind of faith. This is indeed very pitiful. If you want to ruin a nation, you would ruin its culture."

The High-Ranking Official was unusually well-read in both Marxism-Leninism as well as many Chinese traditional classics. He began his own philosophical soliloquy:

> "There is no solution to the CCP's destruction of traditional culture. It has reached a dead-end.
>
> With atheism, there is no god, no divine beings, no reincarnation, no heaven and hell, and no karmic retribution. And with power and money, one dares to do anything.

Chinese people are on the one hand, very lost, and on the other hand, searching for answers. They might be making a lot of money day to day, but they still feel very empty inside. They might hold great power, but they still lack a sense of security.

The Chinese scholar, Mencius, said 2,300 years ago: 'If you do not have a sense of right and wrong, you are not a human being.'

For thousands of years, traditional Chinese culture attached great importance to family ethics and relations.

Chinese people used to say: 'Heaven is watching you,' so people knew they had to be careful of what they did and said because the divine was watching their every move.

Chinese philosophy speaks of heaven, earth and man: 'Man stands between heaven and earth. Man should possess great qualities and stand tall and proud between heaven and earth. In order to do that, a man must be righteous.' This is what Chinese people today lack the most. This is one of the most valuable legacies of Chinese traditions that we should carry forth."

The Professor gave his own philosophical perspective:

"What is the meaning of living and having the ability to think as a human being? The human thought process is to search for the truth, otherwise why would you have the ability to think?"

"Buddhism teaches that humans live in a maze. Then you have the opportunity to enlighten. To enlighten is to jump out of the maze and see the truth. Human nature is designed to search for the truth. But the CCP will let you get lost, and not let you see things. They not only don't want you to become human, they want you to become animals. They think you are an animal now."

I later learned about a prolific Chinese intellectual, Qian Mu, who was considered one of the greatest historians of Modern China. Seeing no future for China under the CCP, Qian Mu bid farewell to his fellow scholars when the CCP took power in 1949. He established a school in Hong Kong and watched from afar, as his worst fears played out in the Mainland when China's intellectuals were forced to "transform" their minds and their humanity during the CCP's tragic campaigns against them.

Qian Mu wrote in his book, *History of Chinese Thought*[66]:

> "The communism that is spreading rampant in China at this moment will at most become a walking corpse. . . . "

It is communist culture and CCP culture that has created China's Walking Dead. A few Chinese with great wisdom had foretold of the tragedy many decades ago, but they were unable to alter the course of history.

Qian Mu (1895-1990)
(Public domain image)

The vast majority had fallen under the spell of the specter and began their slow walk to become the "dead."

Very few of our interviewees were academics or philosophers. Most of them struggled to find the right words to express their hopes, their anguish, their guilt, their shame, and their desperation.

"I had a faint wish that I could survive before my true self completely died," said the former CCP Heart Surgeon, describing his life-changing decision to leave his homeland. "I needed to escape, so I fled China."

He then gave another example of the Walking Dead:

"One time I talked to my brother-in-law in China. I said to him: 'There is no hope for the CCP.' Do you know what he said to me?"

I shook my head. After all these interviews, I still had no answers to the questions the CCP insiders asked me.

He continued:

"He said to me: 'I have to have some hope, otherwise how can I live?' "

The interviewee looked at me. I waited.

"I said nothing in reply to him," he concluded sadly. "He's one of the Walking Dead."

CHAPTER 22
There Is Hope

Entering the world of CCP officialdom was like entering a dark abyss lined with sorrow, terror, apathy, and hopelessness. Coming out the other end, I feel the muddy filth of communist texts and documents and propaganda that I had purposely injected into myself, dissipating and dissolving. It is somewhat a feeling of purification, of being cleansed. It is a form of catharsis, and I'm grateful to be on the other side of this particular journey.

I do see hope for the land of China, but we cannot depend upon it coming from those who have been broken the hardest and penetrated the deepest by CCP culture—the official ranks of the CCP.

There is hope because they are willing to speak, but only if we are willing to listen. They need to be reminded of their own self-worth, which has been desolated by decades of living in the ghostly shadows of Marx and his cohorts.

It takes great courage to face the reality that one's life has been unwillingly formed, controlled, and warped by an evil force. It takes great courage to seek the truth and an even greater humility to accept it. Like any long-term victim, it takes time and effort to cleanse one's internal system of the poison from a captor's lies and harmful behavior.

But I believe there is hope for the Chinese people if they can recognize their captor as a non-Chinese captor and choose to seek out and reunite with their own Chinese culture. The distancing of themselves from the CCP is not merely symbolic, but fundamental to breaking the chains upon them and within them.

In the words of the poet Kahlil Gibran's from his poem *On Freedom* in his book *The Prophet*:

> "And if it is a despot you would dethrone,
> see first that his throne erected within you is destroyed.
>
> For how can a tyrant rule the free and the proud,
> but for a tyranny in their own freedom
> and a shame in their won pride?"

Chinese dissidents, human rights activists and advocates worldwide have not lost hope. Despite enormous adversity and threats of all forms from the CCP, their efforts are contributing to the growing cracks in the regime. The CCP fears them and their hope very, very deeply. Because their hope rallies and bouys the hopes of the Chinese people that the CCP feeds off. Their hopes continue to awaken the people of China and remind them of their humanity.

I share their hope and I hope that you may too.

I also believe there is hope for the Free World to cut through the Marxist chaos by learning—learning to recognize the two skins of Marxism in all its forms and at all its locations, and by piercing its outer layer with truth. Its inner skin may wriggle and writhe, and likely kick and scream too, but like a tantrum-throwing toddler, that shouldn't deter a truly loving, responsible parent.

Ah, these are all touchy analogies in a modern Marxist world of political correctness. They could be labelled preachy, conservative, right-wing, anti-progressive . . . But words are words, unless we give them the power to be more. And as humans blessed with precious faculties of thought and speech, we have also been given the ability of choice, and the ability to shape our language, our culture, and therefore our future.

Most importantly, we have been endowed with empathy and the ability to understand, to help, and to heal. Our humanity is our ultimate hope. It is only a matter of how we each choose to use it.

Thankfully, unlike China's Walking Dead, we are still blessed with the freedom and faculty to choose.

Glossary of CCP Cultural Terms

Most of these terms are euphemisms. They are dishonest terms born and bred by communist culture. They blatantly lie or water down the truth to make excuses for the CCP's brutality and disregard for human life.

For decades, Chinese people have learned to live with the lies. And for decades, the West has fallen for them, repeated them, and wrongly embedded them into our culture and history books.

This glossary is more like a sideshow at a circus—full of curiosities and the unexpected—than a comprehensive listing of serious terms and definitions. It is limited to the terms and phrases mentioned in this book, whose wordplay is yet to be fully explored. However, volumes can, and should, one day be written about the pervasive Marxist-based CCP cultural language—to study its structure, meaning, and impact—to avoid it devastating future human cultures again.

Dishonest, Communist Term	Honest, Accurate Description
Accident; Incident	Catch-all euphemisms for anything negative—from a brutal murder, to a massacre of thousands of people.

Basic principles	The fundamental concepts that cannot be debated and must be followed by all CCP members. This includes the "principle" that the CCP must always rule China.
Beating	Often a whitewashed term for torture.
Bloody lesson	An "accident" or "incident" that resulted in publicly visible bloodshed and therefore caused damage to the CCP's reputation.
Campaign; Movement	A systematic, top-down effort to dehumanize and eradicate a group of people who the CCP has decided to target.
Caused some reactions	If referring to reactions from the public, the "reactions" are a euphemism for expressions of anger, riot, petition, or other signs of discontent. If referring to reactions among officialdom, the "reactions" are usually a euphemism for revenge, demotion, back-stabbing, or other visible or invisible displays of anger.

Correctional institutions	A catch-all administrative term for facilities that house detainees and/or prisoners, including slave labor camps, prisons, reeducation centers, detention centers. The English word *institution* gives the false impression that the facilities are law-abiding, formal, or well-established.
Dark side	A catch-all term for all negative things (things that hurt Chinese people and Chinese society) that the CCP has trained Chinese people to look away from.
Dealing with poverty	A CCP excuse for not dealing with pressing issues facing its people. For example, they may say they are too busy "dealing with poverty" to handle other things. Similarly, CCP apologists praise the CCP for "raising people out of poverty," to deflect attention from the crimes of the CCP.
Defer to	Must be subordinate to.
Democratic centralism	The practice (conceived by Vladimir Lenin) where all CCP members must follow every CCP decision once it is made, and thus no one can promote any alternative view or work against the decision.

Detention	The vague term used to describe the state of limbo for someone who has been forcibly locked up and deprived of their rights, including the right to inform one's family of one's whereabouts. It could be at a police station, a prison, a work unit building, or any other facility the CCP chooses to isolate a person from the rest of their lives.
Disappeared	The act of making a person "disappear," while in truth, they have been secretly put into some form of detention by the CCP.
Disorder; Chaos	The label given by the CCP for any activity that it hasn't approved or doesn't like. The CCP regularly (and falsely) claims that "chaos" would reign over China if the CCP wasn't in power.
Disturbance	An event or situation that interrupts the CCP's agenda. For example, the 1989 Tiananmen Square Massacre is sometimes referred to by CCP officials as a "disturbance."

Elections	A mere formality of announcing new leadership within the ranks of CCP officialdom. It is completely opposite to the concept of elections in the West. These are not "free" elections. The "votes" and "results" are *always* prearranged by the CCP.
Evidence	Can be real evidence or something completely falsified by the CCP to "justify" anyone's imprisonment for crimes that they did or did not commit.
Fog; Haze	For decades the CCP has labeled dangerous industrial air pollution haze or fog, and thus removed the blame from the cause—the CCP and its policies—to a silent victim: the weather.
Forced labor	The requirement of a human being to carry out physical work under inhumane conditions against their will as a punishment for crimes that the person may or may not have committed. Also: slavery, slave labor.
Good handling	The act of a CCP member mitigating negative repercussions—caused by an "accident" or "incident"—from public attention.
Isolated cases; Isolated incidents	A lie used to make widespread suffering caused by the CCP appear to be random, forgettable anomalies.

Merit; Meritocracy; Meritocratic Screening	The CCP claims that its officials rise in ranks based on their *merit*—a meritocracy, based on a system of meritocratic screening—where CCP members are regularly profiled, reviewed, and measured by higher-ranking members who decide if and when they are worthy of receiving a higher ranking position. However, the CCP's measures of worthiness or merit are not carried out in an official, standardized way, as someone from the Free World might assume. Instead, cutthroat corruption and mafia-style techniques are the norm. Without the right financial positioning, social positioning, and connections to the right higher-ranking officials, an official will be without the *merit* they need to rise within the ranks of the CCP.
Mistake	If the CCP is ever forced to admit that their planning or actions were imperfect—including murder and other forms of physical destruction of life and/or property—the admission may be called a *mistake*. No consequences are required for *mistakes*. The criminals get off scot-free.

Natural disaster; Meteorological disaster	A CCP scapegoat. Whenever possible, the CCP lays blame on the external environment so that the CCP will not be held responsible for damages. For example, the dangerously harmful levels of toxic smog caused by unregulated and extreme industrial pollution permitted by the CCP (for the purpose of achieving wealth) has been labeled a "meteorological disaster" by the CCP.
No limit	No moral boundaries or limitations. Similar to the occultist / satanist rule: Do what thou wilt.
Offsetting	Distracting an audience away from an event or issue that would make the audience think negatively about the CCP, and instead, draw their attention to the negative aspects of something else. In other words, it is to shift the blame to anyone or anything else so that the CCP always appears *perfect*.
Ordinary people	Non-CCP members, non-CCP officials. Also referred to as *the masses*.
Overseas job; Overseas work	The work of CCP members overseas, such as in positions of foreign diplomacy. All such work is solely for the purpose of furthering the CCP's agenda.

Peace; policy of peace; peaceful development; world peace; a harmonious world of lasting peace	Decorative terms used to lull the West into believing that communists seek the same "peace" that the West seeks, which they do not. Communists require a constant state of war and struggle, which requires the slaughter of citizens. They may claim that they are in times of "peace," but have, and still do, continue to slaughter during their times of "peace." As Lenin described it in 1915: "Pacifism: the preaching of *peace* in the abstract, is one of the means of duping the working class."
Peaceful Reunification Council; Peaceful Reunification Association	CCP front organizations to infiltrate and influence foreign countries according to the CCP agenda.
Political consequences	If in relation to individuals, the "consequences" are punishment from the CCP for anyone not following CCP rules. The consequences are especially heavy for CCP officials whose livelihoods are completely dependent upon the CCP. If in relation to the CCP, the "consequences" are outcomes that may lead to a negative impact on the CCP and its rule and thus need to be stopped or negated.

Progress	CCP "progress" always refers to "progress" in the direction of the CCP's goals. No other "progress" exists for the CCP.
Publicity department	Propaganda department
Public security	Mechanisms and apparatus for maintaining the CCP's control over the Chinese people.
Red descendent	Someone whose parents or grandparents were considered "good" CCP members.
Red second generation; Second generation red	Second-generation reds have parents or grandparents who held high-ranking positions within the CCP. They therefore have greater access to power within the CCP system than other CCP members.
Reeducation	The psychological process of brainwashing a person so that they no longer hold the same values, beliefs, or morals that they once had, often requiring the person being "reeducated" to betray their conscience and then participate in helping others to do the same. The methods of reeducation range widely, from subtle manipulation to mind-altering drugs, and brutal physical torture.

Research	Collect and analyze data on an individual, including "research" on all their family members, personal connections, and business or other relationships.
Sensitive day	An anniversary of a major event where the CCP harmed its citizens, eg. June 4, the anniversary of the Tiananmen Square Massacre. The CCP implements special strategies to prevent any public memorials or protests around these anniversary dates as part of its practice of making the Chinese people forget about these events.
Stability	Total social control by the CCP.
Stability maintenance	Any action required to maintain total social control by the CCP.
Struggle	To "struggle" is the opposite of working together to achieve a common goal or unity. Karl Marx called it "conflict," the CCP calls it *dou zheng*—to fight, to battle one's enemy, which may be your neighbor, your family, or you. After decades of CCP-instigated, bloody struggles, the meaning now includes "violence" and "cruelty."

That Political Incident of 1989	The 1989 Tiananmen Square Massacre: mass slaughter of students and citizens calling for democratic reform on Tiananmen Square, Beijing, on the eve of June 4, 1989.
The Three Years of Natural Disasters	1959-1961, the largest and most devastating mass starvation in history created by destructive socialist policies. Outside of China it is often called the "Great Chinese Famine," however, other than its vast reach across the nation, it is anything but "Great."
Two skins of propaganda	A control mechanism carried out by the CCP's propaganda machine to dupe the public. CCP's propaganda messages have an outer skin (layer) that presents untruths or distortions of the truth to the public. The outer skin hides the inner skin, which is the truth. The truth is required to be hidden from the public in this way because the truth gives a negative (often damning) impression of the CCP and its policies.
Unspoken fact; Open secret	Something negative that doesn't fit within the image that the CCP wants to publicly portray of itself, but that it allows to exist because it doesn't hamper the CCP's overall goals. For example, environmental pollution, bribery, and corruption.

SAYINGS

Saying	Meaning
Being flexible	Break the law, break the rules, intentionally harm others to achieve personal gains.
Dog Intellectual	A member of the Chinese academia that is paid well by the CCP and treats the CCP as its master—compromising academic standards and ethics to help the CCP achieve its goals. There are said to be a large group of these intellectuals in China propping up the regime.
Exposing too much bone	Revealing too much of the truth.
Go see Marx	False hope in the afterlife, that one will at least be able to be consoled by someone after they die—Karl Marx—since the Chinese ancestral lines have been cut.
It doesn't matter whether it's a black cat or a white cat, if it catches mice it's a good cat	There is no right or wrong. Any means are justified to get the job done.

Serve the people; Smog the people; Serve the renminbi	Mao Zedong's false promise that the CCP will 'Serve the People' has been turned into truthful puns: The CCP fills Chinese people with smog instead of serving them, and the CCP serves the economy instead of the people.
Shut up and get real rich	Close your eyes and ears and mouth to the sorrow of others. Follow the CCP blindly and use money to replace any feelings of guilt.
Soldiers who do not want to be generals are not good soldiers	No one should be content with their existing position, they should proactively and continually contend and fight with their bosses and seek to take their position.
The people have sharp eyes	Be alert, be cautious, be suspicious. Anyone and everyone could be watching you, so you should also be watching them.
Throwing an egg at a stone	A hopeless, useless action.
To kill people like scything flax	To dehumanize any group of people until they are seen as worth less than a blade of grass, then kill them without remorse, and with a clear (yet warped, anti-human) conscience.
Words are no small matter	The wrong choice of words can get you killed.

Acknowledgments

This book could not have been written without the willingness and courage of the CCP insiders who, if they are not already, will be treated as enemies of the Chinese communist state for revealing "state secrets" in these interviews.

There are many insiders who were only willing to speak if they remained anonymous and off-camera. Their testimony, information, and contacts helped tremendously to inform the research required for this book and for our movie *Finding Courage*. Their need for anonymity is understood and respected.

A great acknowledgement is required for all the translators who assisted throughout the process. Without their skills and service, the words of the insiders would have remained inaccessible to a Western audience.

As an author and director who doesn't speak Chinese, but endeavored to tell a story about a foreign people, language, and culture, there may be questions about any interpretations made in the translation process, and I would like to address this point.

Having spent years working with Chinese translators prior to this project, I was acutely aware of how biases and agendas of a translator permeate their translations. I therefore chose translators carefully, reviewing their abilities in casual scenarios before asking for their participation. I selected them based on their lack of agenda and lack of Chinese political knowledge instead of their experience as a translator. In most cases, I chose translators in their 30s or younger because older translators generally had more political awareness and opinion, and couldn't help but put their slant on the content. Thus, for most interviews, I purposely received literal, blunt, and unadorned language translations, with little to no external political framing. I then used another translator to provide a written translation which I could compare with the verbal translation.

The translators, many of whom were volunteers, friends, and friends of friends who enjoyed the idea of being part of making a movie, suffered in the reality of the hard work of translation, dealing with deadlines and accuracy requirements for many hours of heavy interview material. In many cases these interviews were cathartic experiences for the interviewees, laden with the heavy emotions of guilt, remorse, *I've-never-told-anyone-this-before* experiences, tragedy, and awful mental trauma and physical torture. Sometimes there were tears. Other times the translation tasks were seemingly endless lengths of CCP propaganda pieces, official CCP speeches and official documents full of challenging CCP terms and an enormous amount of eye-glazing communist rhetoric. But the translators stuck their course, pushed the sorrow or the monotony aside, and focused on the task at hand—literal accuracy. To them, I am greatly indebted.

I must also acknowledge *China Digital Times* (CDT). I believe this book would be lacking if it did not include the leaked CCP propaganda directives that CDT has persistently gathered, translated, and published on their website for Western readers.

In an interview published on their site, CDT editor and founder Xiao Qiang described their platform:

> "CDT is like a growing coral reef of resistance to internet censorship. One day, the reef will be so big that it will tear into the hull of the dictators' legitimizing discourse."

Like many others, I too look forward to that fateful day.

I wish to thank Louise Stevanovic, Orysia McCabe, and Laurie

Gorham for their painstaking copy-editing and significant improvements they made to the text, and Grace Khmelev and Lu Lu for their ever-ready translation and research assistance.

Thank you to Better World Studios for bringing this book to life with their beautiful design and layout. And thank you to Liberty Hill Publishers for servicing new authors, like me.

And finally, of course, thank you to Paulio Shakespeare, Loren McCune, and Timothy Gerbhart at Swoop Films for their trust and support. And to my dear husband David for being the rock that always steadies my attempts to achieve the impossible.

Endnotes

All weblinks were archived in August, 2020 via the Internet Archive Wayback Machine: https://archive.org/

CHAPTER 1: Meeting the Walking Dead
(1) Kay Rubacek, Paulio Shakespeare, and Loren McCune, "Finding Courage," October, 2020, produced by *Swoop Films*, feature film, www.findingcouragemovie.com.

CHAPTER 4: Department P
(2) Benedikt Tashen, *Chinese Propaganda Posters* (Cologne: TASHEN GmbH, 2011).
(3) Anne Henochowicz, "Propaganda Training for Chinese Journalists," *China Digital Times*, January 15, 2014, https://bit.ly/3lc5N4f.
(4) CDT Staff, "Minitrue: Early Coronavirus Directives," *CDT*, April 17, 2020, https://bit.ly/31kFqBu.

CHAPTER 6: Money-Law and Constitution
(5) The Chinese Communist Party, "Constitution of the Communist Party of China, Issued: Thursday, November 14, 2002," *Congressional-Executive Commission on China*, retrieved from China.com.cn on May 31, 2013, https://bit.ly/3jayoXD.
(6) The CCP, "Constitution of the Communist Party of China, Revised and adopted on October 24, 2017," *Xinhua*, https://bit.ly/3lda7Ay.
(7) The CCP, "Constitution of the People's Republic of China, as amended in 2004," *National People's Congress Observer*, https://bit.ly/3j3H28t.

CHAPTER 7: Little Brown Birds

(8) Frank Dikötter, *Mao's Great Famine: The History of China's Most Devastating Catastrophe, 1958–62* (New York: Bloomsbury Publishing, 2010).

CHAPTER 8: Parasite

(9) Nan Hu, "Communist Party Grows Branches in Foreign Companies," June 12, 2016, by *CCTV*, video, https://bit.ly/32fLRF5.

CHAPTER 9: Dear Mother

(10) Cary Huang, "Sir Alan Donald, British Ambassador to Beijing During Tiananmen Square Killings, Dies Aged 87," *South China Morning Post*, July 21, 2018, https://bit.ly/32gcSIn.
(11) Kay Rubacek, "Deep Dive on The 1989 Tiananmen Massacre: How China's Regime Justifies Slaughter," June 2, 2020, by *Swoop Films*, video, https://youtu.be/668YLJ6XEQs.
(12) Lindsey Hilsum, "Voice of China: Students Tell C4News Why Communism Works," Jan 20, 2011, by *Channel 4 News*, video, https://youtu.be/nRjdJWeCuFo.

CHAPTER 10: Ad Break No. 1

(13) "Combat Declaration," 2016, by *China Military Network*, video advertisement, https://youtu.be/S98yRQf63Uw.

CHAPTER 11: Daughter, Go Watch the Slaughter

(14) Hongzhi Li, *Zhuan Falun* (Taiwan: Yih Chyun Book Co., 2000).

CHAPTER 12: The Wedge

(15) Sarah Cook, Leeshai Lemish, "The 610 Office: Policing the Chinese Spirit," China Brief, Volume: 11, Issue: 17, *The Jamestown Foundation*, September 16, 2011, https://bit.ly/2Eh56WP.
(16) Pete Earley, *Comrade J—The Untold Secrets of Russia's Master Spy in America After the End of the Cold War* (New York: Berkley Books, 2009).

(17) Kay Rubacek, Paulio Shakespeare, and Loren McCune, "Finding Courage," October, 2020, produced by *Swoop Films*, feature film, www.findingcouragemovie.com.
(18) "Historical Facts: Zhuan Falun and Zhuan Falun Vol. II Were on the Best Seller List in Beijing in 1996," *Minghui*, April 22, 2002, https://bit.ly/31h7pSu.
(19) Bin Du, *Vaginal Coma* (Hong Kong, 2014).
(20) "Testimony of Ms. Yin Liping, Hearing on 'China's Pervasive Use of Torture,' " *Congressional-Executive Commission on China*, April 14, 2016, https://bit.ly/2QjbW0t.

CHAPTER 13: Turning Points
(21) Fengjun Hao, "In His Own Words: Hao Fengjun Explains Why He Escaped from China," *The Epoch Times*, Jun 9, 2005, https://bit.ly/3l8MicO.

CHAPTER 14: Chameleon Skin
(22) Robert F. Service, "The Secret to Chameleon Color Change: Tiny Crystals," *Science Magazine*, March 10, 2015, https://bit.ly/2Yq8ozi.
(23) Col. Qiao Liang and Col. Wang Xiangsui, *Unrestricted Warfare* (Vermont: Echo Point Books & Media, 1999).
(24) C.K. Tan, "China Spending Puts Domestic Security Ahead of Defense," *Nikkei Asian Review*, March 14, 2018, https://s.nikkei.com/2FP22BJ.
(25) Paul Bischoff, "Surveillance Camera Statistics: Which Cities Have the Most CCTV Cameras?," *Comparitech*, July 22, 2020, https://bit.ly/3gs73Nm.

CHAPTER 15: Lives of Grass
(26) Max Roser and Mohamed Nagdy, "Genocides," *OurWorldInData.org*, 2013, https://ourworldindata.org/genocides.
(27) "Painless Abortion Bundle," Changsha Tianlun Women's Hospital, online advertisement, accessed August 24, 2020, http://ymsx.com/a/yyzt/renliu480/.

(28) Sir Geoffrey Nice QC, Prof. Martin Elliott, Andrew Khoo, Regina Paulose, Shadi Sadr, Nicholas Vetch, and Prof. Arthur Waldron, "Final Judgment," *The China Tribunal—Independent Tribunal into Forced Organ Harvesting from Prisoners of Conscience in China*, June 17, 2019, https://chinatribunal.com/final-judgment/.

(29) Kay Rubacek, "China Deep Dive Xinjiang, Kazakhstan & Uyghur Muslims Being Killed for Organs with Ethan Gutmann," May 19, 2020, by *Swoop Films*, video, https://youtu.be/dYWCkeyxGs8.

CHAPTER 16: Beans and Bulbs

(30) William Z. Foster, *Toward Soviet America*, (New York: International Publishers, 1932)

CHAPTER 17: Ad Break No. 2

(31) "Who am I?" July 27, 2016, by *China Youth Studio* and *CCTV*, CCP video advertisement, https://youtu.be/DRu2Ka1mnaA.

CHAPTER 18: Bloodlines

(32) "How to Make Leaders (How Leaders are made)—Viral Chinese propaganda video," 2013, by *Revival Studio*, CCP video advertisement, https://youtu.be/M7340_17H_A.

(33) "China's $10bn Annual Spending on Soft Power Has Bought Little of It," *The Economist*, May 24, 2019, https://econ.st/3h0V1pg.

CHAPTER 19: Of Pigs and Fish

(34) Robert A. Rohde and Richard A. Muller, "Air Pollution in China: Mapping of Concentrations and Sources," *Berkeley Earth*, July, 2015, https://bit.ly/3lcCYVr.

(35) N.D. Songjiang, "A Bay of Pigs Moment," *The Economist*, March 12, 2013, https://econ.st/2FG6NgK.

(36) Julie Zaugg, "China's Polluted Rivers Yield 'Cancer Villages,'" *WorldCrunch*, August 23, 2017, https://bit.ly/3ghYAfz.

(37) Little Bluegill, "Ministry of Truth: Vandalism and Water Pollution," *China Digital Times*, Feb 27, 2013, https://bit.ly/3lbc2W0.

(38) Anne Henochowicz, "Minitrue: Liquid Ammonia Explosion in Xinjiang," *CDT*, November 12, 2013, https://bit.ly/32vqr7d.

(39) Josh Rudolf, "Minitrue: Pollution Lawsuit, Smog Classification," *CDT*, January 5, 2017, https://bit.ly/3hoLqi3.

(40) Samuel Wade, "Minitrue: Delete Report on Air Pollution Deaths," *CDT*, February 6, 2017, https://bit.ly/34nsr3R.

(41) "Enabling Nature-Positive Growth in the People's Republic of China's Yangtze River Economic Belt and Beyond—Case Study," *Asian Development Bank*, June 1, 2020, https://bit.ly/3j2jNvC.

(42) Eleanor Albert and Beina Xu, "China's Environmental Crisis—Backgrounder," *Council on Foreign Relations*, January 18, 2016, https://on.cfr.org/3hmSfAP.

(43) Julie Zaugg, "China's Polluted Rivers Yield 'Cancer Villages,'" *WorldCrunch*, August 23, 2017, https://bit.ly/3ghYAfz.

(44) Josh Rudolf, "Phrase of the Week: Smog the People," *CDT*, December 16, 2016, https://bit.ly/3403WDr.

(45) Fauna, "Chai Jing's 'Under the Dome' Documentary—Chinese Reactions," *chinaSMACK*, March 4, 2015, https://bit.ly/3gn6Mev.

(46) Josh Rudolf, "Minitrue: Don't Hype 'Under the Dome,'" *CDT*, March 1, 2015, https://bit.ly/2QdXcQx.

(47) Anne Henochowicz, "Minitrue: Delete 'Under the Dome,'" *CDT*, March 7, 2015, https://bit.ly/2YpoJjn.

(48) The CCP, "Meteorological Disaster," *Beijing Municipal People's Congress Portal*, June 6, 2016, https://bit.ly/2EuWyLW.

(49) Josh Rudolf, "Minitrue: Pollution Lawsuit, Smog Classification," *CDT*, January 5, 2017, https://bit.ly/31jOAoN.

(50) Anne Henochowicz, "Minitrue: Clear Smog from Politics," *CDT*, April 8, 2014, https://bit.ly/2QibDD6.

(51) "Fake Egg," November 17, 2012, published by Seki Seto, creator unknown, home video, https://youtu.be/YsBWIipA-jE.

(52) Anne Henochowicz, "Ministry of Truth: Tainted Rice and Strikes," *CDT*, February 27, 2013, https://bit.ly/3lbtcD9.

(53) Anne Henochowicz, "Censorship Vault: Sit-In Over Pork," *CDT*, October 31, 2013, https://bit.ly/2QgaQ5B.

(54) Anne Henochowicz, "Censorship Vault: High School Food Poisoning," *CDT*, November 14, 2013, https://bit.ly/3hgqVnH.

(55) Sophie Beach, "Minitrue: Focus on Fake News in Food Scandal," *CDT*, March 20, 2019, https://bit.ly/32kzuI1.

(56) Josh Rudolf, " 'Cadmium Rice': China's Latest Food Scandal," *CDT*, May 21, 2013, https://bit.ly/32eRNy9.

(57) "Grass-Mud Horse Lexicon: Ditch Oil," *CDT*, accessed August 24, 2020, https://chinadigitaltimes.net/space/Ditch_oil.

(58) Gao Fei, "Netizen: List of Toxic Foods You Need to Know," *CDT*, September 29, 2008, https://bit.ly/32mYsXg.

(59) Fei, "Netizen: List of Toxic Foods You Need to Know," *CDT*.

(60) "These 10 Toxic Food Items Made in China are Very Dangerous for Your Health," *Top 10 Home Remedies*, April 8, 2020, https://bit.ly/32l4eZ8.

(61) "12 Fake Food in China You Wouldn't Believe Existed," *World of Buzz*, September 11, 2015, https://bit.ly/2Eiscw7.

(62) "10 Fake Foods From China That Will Make You Cringe!" *Juicing For Health*, June 18, 2017, https://bit.ly/2EwfOs7.

(63) "12 Fake Food In China," *World of Buzz*.

(64) Eve Cary, "China's Dangerous Tofu Projects," *The Diplomat*, February 10, 2012, https://bit.ly/2QjnsZL.

(65) Anne Henochowicz, "Sensitive Words: The Poetry Edition," *CDT*, September 5, 2014, https://bit.ly/2YslZoe.

CHAPTER 21: In Their Words

(66) Shi Xiang, "Hu Shi's Thousand Year Sigh," *Minghui*, August 16, 2020, https://bit.ly/31kAPiA.

About The Author

Kay Rubacek has 20 years experience producing award-winning, educational programming in print, digital, and video formats.

She is currently a producer and director for Swoop Films and directed their latest award-winning documentary, *Finding Courage*.

Kay's family members escaped communism in Russia, China, and the former Czechoslovakia between 1918 and 1986, and she was arrested in China in 2001 for being a human rights advocate.

Born and raised in Sydney, Australia, she now lives in New York's Hudson Valley with her husband and two children.

Swoop Films is a New York-based film production company that produces and distributes films across the globe that have a lasting, positive impact on society. Their award-winning investigative documentaries tell true stories and highlight social injustices, as well as courageous efforts to speak truth to power, despite impossible odds.

For more information visit: www.SwoopFilms.com

CPSIA information can be obtained
at www.ICGtesting.com
Printed in the USA
LVHW050744160623
749886LV00011B/1492